More Perfect by Design

The Science of Designing More Perfect Business Processes

Angelo Baratta

iUniverse, Inc.
New York   Bloomington

More Perfect by Design
The Science of Designing More Perfect Business Processes

iUniverse books may be ordered through booksellers or by contacting:

iUniverse
1663 Liberty Drive
Bloomington, IN 47403
www.iuniverse.com
1-800-Authors (1-800-288-4677)

Because of the dynamic nature of the Internet, any Web addresses or links contained in this book may have changed since publication and may no longer be valid.

ISBN: 978-1-4502-7537-8 (sc)
ISBN: 978-1-4502-7538-5 (ebk)

Library of Congress Control Number: 2010917403

Printed in the United States of America

iUniverse rev. date: 12/14/2010

To everyone who longs to work in

a more perfect organization

CONTENTS

INTRODUCTION

Where do we spend the majority of our lives? Inside organizations, of course. At first we spend it inside educational institutions. Then we spend it inside work organizations. Next to the institution of family, the organization has the most profound effect on our happiness and well-being. Organizations are the source of livelihood for most of us. They also produce virtually everything we consume. The proper and productive functioning of organizations is at the core of our standard of living and quality of life.

I began my career in 1970 in the field of Information Technology. As of the year 2000, I had participated in, implemented, and directed more than 100 projects for more than 50 organizations. Implementing projects in large organizations is fast-paced, pressure-packed, gruelling work, at best. After 30 years, it was beginning to take its toll. The work itself was rewarding enough, but the lack of high success rates across virtually all industry sectors was demoralizing.

I could see no reason why we couldn't achieve a project success rate of 80% or more. It seemed as if everyone knew the reasons why projects failed and yet they continued to fail. More and more, it seemed that the problems were increasingly within the business processes rather than with the technology.

So after 30 years, I decided to re-engineer what I did. I turned my attention to business process improvement, believing that there was more opportunity there to help organizations develop and prosper. However, I decided to use a different strategy. One thing I always regretted was that in the competitive corporate environment, we rarely get an opportunity to really think through what we're doing. We have only enough time to cope with the circumstances, but not enough time to change them. So I decided that a good chunk of my time—about 50%—would be spent reflecting, doing research, and developing new approaches. This book presents the results of some of that work.

The title of the book is "More Perfect by Design." It is based on the premise that excellence doesn't just happen. It has to be designed. It is also based on the premise that no matter how perfect a solution looks, there is always a more perfect solution just behind it. We just have to learn how to discover it.

Early on, I looked at what was working in industries—where we had made larger advances. It is in the product-manufacturing sectors that we see the most successes. New products seem to come out almost daily. Each product surpasses its predecessor in quality, reliability, and value. No such sustainable successes are evident outside the product-manufacturing sector. So I asked myself, "What is the key difference?" What is the game changer?

No successful, useful, or reliable product is produced without a blueprint. Products used to be built based on "practices," which were honed over time. Today, products are first specified by detailing the performance needs, including quality, price, reliability, and other measures. Then they are designed to those specifications and documented in a blueprint. Then they are built to the blueprint. This is the key. The blueprint is a permanent memory of the product specification. When we discover a defect in the product, we don't just fix the product; we also fix the flaw in the design or blueprint. This allows us to think through other repercussions. This allows us to continuously improve without regressing. Without the blueprint, we run the risk of re-implementing failed ideas. Without the blueprint, we cannot evaluate new ideas prior to implementation. The blueprint provides all participants with an objective target, an outside focus.

Good organizations take great pains to ensure that they build to the blueprint and that they continuously improve the blueprint. It is in this way that the product itself is improved.

Now contrast that with how we deal with business processes, the key building blocks of the modern organization. When something goes wrong (flaw), we just patch the process. When someone gets a "good" idea, we tack it onto the process. When someone new and with authority comes in and decides that they prefer a different approach, they scrap the process and create their own. This causes processes to devolve, instead of evolve. This causes processes to take steps forward, and then steps backward. Imagine if this happened to a product.

To a customer, what you make is the product. To the other stakeholders and to the employees, it is the business itself that is the product. We put so much systematic effort into designing the customer product, yet we put little effort into designing the business itself. It seems that we would rather spend the effort dealing with the flaws than designing in excellence.

For most organizations, their business processes are so poor that the only way to stay competitive is to either burn out their employees or forever search for cheaper employees somewhere else. Of course, when an organization replaces its highly paid employees with poorly paid employees, they are inadvertently reducing demand. After all, it is the employees who are the ultimate consumers. If they make less, they will have to buy less.

I had originally intended to write a book on process improvement relying on existing knowledge and practices. However, in researching the subject, I found that the bulk (more than 90%) of the knowledge deals with project management or people management rather than process management. There are plenty of books, articles, training courses, and conferences on how to organize for a process improvement project, how to control such a project, and even how to select such projects. However, there is no body of knowledge or sources that describe how to go about designing a business process in a systematic and repeatable way.

And so, I set out to discover and expand that knowledge. This book presents a *paradigm* or *framework* that serves as a foundation for business process design. It is a systematic approach to designing business processes and linking them directly to an organization's strategy. Design is a fundamentally human activity. There is no other entity on earth that designs. Design is about envisioning something different, something more perfect. It is about forming intent and then building something to achieve that intent. And so people are a critical component of this process. It is people who formulate the intent, without which there would be no reason to design anything.

This book is about how to go about creating a business process blueprint. The lack of a blueprint is at the core of our inability to learn at the organization level. If I look back to project management I can clearly see why all those "lessons learned" were never learned, and continue not to be learned. A lesson is only learned when we can integrate it into what we do in such a way that we do things correctly the next time. That means we have to be able to apply the lesson to something concrete. Products advance so quickly because a lesson is applied to the blueprint as follows:

1. The flawed element is removed from the blueprint.
2. The correct element is inserted into the blueprint.

The next time the product is made, we begin with the new blueprint, which allows two things to happen:

1. We forget how to make the flaw because its cause has been removed from the blueprint.
2. We learn how to make the product right because the correct way has been incorporated into the blueprint.

Every time a lesson is learned, we should erase from our memories the wrong way to do things. Contrast this with lessons learned on projects:

1. The blueprint is in our heads, so everyone has a slightly or completely different blueprint.
2. The lesson is documented separately from the method that caused it, so it may not even apply to everyone.
3. When we begin the next project, we will typically begin with the same blueprint. Even when we try to change the blueprint, there may be others who object because they haven't learned the lesson yet. So there is a strong tendency to repeat the same error.

The ideas and approaches in this book do not replace such things as Lean or Six Sigma or BPMN or even your own internal methodologies. We present a methodology-independent framework for designing a process in a systematic way, engaging all subject matter experts while supporting them with process design knowledge, which many don't currently possess. It is an approach based on the following assumptions and principles:

1. Design is a human activity and, therefore, cannot be successfully accomplished without engaging the appropriate people.

2. People want to be fully engaged. They want to be challenged. They want to use their knowledge and their skills to the fullest. When they aren't fully engaged, they lose their motivation for excellence.

3. Designing a process and executing that process require different skill sets and distinct knowledge. Few people can master both. "Jack of all trades, master of none" is a warning. If we are to design more perfect business processes, we need masters in process design. And masters need a body of knowledge to master. Today, process design is an informal practice that includes many "Jacks of all trades" but no process design master. That needs to change.

The framework presented is intended to provide a foundation for a growing body of knowledge for the job of the next decade—*the process design master*.

DEALING WITH COMPLEXITY

This book introduces two frameworks intended to reduce the complexity associated with understanding, modelling, and designing business processes:

- **Strategy-Function Deployment**: This is a systematic, step-wise approach to deploying strategic intent down and across functional silos. It links business objectives, strategy, and functional processes.

- **Relational Process Model (RPM)**: This is a framework for modelling business processes and producing a normalized process blueprint. It reduces process complexity by normalizing (separating out) all the key process components. It simplifies understanding, modelling, and design of business processes.

Together these two frameworks help us to develop more perfect business processes.

The greatest challenge of design is complexity. Every real problem or opportunity has a specific, inherent level of complexity. Some problems may have a low inherent level of complexity while others have a high level of complexity. When we set out to solve a problem or address an opportunity, there are three distinct stages where we get to address the complexity.

The inherent complexity must be totally addressed by the three stages in order for the problem to be solved.

The first stage is the Design stage. This is the stage where we design the solution. The second is the Build stage, where we build the solution. The third stage is the Use stage. This is the stage where we use the solution. Whatever problem complexity is not taken care of during the Design or Build stage will be left to be addressed during the Use stage.

Let's look at a simple example of getting from Buffalo, New York to Boston, Massachusetts. We must deal with at least two things: the distance and the geography. The geography between these two cities contains mountain ranges. These are part of the inherent complexity of getting from one to the other. There are two basic solutions that have already been built. The first solution consists of twisty mountain roads that follow the natural contours of the mountains. The second solution consists of a highway that cuts through the mountains. Let's look at each of these in terms of the three stages.

The scenic drive solution was the first to be built. It was designed and built using engineering principles and construction methods, some of which date back to the time of the Romans. The techniques are based on following the contours of the mountain and building roads using relatively simpler techniques. Those are the Design and Build stages. The resulting solution, however, means that every time we take the journey we have to cope with the remaining complexity of the mountains. We have to be careful and skilled if we want to make good time. We have to negotiate the many curves and the ups and downs. There may also be oncoming traffic just a few feet away. We have to deal with the complexity left in the road every time we make the trip.

Now let's look at the highway. Both the Design and Build of the highway used more sophisticated engineering principles, more complex tools, and people with higher levels of expertise. The Design and Build of the highway required significantly more sophisticated and complex Design and Build stages. But the result is that the remaining complexity is considerably lower. It takes less skill to drive on a highway. It is a shorter distance. Gone are the dangerous curves and the oncoming traffic. The more sophisticated Design and Build stages have absorbed more of the inherent complexity of the problem.

The Design and Build stages for a highway are more complex and more sophisticated than the Design and Build of the scenic road. This is a general principle that applies to solving any problem regardless of the type. It is a crucially important principle, so we will restate it.

The more complexity we want to remove from a solution, the more sophisticated the design approach needs to be.

In order for a problem to be solved, we must completely address its inherent complexity either during the Design and Build of the solution or during the Use of the solution. Whatever complexity is not addressed during the Design and Build stages must be dealt with every time we Use the solution. In order to reduce the complexity during Use, we must find more sophisticated (complex) approaches to Design and Build. I will call this the Law of Solution Complexity.

What if we wanted to make it even easier to get from Buffalo to Boston (Use)? Of course we could fly. What's easier than sitting on a seat and reaching the destination a few hours later? Of course the flight solution requires even greater design sophistication.

In order to improve the Use stage for any problem, we must become more sophisticated and complex in the Design and Build stages. In an organization, we use processes to achieve the objectives of the organization. We have been using the same simple approaches to design processes for decades. This is unfortunate because business problems have become more complex. The result is that business processes have become much more complex in their execution (use). This is because the inherent complexity has risen but the approaches to designing and managing processes have pretty much stayed the same. Our Design and Build sophistication has moved very little. That's what the framework addresses.

Currently process design and management is based on an approach that relies more on art and practice and little on science. We tend to view a process from a perspective that has people as the focal point. We ask or solicit from those people what they "require" to improve *their* process. This is clearly a simple Design and Build approach and, therefore, is destined to transfer much of the inherent complexity to the Use stage. What this leaves us with are complex processes inside complex organizations.

This Relational Process Model (RPM) is a new paradigm. It is an integrated framework to be used during the Design and Build of processes as well as during the Use of the process for continuous progress towards a more perfect solution. The framework is richer than current approaches. It is a bigger, fuller model with new concepts and new terms. Some may prefer to continue with their simple process models, which can be described in a few pages. Of course, their organizations may continue to live with the resulting Use complexity. It is unavoidable that in order to reduce execution complexity, we must raise the Design and Build sophistication and complexity. The Relational Process Model addresses the following central question:

What do we need to change in order to achieve a more perfect solution?

In answering this question, we displace people as the centre of the problem. Instead, people become the centre for finding the more perfect solution. We believe that engaging people is the most important factor in improving the design and execution of business processes. Centre is about finding the most useful model that will help us to understand the behaviour and results produced by an organization.

At the centre of the model is the purpose of the organization as expressed by the process design. We view people as participants in processes, where each process is connected to the purpose of the organization. People are participants in a process. People are not the reason or purpose for which the process exists. Achieving the purpose of the organization is the reason the process exists. Therefore, the Design and Build stages must allow us to build processes that can contribute to the fulfillment of the purpose in an effective and productive way. This drives us to *discover process* requirements rather than *elicit user* requirements. This does not imply that we use people as mere resources and throw them away whenever we wish. A healthy relationship between people and the organization should be part of the purpose of a great organization.

The RPM paradigm is a thinking framework that requires full people engagement. It has as a central purpose and objective the closing of the strategy-execution gap. This model is a way to deploy strategy across functional silos. It is a way to model processes. It is a framework for managing process and performance knowledge. Current approaches focus on the parts, treating people, technology, methods, etc., as pieces that are designed separately and replaced serially. Our framework looks at the parts within the context of the whole through performance. It is an integrated model rather than a parts model.

We can make a positive difference by designing more perfect processes, producing a blueprint, and then **executing the blueprint**.

AUDIENCE AND PURPOSE

A key purpose of this book is to address the general lack of proper and systematic business process design. The model is intended to connect strategy with execution. Therefore, aspects of the model are relevant at all levels of the organization. The model bridges strategic intent and execution delivery. Since it reflects knowledge of the organization, shouldn't everyone have access to it? Relational Process Modelling can and should be implemented incrementally, one process at a time. Also, the framework does not conflict with other approaches to process modelling but, rather, enhances them. It is an incremental modelling system with levels of detail appropriate to the executive level in an organization as well as the execution levels. It brings process management into everyone's focus.

Who should *understand* this framework? Everyone works inside some process. Therefore, everyone in an organization should be able to use the framework to better understand how their processes function. That includes process managers and subject matter experts. It provides them with a more complete framework for continuous process improvement.

Who should *master* the framework? It is a rich and sophisticated framework that won't be mastered by all but should be mastered by some. Anyone who is directly involved in the design and improvement of business processes should strive to master this framework. Since many organizations don't formally design their processes, there are no standard job titles that can be listed. However, the following list will likely capture the majority of job titles currently in use that would benefit significantly both personally and organizationally by mastering the framework: business analyst, systems analyst, process analyst, process engineer, process designer, project manager, and others.

Learning Strategy

A book can be read, or it can be studied. As a starting point, I would recommend that everyone read this book earnestly to gain an appreciation for the different components that make up the framework. The book is divided into four parts. Each part is a unit. Read it a chapter at a time and give the concepts some time to settle in your mind. If you can, find others with whom to share questions and review concepts. Pause at the end of each Part. If some concept isn't clear enough, then consider reviewing it before proceeding to the next part.

> Part I: The Foundation contains introductory material and is a warm up for material that follows. You can read this material anywhere and at a leisurely pace.
>
> Part II: A Framework for Understanding begins to introduce some new concepts. Make sure these concepts are understood before proceeding. You can read this any place where you can give it moderate attention.
>
> Part III: The Relational Process Model contains the bulk of new concepts and will require more time and more attention. You should read this where you won't be disturbed and when you can give the material your undivided attention.
>
> Part IV: Application still introduces some new ideas but they are lighter in nature. Most of the heavy lifting has been completed. It's now time to wind down. You should read this in a distraction-free zone, but it can be read anywhere.

For those whose goal is simply to understand the ideas presented, then you might be done after the first reading. However, consider reading it a second time. A book should not be the same the second time around because you are reading it with new knowledge. You might be surprised at how much was missed the first time. At the least, review any concepts that are not quite clear yet.

For those who want to master business process modelling and design, study is the better option. For you the first reading is just the beginning. Once an initial reading is complete, it's time to put it to use through practice. Chapter 12: Model Maturity Stages presents a systematic and progressive approach to modelling a process. Following that method to model a current process of interest and using this book as a reference during the model development is an effective way to master the material while producing useful work. If this is carried out in a team structure, then learning will take place more quickly and more effectively.

Learning is a social experience that can be both enlightening and rewarding. But remember that developing our minds is no different from developing our bodies. If we want to build muscle mass, we have to *lift our own weights*. The same principle applies to the mind. Struggling is the mental equivalent of lifting weights and is part of the learning journey. Struggle is the challenge. Mastery is the reward. Creating more perfect organizations is your contribution.

There is a saying that "Practice makes perfect." But only "more practice makes more perfect."

It takes *more practice* to make *more perfect*.

PART I

THE FOUNDATION

1

PROGRESS MANAGEMENT VERSUS CHANGE MANAGEMENT

Every man takes the limits of his field of vision for the limits of the world.
Arthur Schopenhauer

Change management is a structured approach to transitioning individuals, teams, and organizations from a current state to a desired future state. In other words, change management is often about getting *other* people to do what *you* want them to do.

Progress management, on the other hand, is about figuring out what needs to be changed in order to make progress for everybody. Progress management comes before change management and it makes change management as easy as it can be, but no easier. The Relational Process Model is a framework that supports progress management.

Quite often we invest time, money, and energy in getting people to change, but when all is said and done, little or no progress is made. Change all too often results in little, negative, or no progress. Although progress requires change, most changes do not result in permanent sustained progress.

At any given point in time there is at least one constraint that limits an organization's performance relative to its goal. Finding that constraint and dealing with it is a key management activity and is the heart of progress management.

Consider a couple of statistics:

1. More than 90% of all improvement initiatives fail outright or aren't sustained beyond a few years.
    - 100% of those that failed initially believed they would be part of the 10% who succeeded. So it seems that we can't effectively predict success.
2. More than 50% of all software projects fail to deliver expected business benefits.
    - 80% of the issues stem from poor or wrong requirements. So it seems that we can't effectively state what is needed.

Organizations are constantly plagued with problems. But do we see problems as a problem? Some people, myself included, make a living solving other people's problems and so, perhaps, we might come to the conclusion that having a steady stream of problems is a good thing. But solving problems requires resources. And while the problem exists, we are leaking value. Therefore, we are paying a great price to live with and solve these problems. In today's highly competitive global environment where labour rates are always lower somewhere else, we can no longer afford to absorb the high cost of "problem" waste.

Why does it seem that organizations always have an unlimited supply of problems that need to be solved? Why is it that despite the fact that we have solved so many, we still have so many more? And why do they seem to get more complex?

If you have children, or know someone who has, then you've probably visited this popular pizza and games joint that has a mouse as its mascot. They have a game referred to as "Whack the Mole." The rules of the game are simple. You get a padded hammer, which you use to whack. There are a number of holes out of which a mole will pop. But you don't know which hole it will pop out of. As soon as a mole pops up, you whack it. If you whack it hard enough, it will go back into its hole, but then another will pop up from a different hole. The object of the game is to whack as many of those hole diggin' varmints as you can in the time allotted.

Does your organization sound even a bit like this? Solving business problems is similar. You get credit for solving a business problem (whacking a mole). The more problems you solve, the more credit you get. If, when solving one problem, a mole pops up somewhere else, then that becomes someone else's problem. It is only your problem if it pops back up in your area. And therein lies the problem. All we need to do to be personally successful is to stop at the first solution that does not cause the mole to pop up in our area, during our watch. Let's repeat that so we understand. If a result of whacking the mole is that it shows up in someone else's territory, then from a personal perspective, we have solved the problem. Also, if it pops back up in our territory, but at some future time so that it appears unrelated to our whack, then we are still seen as having solved the problem.

But how does it look from the perspective of the organization? If a problem solved in one area causes another one to pop up in a different area, then is that of any benefit to the organization? Of course it isn't, because the organization is affected by all of them, no matter where they pop up. So we could conclude that people may have become quite good at solving problems, while organizations have not. That's because people are solving their functional problems, not enterprise problems.

**The number of *functional* problems solved *far* exceeds
the number of *enterprise* problems solved.**

Let's explore an alternative definition of a problem within the context of an organization.

A problem is an undesirable side effect caused by the current solution.

For every problem there is a more perfect solution. No implemented solution is perfect. As such, every solution will have side effects. Anyone who has ever been on a medical drug, or undergone a medical treatment, or seen an ad for one, understands the concept of side effects. Some will be benign and have little impact. But some side effects can be worse than the cure, as far as the organization is concerned. We seem to be in an endless cycle of problem solving with no end in sight. Many problems have accumulated as a result of previous solutions. Organizations are investing resources in training people to become better problem solvers. But we don't need better problem solvers. We need *more perfect* solutions.

Instead of solving a problem, create a *more perfect* solution.

Problem solving is a highly focused activity aimed at eliminating something specific. As long as the undesired effect is eliminated and nothing obvious is created during the time when we are looking for the side effect, then the problem is solved. We have had thousands of years to improve our problem solving abilities. And we have gotten better. But continued improvement will not achieve better results because the root cause of the problems is the problem solving paradigm itself.

The biggest source of problems is the *current solution.*

The problem solving paradigm has its roots in functional (local) thinking. This book presents a framework for specifying business solutions in the form of a business blueprint. The process blueprint is a description of the full solution. The idea of a blueprint is not new.

Wherever a blueprint is applied, we can see constant forward progress. Virtually all reliable products and services are based on having a current blueprint that describes in detail the best known way to produce that product or service today. A blueprint allows us to retain all the desirable aspects of the current solution at any time. Without a blueprint, the solutions end up going around in circles, reintroducing problems that had been previously solved. So what is the alternative paradigm to functional problem solving?

A More Perfect Solution

The objective of this alternative approach is to discover more perfect solutions. And what is a more perfect solution? It is a solution that has the following properties:

1. It is better than the current solution for at least one aspect.
2. It is as good as the current solution for all remaining aspects.
3. It is inferior to the current solution for none of the aspects.

The context for a more perfect solution is always broader than the context for just solving the problem. But you might be thinking "that's all well and good, but I still have functional problems to solve." And that's true. We must still solve the functional problems. However, when a functional problem is solved somewhere else, we don't want any problem to pop up in our area as a result. Therefore, we must ensure that whenever we solve one of our functional problems, there is no problem created anywhere else. When a functional problem is solved in one area, and when solving that problem creates no new problems anywhere else, in the present or in the future, then we have achieved a *more perfect solution*, one with higher performance, less risk, and fewer problems. That's the goal.

In order to reduce the volume and complexity of problems, we should seek to discover a *more perfect solution*.

In order to discover a more perfect solution, we need two sets of constraints: those relating to the problem, and those relating to the higher context of which the problem is a part. The solutions that are more easily and more quickly found are those that solve the problem while creating undesirable effects elsewhere. In order to reduce the number and complexity of problems in an organization, we need to identify and eliminate these zero sum solutions. That means that we have to have a way to identify or measure any performance decreases or risk increases, external to our focus, that result from any proposed solutions. If we can achieve that, then we can be assured that every time we solve a problem we are also moving towards a more perfect solution. But in order to do that, we must know what the perfect solution is.

We need to solve the functional problem AND move towards a more perfect solution.

THE ROLE OF COMPLEXITY

We are faced with ever increasing complexity, of which there are two kinds. There is the *core* complexity, which reflects the nature of the problem. The degree of core complexity is dependent on the problem to be solved. Then there is the *solution* complexity, which is of our own making. When we try to solve a problem we have to deal with the product of the two. I say product instead of sum because combining complexities has an exponential effect on difficulty. Unfortunately, we are not experiencing an exponential increase in our raw intellectual capacity. But we have something not available to any other creature on the planet—our ability to design tools that help us to deal with situations that are outside the human capacity. We can design physical and mental tools that can increase our capability. Most of the current **technology** was developed to increase our physical capacity to produce more **volume**. What we need now is to focus on producing more **value**.

We want to make value and complexity more visible so that we can produce more of one and less of the other using current capacity. In the physical world, we have taken the approach of using tools that extend our physical power. If you want to lift something that is twice as heavy, you need twice the power. But if you want to solve something twice as difficult, you need more like four times the mental capacity. I don't know for sure if complexity increases as the square of the difficulty, or by an order of magnitude (10X). I only know that it is not linear. And, therefore, it is more difficult, perhaps impossible, to devise tools that would extend our mental capacities exponentially. But we can achieve the same effect by taking the opposite approach. Instead of trying to invent technology to increase our mental capacity, what if we devised ways to reduce the complexity of the problem by breaking a problem into more but simpler problems?

Our framework is about creating a business blueprint that can reduce the complexity of the work that goes on in the organization.

The volume and speed of changes far exceeds the amount of progress. Complexity is holding us back.

The past 100 years have been devoted to designing and building tools that extend our physical capabilities. We have built machine counterparts to replace our muscle power. And these have allowed us to build things that could not have been built otherwise. But we seem to have reached the limit with these "tech" muscle extensions. Unfortunately, in the process, we have created greater complexity around us. So now we are in peril of regressing—not because we can't build better machines, but because we don't seem to be able to solve one problem without replacing it with another, more difficult one.

EXERCISE

Let's explore our ability to solve problems with this number sequence puzzle. Please spend at least five minutes on this puzzle before proceeding to the answer.

The challenge is to figure out the pattern behind the sequence and to use it to determine the next number in the sequence. The sequence is:

1, 1, 2, 2, 4, 4, 5, 7, 7, 11 …

As a hint, you can try adding, subtracting, multiplying, or dividing.

OK, go ahead and give it your best shot.

Have you spent at least five minutes?

No! Then go back and give it another shot.

Once you've devoted an honest five minutes, you may continue.

....

....

....

OK, did you figure it out? If you did, then congratulations! I don't know anyone who has figured it out. But let's not go to the answer yet. Perhaps you are truly motivated to solve this problem. So let's do a couple of really easy ones to build our confidence before we try again.

Alright, let's try this simpler sequence: **1, 2, 4, 7, 11…**

Write down the pattern. Then figure out the next number in the sequence. This one should take you only a few minutes. When you're done, we'll go to the next one.

....

....

OK, let's do one more before returning to the more challenging problem.
Here is the sequence: **1, 2, 4, 5, 7…**

Are you ready for the answers?

.

.

.

.

.

Alright, let's look at the answers to the two simple sequences.

First sequence: **1, 2, 4, 7, 11 ... 16**. The pattern is: [+1, +2, +3, +4, +5 ....]

Second sequence: **1, 2, 4, 5, 7 ... 8**. The pattern is [+1, +2, +1, +2, +1 ...].

If you gave this one an honest try, you probably had little difficulty, unless you happen to be math challenged. Don't worry, many of us are.

Now that you're all limbered up, maybe you want to try the original sequence again. Let's repeat it here:

1, 1, 2, 2, 4, 4, 5, 7, 7, 11

Still stumped? Did you notice anything familiar about this string? Still can't see it. Let's give you a little help. Let's reframe the string two different ways so we can see the pattern better.

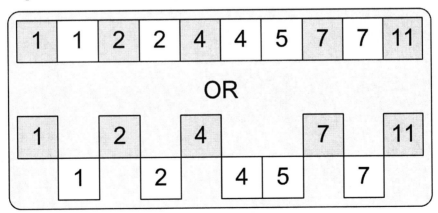

How about now? It should be much clearer. What we have are two simple sequences mixed together. What we have are two otherwise simple problems, which can be solved in a matter of minutes. But when we combine them, we get an exponential increase in complexity and difficulty. When we combine the two, they effectively hide each other's pattern so that we can't see them. And until we can see that we have two different problems, neither is likely to be solved.

You might be asking, "What does this have to do with business?" Well, let me tell you. Many times when we think we are solving one problem, we are really trying to solve two or three or more problems simultaneously. This increases the complexity and often puts the issue beyond our ability to understand, let alone solve.

In the functional silo paradigm we often get the opposite problem as well—that of a partial problem. Imagine that instead of the following sequence

1, 2, 4, 5, 7, 8, 10

we got **1, 4, 7, 10**. In other words, we got a sequence with missing elements. Again, what is a simple problem can become unsolvable, or we can end up solving the wrong problem. In this example, the problem is solvable, but the answer is incorrect relative to the original sequence (+3, +3, +3 …).

So we have the following possibilities:
1. Combining simple problems can yield problems where it is beyond our ability to produce effective solutions.
2. Getting only a partial problem can either provide a problem that is difficult to solve, or one that is easy to solve, but gives the wrong solution with respect to the higher context.

The current functional silo paradigm tends to give us both. But wait, we aren't finished yet. Remember the Whack the Mole game. Imagine that each mole hole is a different functional silo. When you whack a mole from one hole (functional silo), it may simply pop up in another hole (functional silo). This is another effect, where solving a problem in one area isn't really solving it. It is simply moving it out of your jurisdiction into someone else's. You might be thinking that a good way to get rid of a monkey is to move it onto someone else's back. The problem is that while you are moving your monkey, someone else is moving theirs. *The end result is that everyone is working harder, but overall, there is no progress.* And, of course, those nasty moles are busy procreating, making new, stronger, and more resistant moles. Unfortunately, and especially in a highly political organization, getting the mole (monkey) off your back and onto someone else's can be rewarding.

Putting an end to this situation requires a new paradigm, with new ways to see. It doesn't require new skills, necessarily. It merely requires that we apply the skills to different and complete problems. Being able to see these different problems are what the framework addresses. Its goal is to help us to *discover more perfect solutions.*

FUNCTION AS A KEY ORGANIZING PRINCIPLE

Organizations can be large and complex so we need to chunk the work of the organization into more manageable pieces. Since the beginning of the industrial revolution, we have organized ourselves according to skill sets dictated by the many technologies that we have invented and developed. We have then grouped people with the same or similar skill sets into separate functional areas. These functional areas became functional processes that, in total, make up the organization.

There are many obvious advantages to this. In theory, people in a functional group can improve their skills and learn from each other. They can communicate more easily with each other because they have a common base. We can easily administer both the carrot and the stick. All we need to know is where something went wrong. Was it in Accounting or in Information Technology? Was it in Sales or in Production? The appeal of the functional organization lies in its apparent simplicity when it comes to management. The key is to always know who is accountable for what. And this seems easy to accomplish. We simply put people in charge of various functional silos. Then when things go wrong, we should know exactly who is accountable. Thus, the holy grail of the functional organization is personal *accountability*.

The holy grail of the functional organization is personal accountability.

Personal single-point accountability is based on the notion that success or failure is strictly due to who is in charge or who is executing and that the cause of a problem is to be found wherever the problem pops up. Therefore, when something goes wrong we want to quickly find out who was in charge so that we can quickly assign blame. Then we can act and move on. If you don't think this is so, then listen carefully at work. Listen to the news, watch election campaigns. Personal accountability implies that the quality coming out of a function is strictly due to what happens inside that function. Fifty years ago that was an OK model. In today's highly linked organizations, this is no longer that clear.

We often hear people lamenting about the lack of accountability in organizations. What is usually meant by that is that no one wants to accept the blame when something goes wrong. The fact that it is so difficult to fix (attach) the blame should be telling us that perhaps the way that the work is managed only lends itself to single-point accountability. Unfortunately, organizations have become more complex so that today, more and more problems have multiple root causes for success and for failure. Any approach that tries to find a single point of cause will not succeed. So perhaps we need to shift our view of accountability.

The most popular view of accountability is based on fault. We will often hear the question "Whose fault was that?" Perhaps we need to change the question. Perhaps we should consider the following mental model.

It may not be your fault, but it is your problem.

A person may contract a disease through no fault of his own but it is important that he act immediately and appropriately to get himself back to health. It wasn't his fault but it is his problem. When we operate in an organization we seem to take the attitude that "if it's not my fault, then it's not my problem." And, of course, no one ever sees anything as being their fault. What is the problem with that attitude?

There are many effects in an organization that aren't the fault of any one person. They may simply have been caused by some combination of internal, external, personal, and other conditions. We may not be able to find out "who is at fault" because no one person is genuinely and uniquely at fault. Nevertheless, we cling to the idea that someone has to take the blame. In politics that's what a scapegoat sometimes is. It isn't the person who is actually at fault but it is the person who will absorb the blame so that people will have the illusion that the problem is gone. But is the problem gone? Of course it is not. But since we believe it is, we can't work on solving it because it's not supposed to be there anymore (kind of like *The Emperor's New Clothes* by Hans Christian Anderson).

In an organization, there are many problems that can't be attributed to a functional group. We need to establish a way to ensure that those problems will be looked after regardless of fault. We need to put the solving of the problem ahead of the attachment of fault. In fact, fault should only be attached at the end when we have developed a more perfect solution. Only then are we in a position to assign fault, if fault needs to be assigned.

There is also another side to the fault problem and it has to do with taking credit. When things go right, there are some people who are good at taking (literally) the credit. They were not necessarily the reason why things went right but they positioned themselves to be in the neighbourhood when it happened and so they take the credit. Aside from the fact that this destroys morale, it contributes to promoting people who promote themselves rather than promoting those who can move the organization forward. That is not to say that we should be shy and humble about our accomplishments—quite the contrary. But an organization must be better able to tie actual results to actual causes. The functional model is no longer sufficient for us to achieve that objective.

The expression "not on my watch" is a testament to the personal accountability mental model. One of the biggest roadblocks to effective change is success. The success of using function as the predominant organizing principle and personal accountability as the basis for management is precisely what is making change so difficult today. As a society we have been successful using this paradigm. But all paradigms have limits. The key is to understand where we are with respect to those limits. The world is more complex now and there is more than a single factor responsible for the achievement of results. We need paradigms that help us to understand what the major contributing factors are. Personal accountability is still necessary but it is no longer sufficient.

This organization-chart view allows us to see the organization as a series of boxes (jobs) within silos (business units). It is essentially a command and control structure view. It is primarily about seeing how people relate to each other in the command structure and to what general skill box they belong. It is a useful view going back centuries. It is also a view that leads to significant personal biases and gaps. If something doesn't seem to fall inside a particular box, then the risk is that it will be ignored (white space on the organization chart) by everyone. What one sees depends not only on the silo one is a part of but on one's hierarchy within the silo. From this vantage point, there are almost as many interpretations of a particular thing as there are people.

The biggest and most damaging effect of the predominance of the functional view is employee disengagement. For the past 100 years we have done well using a parts-swapping approach. We swapped the horse and plough with a tractor and the improvement was huge. We swapped the horse and carriage with a car, the hand drill with the electric model, the fireplace for the stove, and so on. This approach of swapping parts worked because of the enormous difference between the pairs of parts. But now we have good parts in almost all processes. So when we swap, we no longer have a large improvement because the parts are no longer the constraint. It is the way all the parts (people skills, method, technology, etc.) are structured or designed to work together that is the constraint.

In the parts swapping model, we needed people to disengage. We just wanted them to use the new part and move on. Sometimes the people were the parts. In a world where integration of the parts has become more important, we now need people to be re-engaged in their work. Why? Because people are the integrators. Unfortunately, many haven't noticed the changed conditions and they are still on the parts swap road. So, most still work within the functional organization mindset. The results of that are all around us.

Some of the other side effects are:
1. Isolationism—The tendency not to care about other boxes (units) or the people in them.
2. Resistance to change—If my box is made smaller, then I will be less important. Or if stuff is added to my box, then I will have to work harder. So I should hold on to the status quo, no matter what it is. The implication is that every function must be perfect since we should neither reduce nor increase any of the functions.
3. Limited view—People only see things from inside their box. They don't see or care about other impacts.
4. Externalities—the tendency to push risks to other functions or to future times.
5. Weak customer focus—I do my job and someone else takes care of the customer.

Using function as the key organizing principle and using personal accountability as the key change tool does have advantages, the principle one being simplicity in organizational design. What could be easier than knowing where to point every time something goes astray? Unfortunately, this simplicity comes at a great price. For one thing, less than 15% of organizational issues have people as the single contributing factor. That means that using this as the primary method for determining change will only be correct about 15% of the time, at best. And even when we are correct about assigning blame, we still run the risk of having the situation repeat itself. Why is that? Because what we really need to know is what actions the person took, what decisions they made, and what conditions were present that may have led to the situation. Without knowing that, the risk is that the situation will be repeated by the next person. Of course time will pass before we notice the repetition. Perhaps enough time will pass that we don't even recognize it as a repetition.

OUR FUNCTIONAL NEIGHBOURHOOD

We live in functional neighbourhoods. Our neighbours are people like us. They have the same language as us. We occasionally interact with the neighbourhoods on either side of us but only along the boundary. They give us stuff and we move it along. Sometimes we take great care to make sure that the stuff we pass along is of the highest quality but other times we just try to move the stuff through as quickly as we can. As part of a functional neighbourhood, we tend to have a local (narrow) focus. We strive to achieve functional and personal objectives because that's what we're given. And, of course, we are protective of our neighbourhood and of our particular house (job) in that neighbourhood.

Fifty years ago this worked relatively well. Then the world was different. When you set up a particular functional structure it would be relevant for years and decades. We could happily make local improvements and those improvements would translate into enterprise improvements.

What we need to recognize is that we have reached the limit of local improvements. We have reached a point where local changes can rarely be made without impacting some other function. That means that we have to go beyond the local functional needs. If we don't, then we are wasting resources and energy to simply fight each other's changes. This is the critical point in any paradigm. If you can't see that you have reached the limit of that paradigm, you tend to work harder at doing what you've always done before. All this does is consume energy, create stress, and drive everyone mad.

The conditions that made the paradigm work in the past were the following:
1. We came from an individual-based manual society.
2. We had a largely uneducated and unskilled workforce.
3. Doing the core work (tilling the soil, cutting the tree, building the house) took all of our energy.

4. Technology, in the form of machines and computers, represented orders of magnitude improvements over the manual methods. What took a person a day to do manually on the farm, for example, only took a few minutes with a tractor. What took a person an hour to manually compute takes a computer only nanoseconds.

5. We went from a period of scarcity to a period of great abundance. This has led to being wasteful in our practices. In many ways we have been wasteful on purpose, designing jobs not to be efficient but to consume resources in order to spread the wealth. It is no longer necessary, nor useful, to be wasteful. Since there are so many needs that are going unfulfilled, we could easily become more efficient without any personal wage (not job) losses whatsoever.

6. Before the world moved slowly and locally. Changes were local and we had time to adapt.

The conditions today are different:

1. We are now an automated society.
2. The workforce is highly educated and skilled.
3. The core work has become a small fraction of the total effort, ranging from 5% to 20% of the total effort. The remainder goes to handling failures, implementing controls, and organizing the work. Fighting obstacles to doing the work often takes more energy than the work itself.
4. Technology is all around us. There are few areas where technology can provide anywhere near the boost it did 50 years ago.
5. We live in a period of abundance. But we squander much of that abundance and, therefore, we get no value from it.
6. The world moves quickly. Changes are global. We have less time to adapt.

Because the world has shifted, we must shift as well. But in what way does the functional process focus get in the way? After all, it is a model that has served us well for many decades. In the old world, when things changed slowly, we could design a process, establish a functional model to support it, and simply let it improve over the years through the use of technology. It was all about improving the components. We know that these conditions no longer apply. Let us explore the world of the Functional Organization a little more through a hypothetical example.

THE WORLD OF FUNCTIONAL SILOS

The functional model is driven by functional and personal objectives. It is defined by specific boundaries, well-defined work that happens inside the boundaries, and not so much coordination between functional boxes. It is based on the assumption that when we improve things locally (in our box), these improvements will translate into enterprise level improvements. It assumes that when things happen faster—for example, inside each box—then the whole process becomes faster too. This was certainly true 50 years ago. There is no doubt that when you replaced manual labour with a machine that produced 100 times faster, this did translate into enterprise level improvements. When we move from one paradigm (manual) to a significantly more productive paradigm (technology), we can make great strides without much effort. But now we are far into the technology automation paradigm and, therefore, introducing better technology simply doesn't have the same impact. Too often it has no impact at all—it just has cost. Why is that? Basically it's because task performance and physical energy are no longer the constraint. The new constraint is process performance and mental agility, which are quite different. And yet, by and large, managers are still focused on task speed and task cost.

To understand the difference between task performance and process performance, let's explore the difference through an analogy as depicted in the diagram below.

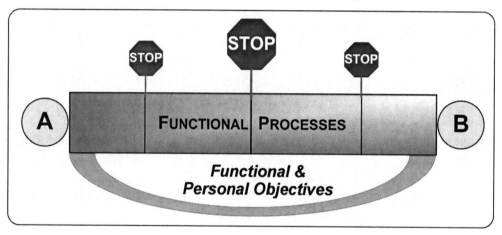

Imagine that we need to take a passenger from Point A to Point B. The road that joins the two points is a series of long city-like blocks. At the end of each block there is a stop sign and a police officer to ensure that we come to a complete stop before proceeding. The stop signs in the diagram represent the end of one long block. If we don't stop, the police will pull us over and we will be ticketed, which will take additional time. We can go as fast as we like within the block as long as we come to a complete stop at the end of each block. So we race, accelerating quickly and braking hard, come to a stop and then repeating until we reach Point B. Although we might attain a relatively high top speed somewhere within the block, what will be the average speed over a single block? Of course it would be quite low compared to the top speed. And what about the average speed over the trip? It would be lower still because of the time taken to stop, to accelerate, and to decelerate. The average speed from A to B is the process speed. Now imagine the stress that this puts on both the car and driver. Even though the overall speed is fairly low, the stress will be quite high. The driver will be frustrated by the fact that he or she is being forced to underachieve. This is what it is like to be in a functional process in your typical organization. We consume enormous amounts of energy and are subject to high levels of stress while achieving at a relatively low level. Yes, we can buy a faster car and we can train the drivers, but we will reach a point where the task speed no longer matters. It is the stops and their impact that are killing us. It is the design of the trip that is the constraint.

Now let's take the analogy further. Imagine that the purpose is to get a passenger from Point A to Point B. Further imagine that each block is a different functional process or job. Each block has a separate car and driver (different job). You can only take the passenger to the end of your block (end of your function), then you return to pick up the next passenger (next transaction).

Let's follow this process:
1. The passenger gets into the first car at Point A.
2. The driver races to the end of the block, comes to a complete stop, and lets the passenger out.
3. The driver races back to pick up another passenger.
4. The passenger then walks across the street. Maybe the passenger needs assistance (more effort).
5. The passenger enters the next car or waits until it arrives and then enters.
6. That driver then races to the end of his or her block, where the passenger repeats the process.
7. This continues until the passenger has arrived at Point B.

Now how long will it take the passenger to get to Point B?

But wait, we're not done. In order to make things more efficient functionally, let's put three passengers in the car. Now we need to wait to get three passengers. Once we have three passengers we can begin. But now at each block we have to wait for all three passengers to get out, walk across the street, wait for the car to arrive, and get into the next car. Naturally, if one passenger is a little slow, then all passengers must wait. If you are the fourth driver in this long line you probably have no idea what the passenger is going through because you have no idea what the overall purpose and performance is or what it should be. All you can do is focus on making your little part better, whatever that means to you. You aren't aware of what impact your functional decisions have on the overall process, let alone on the organization's purpose.

Imagine that the driver for the middle leg makes a case for getting a faster car. So now that leg of the journey is a little faster. But will passengers get to Point B any faster? Think about it.

No, they probably won't! Because the drivers before and after are no faster than before. So passengers will simply trade time in the car for time waiting for the next car. At the same time, the driver of the faster car will simply end up spending more time waiting for passengers to arrive because the car before him is slower. So the overall process speed won't have changed one bit. In other words, the overall process speed, as seen by the customer, will be the same even though it would seem to the driver that things should be going faster. The driver is likely to think, "Oh well, the problem must be with some other function." That's the issue with a strict functional focus. We often think that the source of a problem is somewhere else. And because everyone thinks the same thing, no one takes action.

Of course, we see that the passenger is the customer and getting them from A to B is the product or service that we are trying to deliver. We can begin to see that at some point it is no longer the content of the process that dictates speed and cost but rather the flow of the start-to-end process. And in order to understand the flow of the process we need to go up a level. But is there anyone who has accountability for speed, service, or cost of that overall start-to-end process? Is there no one we can point to and say, "Hey, do something!" Often there is no one other than the CEO and that's way too high in the organization chart. We have reached the point where functional improvements are no longer meaningful on their own. In fact, the last improvement of taking three passengers at a time may have made the process slower still.

In the functional world the talk is all about "who does what tasks"—task responsibility. In the new world it's all about connecting to the strategy so that we can deliver to the business objectives. And so, if we are to make progress, then we must take a different view of how we can get the strategy deployed across functional silos. We need a framework that allows us to see the performance in context, rather than just locally. Perhaps it's time to change *our field of vision*. The Relational Process Model helps us to improve our field of vision.

SUMMARY

Every day someone in our organization solves a functional problem. Despite this, there are always more problems to be solved. The problem is that solving a functional problem doesn't always solve an organizational problem. Quite often all we do is move the problem around the organization. The end result is the number of functional problems solved far exceeds the number of organizational problems solved.

We work in organizations that are highly functionally organized. So our field of vision tends to be functionally constrained. Problems appear complex. Sometimes they are, but other times it isn't the actual problems that are complex. It's what we see or don't see that makes them more complex than they are. At one end we tackle incomplete problems and come up with incomplete solutions. At the other end we tackle multiple problems simultaneously as if they were one. The result is a level of complexity that we can't deal with and so these problems go unsolved.

Over the last few decades the workforce has become more educated and more demanding. In the past we needed skills—disengaged muscle. But today we have the opportunity to engage the whole individual and thus increase stakeholder value delivered. But to achieve this requires a new field of vision. It requires a more holistic, more encompassing view that allows us to more clearly see why organizations behave as they do. We need a new framework to give us this new field of vision. That's what this book presents and explores.

2

TO LEARN—ESSENTIAL CAPABILITY FOR PROGRESS

There are three things extremely hard: steel, a diamond, and to know one's self.
Benjamin Franklin, *Poor Richard's Almanack* (1750)

At any given point in time there is at least one constraint that limits the performance relative to the goal. For an organization, continuously finding that constraint and dealing with it is *the* key management activity.

After a long journey of material progress, we seem to be at, or may have passed, a crossroad. Since lack of strong functional capability was the constraint, a functional focus in both thinking and structure has worked well—at least until recently. We should not be surprised that an organization divided into functional units would result in functional improvements and functional progress. But now it's time to move forward. Although we still need functional progress, we also need cross-functional progress.

There are many who criticize functional silo thinking as being the cause of many of the current troubles. I would submit that it is not the presence of functional thinking that is the problem but rather the *absence* of higher systems thinking to provide context and direction to functional thinking that is the problem. It is not a question of replacing or removing functional thinking. Instead it is a question of adding cross-functional thinking as well. A system progresses by growing, by becoming more sophisticated and, yes, more complex, and not necessarily by simply swapping out one component for another. Such a conclusion is the result of pure functional thinking.

It is the *absence* of higher level cross-functional thinking that is the constraint, not the presence of functional thinking.

Cross-functional system thinking is integrative. And so, in order to pick up the rate of progress in organizations, we need to be able to integrate and link a number of currently separate and disparate parts. We need a framework that will allow us to make this jump to the next level of sophistication. And what do we need to integrate and link? Some of the key problems that need to be addressed and solved are:

1. Link strategy to functional processes (execution).
2. Measure value and performance.
3. Integrate risk, capability, and optimization.
4. Align participant stakeholders to the organization.
5. Link processes and projects.
6. Increase engagement of employees.
7. Unlock the change challenge.

We need to dramatically increase the organization's ability to **LEARN**. Constant progress requires constant learning. The faster we learn, the faster we can progress.

FUNCTIONAL COMPLEXITY

Functions are characterized by specialization. A function is an organizational tool for putting together people and/or machines that do like things. Functional organization is a strategy for optimizing the efficiency of a task. When we went from manual labor to mechanized labor, it seemed to make a lot of sense and it worked quite well for a long time. We have made tremendous progress with this paradigm. But now we are stalling and we need to open ourselves up to exploring other options. But we have been living so long with this option that it is difficult to even visualize other options. We have become functionally constrained thinkers.

But functional thinking is not bad. It is, in fact, essential. We can't do without it. We still have to be able to make engines and write software and bake pizzas and interpret laws. Functional thinking is about making better parts or components. And even the most complex machines and systems are fundamentally made up of components. So what is the next stage if we want to break through the ceiling imposed by functional thinking?

The key capability of systems thinking is design. Design is the art, practice, and science of putting parts together to create new capabilities. Design is the most human of all characteristics. All other species rely mainly on instincts, which can be seen as predefined blueprints for how to behave. Humans are the only species that are given a free slate. Rather than having to rely only on instincts based on a given blueprint, we can develop our own blueprints for how to behave and live. *Our ability to design all aspects of our lives, I believe, is the most distinguishing characteristic that we possess.* We have the ability to design *paradigms and frameworks* that allow us to understand the world as a system. That's what science is essentially all about.

Whereas functional thinking leads to practical (practice) solutions, systems thinking leads to principles or laws that must be engineered into solutions. Functional thinking is about finding a solution that works. Systems thinking is about finding principles that permit us to design and engineer solutions that would otherwise not be visible to us. Science is the search for principles. Engineering uses those principles to design solutions. None of the practical advances in engineering—from the automobile to MRI machines—would have been possible based solely on direct discovery of practical solutions. Unfortunately, this principle has yet to be discovered by modern organizations, which still operate primarily on practices. A practice can make surface discoveries but can't find solutions buried deep beneath the surface.

Designing with blueprints is the key to the success of engineering. Organizations have been put together primarily based on practical approaches of what worked without necessarily understanding why or under which circumstances they worked. In a slow moving world this is acceptable. But in a fast moving world there are two problems with this approach. The first is that it takes a long time to get to a working best practice. Many management practices that we are exploring today, such as Lean, had their beginnings more than 50 years ago. The second is that without understanding the conditions required for a particular practice to work effectively, we are unable to see when those conditions change. So we may not notice when conditions have changed such that the practice is no longer optimal. Of course we do finally get it, when things start to fall apart. But by then it may be too late.

So the capability to design the business, rather than just the products of the business, is at the heart of moving to the next stage of organization evolution. But designs require blueprints because the designs need to be shared across functional silos. And a blueprint is nothing more or less than a framework. Blueprints for computers have a different framework than do blueprints for a building, for example.

The Relational Process Model (RPM) is a framework for designing a business regardless of the purpose of the business. More specifically, it focuses on producing blueprints for an organization's value-producing processes, which are key building blocks for any organization. The main objective of the framework is to boost an organization's ability to learn and to produce stakeholder value.

A LEARNING ORGANIZATION GATHERS LESS WASTE

Waste can be simply described as anything that drains away value from the organization for one or more of its stakeholders. There is an old saying that "a rolling stone gathers no moss." Similarly, we can say that the learning organization gathers no waste. That's because a learning organization is always moving forward or progressing. Since an organization is meant to facilitate the exchange of value for the benefit of all participants, we don't want to have a buildup of waste. And that means that an organization must continuously adapt itself. And that means it must continuously learn.

The LEARNing organization gathers no waste.

Learning is not evolutionary, or a straight line, but rather revolutionary. Many will react to this and say "I disagree." Revolutionary in one sense implies some sort of violent change. That's not what we mean here. With respect to learning, revolutionary has another meaning. It means that there is a cycle to learning. With every revolution or cycle, we have an opportunity to learn and adapt. And the shorter the cycle, the more rapid the learning. So let's look at what a LEARNing revolution or cycle might look like. Luckily the word itself is its own acronym— LEARN.

Listen
Experiment
Adapt/Adjust
Realign
Normalize

The first step in learning is to *L*isten, to get feedback, to know where we are. Of course, the volume of data that we could listen to is always greater than our capacity to hear and process. And so, the framework will need to specify what and whom we need to listen to and with what frequency. Some examples of external stakeholders to whom we should be listening include customers, employees, shareholders, and suppliers. But we also listen to the organizational internals, the business processes. Business processes are like organs. They all have healthy vitals to which we should be paying attention. Part of learning is to discover what the vitals are and what their value (reading) should be. So the framework must allow us to attach vital statistics to a process.

The second step is to *E*xperiment. When we listen we gain new knowledge, but sometimes the knowledge we need isn't readily available and we may need to experiment to find that new knowledge. Experimentation is essentially simulating something in a carefully controlled environment in order to generate data that we can listen to.

Next, we *Adapt* or adjust the current process or framework based on listening and experimenting. Constant adaptation and adjustment keeps an organization on the road to progress.

But we can rarely only change one thing. And so whenever we change one thing, we should ripple out to see what else needs to change in order to maintain alignment. An adjustment is a change. We can compare its impact to the impact of throwing a stone into a pond. We don't just get a splash where the stone lands. We also get ripples. Sometimes we only get a few ripples. Other times we get many. So we need to examine the ripples that will be caused by a change and *Realign* the whole process and beyond.

The last step is to *Normalize* the new adjusted process—to make it the new normal way to operate. Then we return to listen to the changed process, to determine if the new process has led to progress, and to validate the adjustments. If it hasn't, then we revert back to the current process and re-examine. Learning implies progress. Learning is different from knowledge acquisition. We certainly do need knowledge to learn, but acquiring knowledge is not the end game. Learning has only taken place when a change is made, and that change results in progress, however you have defined it. There is a difference between a lesson truly learned and one that is simply recorded.

We could argue that of all the business processes in an organization, the "LEARN the business" process should be among the most critical of all processes. It should be at the core of any organization because without it, we are condemned to repeat the mistakes. For an organization operating in a competitive environment, that means the risk of going out of business. For public organizations, lack of learning can mean placing an unnecessary burden on citizens and reducing the quality of life for all.

FRAMEWORKS: RAISING ORGANIZATION IQ AND EQ

Why are frameworks central to learning, especially for organizations? We know through experience that organizations have a difficult time learning. We mistakenly believe that training and education of employees leads to organizational learning. And so, when organizations don't learn, we conclude that it has to do with their level of spending on employee training, or because people don't want to change. But personal acquisition of knowledge and skills doesn't automatically translate into organizational learning and progress. In fact, quite often, the only thing it leads to is frustration. Let's imagine that you attend a course on Six Sigma and you see applications of the methodology in your group that could lead to significant improvements. But your boss and your colleagues who haven't undergone the training are not convinced by your enthusiasm. As a result, you get no opportunity to apply it. Even though your knowledge has gone up, the organization has learned nothing. Individual knowledge acquisition does not automatically translate into organizational learning. We could say that a process is only as smart as the knowledge it actually uses. So a process can be smarter than the smartest individual, but it can also be less smart than the least smart individual in the process. That gives us quite a large variation and a significant opportunity. The same holds true for discipline, an EQ (Emotional

Quotient) component. A process can be more disciplined than the individuals in it, or less disciplined than the individuals in it. The purpose of a framework is to help us structure the organizational knowledge into blueprints that can be used for design and execution.

Let's explore the idea of a framework. A knowledge framework is a structure that allows us to organize, share, and *retain* organizational knowledge. A framework allows us to convert individual knowledge into organizational knowledge. Through the leveraging power of processes, we can convert individual progress into group progress. A framework increases the likelihood of reaching insights that we would otherwise miss. A framework enhances an organization's ability to learn, to progress, and to retain knowledge across people, functions, and time. An excellent framework will reduce the negative impact of knowledge loss when people leave. This is more important today, when turnover is high, than it was 30 years ago, when people had a much higher tendency to work for a single employer throughout their career.

Let's look at a simple framework: the list. Many people will use a list when going grocery shopping. Here is an example:

Grocery List
1. Milk
2. Toast
3. Orange juice
4. Cookies
5. Chips
6. Hot dogs
7. Frozen pizza

We utilize lists for many different purposes. Lists are easy; they don't require any special tools or resources and we can even create lists in our heads. But lists have little structure and, therefore, little intelligence, because they are the simplest of structures. Structures provide intelligence, which increases our personal abilities. So how might we upgrade the list to a more intelligent framework? Let's look at an example:

VEGGIES & FRUITS	GRAIN	MEAT & ALTERNATIVES	DAIRY PRODUCTS	TREATS/JUNK FOODS	HEALTHY SNACKS
	Toast		Milk	OJ	
				Cookies	
				Chips	
				Frozen pizza	
				Hot dogs	

We have converted the list into a table. The table contains some categories. When we look at the Groceries table, we can get certain insights. For example, seeing the vegetables column empty might remind me that I really need to pick up some lettuce, and, oh yes, the kids are out of bananas. With a simple list, I have to rely on my own memory. There is nothing in a list that might prompt me. Another thing I might notice is that the junk food column seems to have more items in it than any other. Since I'm trying to eat more healthily, perhaps I should remove some items from that column and replace them with better choices in the healthy snacks column.

This simple table is a framework. It can, of course, be augmented. I can add some standard items to make sure I don't forget them, like the milk, toast, cereal, etc. And yes, that reminds me, I need to add cereal because we are running low.

But a framework is not a methodology. It doesn't tell us what to eat but it does make it easier to be aware of what we eat. And awareness is the first step to progress. Let's look at another example of an everyday framework to make this point: the closet organizer. Any two people might have different preferences for clothes and different approaches to buying them. Naturally, each person might end up with a radically different wardrobe. But regardless of how each person acquires clothes, each could use the same closet organizer system, or framework, for organizing and storing clothes.

And how are most closet organizer systems organized? All the ones that I have seen are organized functionally—shirts go together, pants go together, ties go together, shoes go together, etc. Isn't it interesting that the functional paradigm is so pervasive that it is everywhere in our lives and we don't even notice?

"So what?" you may ask. The functional closet organizer is easy to use and it looks organized. It is also simple and easily understood. It just seems to make so much sense. And, of course, when people had few clothes, it did make sense. But the point of clothes is not to put them away. The point is to get a certain look when we wear them, to create a certain impact when people see us in them. Does a closet organizer help with that?

Each component—shirts, pants, ties, shoes—is meant to be part of an outfit. It is the outfit that makes the impression, not the sum of the individual pieces that make up your entire wardrobe. Can you tell from looking at individual pieces how many different outfits you have? Can you evaluate each outfit? Maybe you can but most people can't. A functionally organized closet does not give visibility into what the outfits are like.

Imagine that you were so rich that you had employees working for you to buy the various components. So you had different people to buy pants, shirts, ties, etc. You might give them each some guidance on how to buy, but basically they bought items relatively independently. You didn't have anyone responsible for ensuring that outfits were optimally matched. As you get ready to go out, each unit provides you with one item (pants, shirt, etc.). But the individual functional units may not be fully aware of what the other units are providing, nor are they necessarily aware of the precise impact your are trying to achieve—formal, business casual, casual, etc. So you might find yourself with the following:

- Solid blue suit
- Green socks
- T-shirt
- Striped green tie
- Running shoes

You put these clothes on and look in the mirror. You're not happy because these items clearly don't give you the look you were after. And yet, individually, all the choices can probably be defended. In this case you are the customer and unfortunately the total impact is only seen by the customer and not by the functional buyers.

Companies are organized much like the closet organizer. There is a section for each skill set. When a transaction executes, each functional unit applies its expertise. But the individual units aren't always aware of the total performance that needs to be achieved. In a functional organization, the functional design choices can usually be defended on their own even though together they produce poor customer results. This is central to current organizational issues. And the closet organizer suffers the same drawback. The clothes are organized by function. But they are used by outfit, where an outfit can be defined as a set of functional components that go together to achieve a particular effect.

By organizing the clothes functionally we don't get a sense of whether they are well suited or not. Let me give you a personal example. I was shopping just before Christmas with my wife and daughter when we came upon a tie display. The ties were beautiful so with the help of both my wife and daughter we picked out two ties for me. I loved both ties. About a month later I was dressing up in my suit for a business meeting and I thought of wearing one of my new ties with the suit for which I had purchased them. So I put on the first tie. But to my surprise it didn't match well. So I tried the other tie. And I was disappointed when it too didn't match my suit. I had made a purchase which seemed perfectly appropriate functionally but didn't lead to any progress with regards to my outfit. And upon reflection, I had to admit that I already had four really nice ties for that particular suit, but only one shirt. So why did I buy two more ties and no shirt? Well, I happen to like ties.

That's what happens in a functional world. We make choices which may make sense functionally but that do not lead to progress. If I could have seen those ties in context with the suit, then at least I would have had the opportunity to make a better choice.

And there are other issues. Imagine you hire a personal dress consultant. She comes in and looks at your wardrobe and determines that it isn't Hip. And Hip is the current best approach to dressing. So she purchases all new clothes on your behalf and throws your current clothes out. Imagine that you could arrange all your old clothes and all your new clothes in separate functional organizers facing each other. Could you tell if there was an improvement in your wardrobe by looking at the two sets of clothes organized functionally? Again, most people would look at the individual pieces and they might conclude that the new wardrobe was better but how could you really tell?

So is there another way to organize the closet that comes closer to the purpose of wearing clothes? Ask any woman and she'll talk about outfits and combinations of items to achieve a particular look and purpose. A woman doesn't wear clothes. She wears outfits. So what might be another way to organize the functional clothes? Think about it.

What if the clothes were organized by outfit? So when you looked into the closet you would see them already laid out together. What if we went even further and put the outfit onto a mannequin made in our exact likeness. So imagine you opened your closet and in it were a series of mannequins dressed in separate outfits. Perhaps, if we had more than one tie or shirt for a suit, we could have the primary combination on the mannequin and the alternative ties and shirts right next to it. That way if we had a fetish for ties, we could immediately see that we had too many ties. Then all the ties that we had bought and could not match would be a visible reminder that we don't need any more ties. Another bonus of such an approach is that we might no longer be asked, "Does this make me look fat?" All you have to do is look at the mannequin made to your exact likeness and answer for yourself.

Of course, I have never seen such a closet. The functional closet is simpler to build and simpler to use. But it fails in the most important point—helping us put together better outfits, and keeping the outfits optimally designed as we replace pieces. As we purchase new functional pieces to replace worn ones, we can always ensure that the outfit does not degrade. Naturally, it might be both expensive and difficult to organize the closet according to outfit. But what if we had a visual blueprint of each outfit, perhaps a kind of virtual image while the pieces were still organized functionally? What if we selected an outfit first and then pulled the individual pieces from the closet for that particular outfit? What if the outfits were professionally designed to achieve maximum impact? If we had such a framework we could see how many outfits we had in total. We could tell if we had too many outfits designed to achieve a particular impact and if we had no outfits for a particular impact. We could tell if we had too many ties for a particular outfit, or too few shirts for another. Such a framework might be useful, especially for people who weren't particularly good at matching (design). After all, design is a skill and a discipline. A good framework allows us to see what we have, and what we may be missing. The closet organized by outfit would allow us to see what we have, which outfits are fine, which need to be augmented, and which need to be overhauled. They also allow us to see which items we really don't need more of.

We can compare the functional nature of an organization to the closet organizer. Some organizations may be organized simply and others may be more like the ultimate walk-in closet. But they are virtually all organized by function. Sometimes we refer to the units as functional silos. We organize functionally because that's the easiest way to *store* people and their skills.

Each organizational unit designs its function without truly knowing what the greater objective is. They don't have the context to determine if a change they are contemplating will result in progress or just change (like my new ties).

We need the equivalent of the outfit concept for processes so that we can see the design and performance within the greater context. This way we can see which functional processes need our attention and which do not, as well as which changes will likely lead to progress (greater value) and which will lead only to change (more cost).

We need to break the cycle of going from one methodology to another, from business process re-engineering to Six Sigma to Lean and others. Each time we switch methodologies we redo the processes, throwing away certain elements and replacing them with other functional elements. But are we making progress? This is like throwing away one set of ties for another set of ties without being able to compare outfits. We need a framework that allows us to determine progress.

The RPM framework does just that. And because it's a framework, it doesn't matter which methodology you use. It doesn't matter how you choose your clothes. The mannequin allows you to see the impact of your decisions. We propose a framework that allows us to see the impact of our functional decisions on the value received by each stakeholder. It doesn't dictate what you should do. It doesn't tell you to throw away or abandon your current practices. It simply gives you greater visibility into your current capabilities. You are still in charge, not the methodology. It is based on the philosophy that you should get to know yourself (the organization) better before you burden everyone with large painful changes.

The bigger and more complex the organization, the greater the value that can be derived from having a good framework to help us understand and advance the business. Frameworks are at the core of communication. Sometimes we focus on content in communication. And that's important. But if we each have our own paradigm framework, then we will all interpret what we hear, see, and read in a different way. A common framework improves communication by reducing misunderstandings. A good framework should also allow us to begin slowly and locally or proceed at a faster pace. It should permit us to proceed at whatever pace the organization can absorb.

THE FRAMEWORK—CONTEXT AND OVERVIEW

In order to understand organizational performance, we need a powerful framework. The framework presented has the following main elements:

1. An organization is a Socio-Technical-Economic system. Businesses are organizations created for the primary purpose of exchanging economic and social value. But they are also Socio-Technical systems. So we must explore and separate these three perspectives to better understand why an organization performs as it does.

2. An organization exchanges value among independent stake**holders.** The purpose of the organization is different to each of these stakeholders and each measures value differently. So we need a strong mechanism for measuring value and clarifying accountability from each perspective. We will use the concept of a Chart of Accounts as the framework for measuring value.

3. At the top we have intent, objectives, and strategy. At the other end, we execute inside functional silos. At the top we measure value delivered. At the other end we measure capability to deliver. We need a systematic way to deploy the intent down to the executable functional processes. We need a systematic and reliable method for deploying the strategy across functional silos. This is strategy-function deployment.

4. Value is delivered horizontally across functions during the production of a specific output. Skills are exercised inside individual functions. We need a new construct that encapsulates both value delivered and associated costs. We need to make visible those cross-functional processes to which we can attach and measure value. This is the valueflow process construct.

5. At the intent level we have outcomes. At the execution level we have capabilities. We need a tiered process model that allows us to begin at the outcome level and that will allow us to design capabilities to achieve those outcomes. This is the Three-Tier Perspective.

6. Not all work is created equal. There is the core work required to transform a set of inputs into the desired output. Then there is the work required to correct or handle failures. Lastly, there is the work required to attempt to reduce or prevent failures. We need to distinguish these different work efforts. We need to see them as separate while still seeing how they are related. This is the Three-Stream Perspective.

7. At the end of the day, design is about organizing components in such a way as to produce something that is different from the components—the whole is different from the sum of the parts. But what are the components? This is the Process Components Perspective.

The framework contains all of these. It is a framework for managing an organization's processes so as to achieve its strategy. It describes in detail each of the aspects of the process framework, without requiring a particular methodology. We will explore each of these concepts and how they work together to allow us to develop *more perfect organizations by design*.

SUMMARY

Organizational learning is the ability to adapt and change so as to produce greater stakeholder value. In the past, most of the learning was functional learning. Functional learning is based on **OR** thinking and has led to better parts or functions. The industrial revolution was a parts revolution. We traded human parts for faster, stronger, cheaper machine parts. We traded one part for another. And so we placed value on people based on the parts we used. We hired one person for her arms and a different person for his legs. We disengaged the person from the skill required to do the work because we only wanted to pay for the parts we used. We avoided using both the arms and legs from the same individual. Organizations preferred to hire ten people for their arms at $10 per hour and a different 10 people for their legs at $12 per hour. If they simply hired twenty people to do both, then they would have to pay them all $12 regardless of the part used. In other words, if they hired people to do both it would cost them an arm and a leg. This practice required people to be disengaged and to just do their job. If you were hired for your arms and you also used your legs then you might be stepping on someone's toes. Where do you think all these expressions come from?

Because parts replacement has been so successful, we are now plagued by **OR** thinking. We made progress by swapping out parts for better parts. And so **OR** thinking has become pervasive.

But of course parts don't learn. People learn. And so we have reached the limits of what's possible with this kind of functional thinking. But because parts-thinking is so ingrained in us, many have concluded that functional parts-thinking (functional silos) is the great evil in today's organizations.

But this is a false conclusion. Functional thinking is neither evil nor is it the roadblock preventing progress. It is **OR** thinking that is the problem. In order to progress to the next level we need to embrace **AND** thinking. What's the difference? **OR** thinking is about replacing one part with another. **AND** thinking is about adding parts that aren't there while retaining at least some of the parts we currently have. **AND** thinking is about creating more sophisticated—and yes, more complex—structures. So it's not a question of eliminating functional silos and functional thinking. It is a matter of adding cross-functional thinking on top of the functional thinking.

It is the absence of higher level cross-functional thinking that is the constraint, not the presence of functional thinking.

**It is the *absence* of higher level cross-functional thinking that
is the constraint, not the presence of functional thinking.**

AND thinking is what is required for learning. Organizations have focused on helping their employees to learn. But it is not enough for employees to learn. The organization must learn as well. Progress requires that both the employees **AND** the organization learn. We have developed ways to capture skill or individual learning. Now we also need a framework to capture and retain organization-level business process knowledge. Organizations work well when they successfully deliver value to all stakeholders in a way that is seen or accepted as fair to each stakeholder. So the key is to design business processes that successfully deliver to this objective.

We will explore a framework that provides us with a model that increases the transparency of the work taking place in an organization. Rather than a single tier model based on tasks, we present a three-tier model that links outcomes, outputs, and tasks. This allows us to build our view of the organization incrementally from intent to execution. The model also separates the work according to its purpose. We have the work that directly creates value. We have the work required to deal with failures and realized risks. And we have the work required to prevent failures and risk events. The ability to segment the work of the organization helps eliminate unnecessary complexity so that we can solve more organization-level problems.

Our framework integrates stakeholder value with accountability, a much lamented gap in many organizations. The framework makes it easier for us to understand and separate the impacts made by different components of the business process designs.

3

The Organization—A Socio-Technical-Economic Mechanism

An organization is like a puppet with many puppeteers, each pulling on their strings.
To understand the organization, we need to understand the puppeteers.

Put several people together to pursue some purpose and you have an organization. A book club is an organization. So is IBM. Our focus is those organizations that are private or public businesses; although the framework will apply equally well to any organization unit, including the book club.

Most business books are written about how to manage a business. And few books distinguish between the business and the organization. So let me start with that. In a capitalist society, most businesses are owned by someone. It might be owned by a single person, a partnership, or by shareholders. And, of course, ownership has its privileges, especially when it comes to sharing profits. So although a business may be started in order to deliver a product or service in exchange for money (economic value), an organization must be designed in order to achieve that purpose. The organization needs to meet the business goals but it must also meet the goals of the other participating stakeholders. So an organization is more than the business. It is a mechanism for exchanging value among participating stakeholders.

**A business is a view of the *organization* from
the shareholders' perspective.**

An employee exchanges his or her skill-time for money. A shareholder exchanges capital for the opportunity to make more money. A customer exchanges money for a product or service that he wants or needs. Although someone can be said to own the business, no one owns the organization. It is a mechanism for willing, but not always enthusiastic, participants to come together to exchange value. The attitude that "it's my business" will only get the owners so far. If customers aren't willing to buy their product, then they won't be getting value. If employees only provide minimum effort, then the organization won't generate maximum value. To understand what drives the organization it must be understood as something different from the business per se, which only presents one perspective. But there are other perspectives that are just as important to understanding the organization's behaviour and performance. Each participant has some stake in the organization and acts like a puppeteer pulling, sometimes tugging, on their strings. So we need to understand who each of the **stake–holders** are, and the nature of their stake.

This book is not about how to manage the business, but about what to manage in the organization. And so all the skills and knowledge you already have about the how are still all useable. Where the framework truly shines is in its ability to help you see what and where your focus and resources can be applied to generate even more value.

Socio-Technical-Economic Mechanism

But why do we say that an organization is a Socio-Technical-Economic mechanism? Although a business is primarily an economic concept, it requires additional stakeholders, in addition to the shareholders, to participate. In the past, this economic perspective dominated because of the scarcity of capital (money) that was required to start a business. Although capital is required to get the business going, it is not sufficient to make the organization thrive. Balance sheets and profit and loss (P&L) statements are all about describing the economic situation of a business. But they don't adequately describe the socio and technical aspects that are key to getting an organization to not merely survive but also to thrive.

An organization requires processes, methods, procedures, technology, and other resources in order to operate. It requires people with skills, space, raw material, and other resources. This is the technical aspect of the organization. It looks at an organization as a machine with no emotion or motivation. As important as it is to understand this perspective, it is also not sufficient. Many, if not most, methodologies focus primarily on the technical components. Six Sigma and Business Process Engineering/Reengineering are examples of these. Even Lean, as practised outside Toyota, tends to focus mainly on the technical.

All organizations require financial resources in order to operate. So understanding the economic perspective is also necessary, but not sufficient.

Organizations are stakeholder-centric mechanisms. And, eventually, stakeholders translate into people. And people don't participate just for money, but rather for what the money can provide. People are interested in how the organization impacts their quality of life in general. Employees also care about the impact on the quality of their work life in particular. A poor work life will impact on employees' enthusiasm and their ability to exercise their skills to the best of their ability. Understanding the non-economic factors and being able to work them into measuring value is important if we want our organizations to produce even greater value. This is part of the socio perspective.

As important as each of these perspectives is, it is the interaction among them that must also be understood. At any time, any one of these may be the limiting factor. And it's important to know which one it is. If an economic factor is limiting progress, then we must address that rather than spending time and resources in the technical area. It is the nature of a constraint that it must be dealt with first, before other factors. If your car is out of gas, there is no point in investing in a tune-up, regardless of the perceived benefits. You need a fill-up first for the tune-up to do any good. What happens quite often is that we work on the areas where we are comfortable rather than on the areas that need attention. The paradigm of picking the low-hanging fruit first is based on comfort and ease. This makes sense for a fruit tree because each individual fruit has the same value. However, on the tree of business there are fruits with very different values. So picking the easiest isn't always the wisest move. Analogies can sometimes get in the way of progress.

Since each aspect is important, there is no shortage of people—often consultants or vendors—telling us to buy their product or service. Because organizations are always imperfect in each of the three categories, they are often fooled into investing in areas where they could be better, but which are not current constraints. I like ties and so I was fooled into buying two new ties. Not only did I not need any new ties but the ties I bought didn't match the suit for which I bought them. Of course, if my clothes had been organized by outfit, I would have been less likely to have made that unnecessary purchase. A good framework must be able to help us determine where the current constraint is and what kind of attention it needs.

When we focus exclusively on the technical, we treat the organization as if it were a machine. And for many things this is true. And it's important that we understand what the technical behaviour of an organization is. However, every organization includes people. And people, unlike machines, make choices according to what they value. You might be thinking that machines make choices as well. But I would argue that they really don't or that at least the choices are different in nature.

Let me illustrate with an example. Suppose you are driving with your significant other to New York City, and you reach a crossroads, a T-intersection. There is a sign at the intersection that points left for New York City and right for Chicago. Is this a choice? It isn't really a choice.

It's a question of routing. Since we are going to New York City, there is no choice. There is only the route and so you go left.

Now suppose you are driving with your significant other to get away for the weekend to have a good time. You reach the same crossroad—New York City to the left and Chicago to the right. Now you have to make a true choice. Choices always have probabilistic outcomes—outcomes that are not guaranteed. And outcomes may be interpreted differently by different stakeholders. You might decide that it would be great fun to see some plays and based on your knowledge you figure that New York City is the better choice because the theatre is strong there. And so you go left. In this case you aren't driving to New York City per se. You are driving towards the place that you believe will provide you with the greater opportunity to see plays, and thus have a good time.

The first decision was a technical routing decision. The second was a socio choice decision. Actually, we shouldn't call the first one a decision. It's more like a selection. An organization has to be designed from both perspectives. We can design processes so that the technical selections are made correctly. But we should also design from a socio perspective because people will need to make many true choices. And we want to make the correct choices as often as feasible. In essence, when we design an organization we need to combine the technical architecture with choice architecture (Richard H. Thaler and Cass R. Sunstein, *Nudge*, Yale University Press, 2008). We want to design the organization so that we nudge, not force, people into making the optimal choices in order to deliver stakeholder value. And in order to do that we have to know who the stakeholders are and how to measure value delivered. We need to know the equation each stakeholder uses to measure what value means to them.

STAKEHOLDERS AND ORGANIZATION TYPES

What is a stakeholder? In simple terms it is someone with a stake—something that is emotionally important to us and that we put at risk in order to gain an advantage or benefit. Stake is about motivation and engagement. An unmotivated participant will cease to participate, or at least will reduce her participation to the minimum acceptable level.

Many businesses are failing or at least no longer thriving because they have hit a ceiling that can't be moved because they only followed the *technical* track. Many governmental public institutions are delivering reduced services coupled with increasing costs. Why is this happening? Could it be that they don't quite understand which puppeteers are pulling what strings? Both types of organizations continue to address the issues by trying to change the technical aspects of the organization without fully understanding what is at stake. Let's quickly review some typical stakeholder categories.

1. **Consumer**: This is the person or entity that directly benefits from the use of the product (good or service). The person who eats the pizza is the consumer. The person

who has the hernia operation is the consumer. The person who attends the concert is the consumer.

2. **Payer**: This is the person or entity that pays for the product (good or service) that is consumed. In Canada, the Ministry of Health might be the payer of the hernia operation. In the US it might be an insurance company or it could be the consumer.

3. **Customer**: When the consumer and payer are the same person or entity, we can use the shortcut name "customer." For most profit businesses, we have a primary external recipient of the product who also pays for the product.

4. **Employee**: These are the people whom the organization employs in one capacity or another to make the products or deliver the services. This includes people at all levels of the organization. Even the president falls into this category.

5. **Suppliers**: These are external people or organizations from whom we purchase products, raw materials, or services required to make the products or deliver the services. Sometimes we use an external supplier to deliver a service identical to what an employee would deliver, but we treat them as an external supplier.

6. **Funders**: These are people and organizations that provide funds to begin or maintain the existence of the organization. For a for-profit organization, we usually refer to them as the **shareholders**. We will use the term shareholders going forward. But we mean whoever the funders may be. For government-provided services, it is the taxpayer who can be considered the funder.

Of course, these are roles played by stakeholders. A particular person or organization can sometimes play multiple roles. So an individual can be a shareholder and an employee at the same time. Each role must be understood. And they can be best understood in relation to the organization and the transactions in which the role-holder participates.

Organizations are sometimes divided into for-profit and not-for-profit. This classification may be useful for tax purposes, but I don't believe it is as useful for understanding behaviour. There are many ways to classify organizations to help us understand behaviour.

Below are two models. This doesn't mean that they are the only two, but these are two that appear quite often. The first we will refer to as the Customer Business; the second we will refer to as the Consumer-Payer Business.

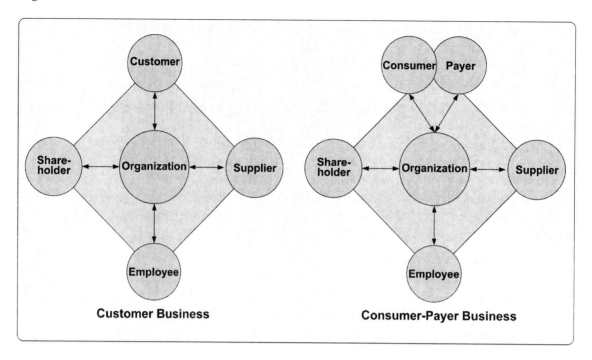

The **Customer Business**, whether it is for profit or not, may behave quite differently than the Consumer-Payer Business. Why is that? Basically, it's because the stakeholder roles are slightly different in the two organizations. Let's look at each in turn.

There are a couple of distinguishing features in this model. The first is that the customer is the consumer of the product or service, and the customer also pays directly for the product or service. So, in this model, the customer fills both the consumer and payer roles. Since the customer is both receiving and paying for the product, the customer has to determine whether or not he wants to participate in the transaction by determining the value of the transaction. Let's imagine that the formula is as follows:

$$Net\ Value = Gross\ value - price$$

Without getting into a discussion of how to determine what the gross value is, we can say that, in order to buy, the customer in this case must reach the conclusion that the gross value exceeds the price. So, the price represents a value hurdle that must be surpassed by the product. Of course, if the customer decides to buy and later finds that the value did not surpass the price, then hopefully he will have learned a lesson for next time. The point here is that the price acts to control demand from the customer. If the price rises, demand is likely to fall, and vice versa.

The second distinguishing feature is that the shareholders provide the initial capital for starting the business but it is the customers who fund the ongoing operations through profits. That's important. The shareholders put up a certain amount of money upfront. We could say that they prime the pump. But once the water starts flowing (revenue starts coming in), then the capital is replenished from the sales revenue. So as long as there is some profit, the organization can continue, at least at current levels, without further shareholder input.

In a customer business, the customer has a demand limiting device in the price. The price imposes self-control on the customer and that puts a limit on demand. In this kind of business, the organization, on behalf of the stakeholders, tries to increase the perceived value of the product. This makes it easier for the customer to buy.

By contrast, in a **Consumer-Payer Business** the consumer uses the product or service but does not directly pay for it. So the value formula for the consumer is:

$$Net\ Value = Gross\ value - \$0$$

The price hurdle here is much lower and sometimes it's zero. So the gross value doesn't have to be large. In addition, the gross value doesn't even have to be real. It can be perceived. As long as the consumer thinks the product might be worth something, then it's worth more than zero. So the self-control is largely removed. Now you might be thinking, "Sure, but just because I'm not paying, that doesn't mean that I'd go ahead and get an operation if I didn't really need it." You'd be surprised. There are many unnecessary surgeries done every year. There are millions of dollars spent on prescriptions that might not be required. By removing the self-control, we tend to lower the standard by which we make our choices. And so, in a consumer-payer business we really can't rely on the consumer to help with demand management.

In these businesses, the payer is different from the consumer. Take the example of the Canadian hospital. The tax payer pays for the services, not the patient. In this model, we don't have shareholders; we have what we might call sharefunders. These are people or entities that fund the initial start-up *and* ongoing operations. They share the total ongoing funding, rather than the profits.

From the payer's perspective the value equation might look like this:

$$Net\ Value = \$0 - cost$$

To the payer, everything might look like a negative value, because she doesn't see or experience the value. Actually, she may not directly experience the cost either. So the payer isn't in a good position to judge value either way. And so payers are not effective in managing demand.

The key to understanding the difference between the two models lies in understanding the socio-economic behaviour rather than the technical behaviour. The reason this kind of organization continuously worsens is not that the managers have no business sense. It's that they are treating it like a Customer Business when in fact it isn't. The key problem is not one of productivity, although that may be an issue. The key problem is more likely to be about who's managing what, especially demand.

In a Consumer-Payer Business, the distinguishing feature is that the consumer of the product or service does not pay directly for the product or service. Someone else does. So in essence the consumer here is a customer who is getting a product at zero cost. So he is highly motivated to consume. Continuing with the Canadian example, since Canada has universal healthcare, the "government" pays while the patient receives the service. Why is this important? In a Customer Business the customer has a large impact on controlling demand based on her view of the value received for the price. In a Consumer-Payer Business, since the price is zero, virtually everything appears to have value. And so there seems to be an insatiable appetite for the product no matter what it is. In other words, demand may be exaggerated.

The point is that to understand an organization the starting point needs to be with the stakeholders. Clearly identifying them is a good start. Determining which of the two organizations we have is also useful. The two types can be viewed as being opposites in many ways. Your organization could conceivably be a hybrid of the two.

All organizations have a purpose. But the purpose is different for each stakeholder. So we can't really understand the purpose without reference to the stakeholders. But who are the stakeholders? They are not the "internal functional units or their representatives." We mean the external stakeholders we discussed previously.

So far we have depicted the four main stakeholder groups: customer, employee, supplier, and shareholder. But we should also add a fifth, which is a conceptual stakeholder—the organization itself. Because an organization is a system, it will behave as if it were a stakeholder. For example, an organization needs to survive, which is something quite apart from the individual stakeholders. For now, let's take it on faith that having the organization as a separate stakeholder will help us to better understand behaviour and performance.

MEASURING VALUE RECEIVED—THE CHART OF ACCOUNTS

In order to understand and gauge stakeholder motivation, we need to measure value delivered in the same way that each stakeholder would measure the value. Having identified the stakeholders, we then proceed to determining what they use to measure or evaluate their level of satisfaction with regards to their participation. Of course they will evaluate both the economic value and the socio values. So we need to account for both.

A common approach to measurement is to construct a dashboard, which might contain such measures as profit, price, revenue, salary, customer satisfaction, etc. Dashboards sometimes give a heavy weighting to shareholder economic factors. But there are many other factors that can be measured or evaluated, though not always in economic terms. We can measure how fast a transaction is completed, for example, but we can't always put a precise dollar value on it. That's how Domino's Pizza made its name; they were able to deliver in "30 minutes or less." We can think of each of these value items in terms of measurements and incorporate them in a dashboard. Many methodologies advocate the use of dashboards and there are plenty of software tools to help us. But, again, this has more of a technical leaning.

Take a few seconds and think of a dashboard and the things you associate with it. What did you picture? Did you picture some sort of instrumentation on a machine? We tend to think of dashboards as instruments on a machine. A dashboard is a technical concept that lacks emotional connection.

But there is another way to view measurement. We can view it from a socio-technical perspective. It is just as systematic, but also incorporates the socio aspect as well. Imagine that for each value we set up an account. Now take a few seconds to think of an account. What did you think of?

Some people thought of their savings account or their vacation account or their retirement account or perhaps their mortgage. We can replace the concept of a dashboard with the concept of a Chart of Accounts. We can have a gross revenue account, a cost account, and a net revenue account. There is also a relationship among these accounts. We can have account executives and account managers. We can have processes drawing from an account or feeding into an account. Some people will be more interested in one account than another.

Our framework uses the concept of a Chart of Accounts rather than a dashboard.

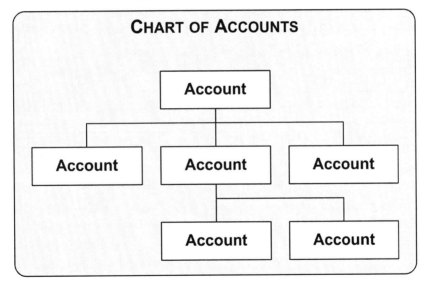

An account can represent a socio, technical, or economic measure. Some accounts will only be of interest to one stakeholder. For example, a revenue account is likely to be of interest to the shareholder but not to a customer. Each stakeholder will have either a formal, explicit Chart of Accounts or an informal, implied Chart of Accounts, which they use to assess their participation within an organization. Employees, customers, suppliers, and shareholders are all constantly evaluating their Chart of Accounts and will base their actions on their perception of the status of their account. A fully defined Chart of Accounts may contain a subset for each stakeholder group, and even for a specific stakeholder. We should think of a Stakeholder Value Chart of Accounts as representing the stakeholders' value formulas.

Why is a Chart of Accounts a potentially more useful concept? Accounts have to be managed. Measures don't. An account implies that there is someone feeding into it, or drawing from it. It implies that someone is monitoring it and managing it. The Chart of Accounts can be used to implement clear, transparent, and explicit **account**ability. The Chart of Accounts gives us the ability to account for impacts. Accountability begins by identifying and specifying which accounts need to be managed and how accounts are related. Then we can use the Chart of Accounts to help us design an actual organizational structure based on those clear accountabilities. We will further explore this concept of accountability tied to measurable value outcomes in a later chapter.

SUMMARY

The organization is a socio-technical-economic mechanism for exchanging value among stakeholders. A business process must address all three aspects if it is to be productive. To view an organization only as a business is to view it from the perspective of the shareholders alone. But an organization has other participants without whose participation it cannot survive. And so we need to understand what each participant's stake is with regard to a particular transaction. That understanding will allow us to design more perfect processes.

All too often we focus on the technical aspects of a process, drawing process maps and drafting specifications. But what about the socio forces within a transaction? To understand these, we have to know who the stakeholders are and what their stake is. The ability to measure how a transaction contributes to the stake of each stakeholder goes to the heart of understanding motivation, a socio factor.

In any organization there are a handful of stakeholder groups. There is always a consumer who receives and uses the product of the organization. There is also someone who pays for the delivery of that product or service. When the consumer and payer are the same entity, we refer to them as the customer. The employees are another stakeholder group present in every organization, as are the suppliers who provide raw material and other resources. Finally, there are those who fund the start of the organization and sometimes its ongoing operation. These are the shareholders or sharefunders.

We can distinguish between two different kinds of business operations based on whether the consumer and payer are the same entity or different entities. Such organizations tend to work in a fundamentally different way. When the consumer and payer are the same entity we refer to it as a customer business. In a customer business, the customer experiences both the value of a product or service and its cost. So a customer can make both an economic and a socio evaluation of the desirability of the product. As such, a customer can act as a demand manager. In other words, a customer tends to limit the demand when the value is seen as inferior to the price. On the other hand, in a consumer-payer organization, this demand-limiting function is effectively eliminated. To the consumer who pays nothing, almost any value seems worth the price of zero. To the payer, who gets no value, any cost appears undesirable. In such an organization, the consumer will tend to push demand up without limit. The payer, on the other hand, is often paying indirectly and so is unable to act to limit demand. The end result is that these—often governmental—organizations have escalating demand with increasing costs and often diminishing value. Such organizations must be managed differently. Putting a "business person" to improve the operations of a "consumer-payer" organization can make things worse.

Since the purpose is to deliver value, we need a mechanism to account for value delivered. We introduced the Chart of Accounts as a tool for defining the accounts to be measured and as the basis for establishing accountability.

Part II

A Framework for Understanding

4

Deploying Strategic Intent across Functional Interests

Strategy without tactics is the slowest route to victory. Tactics without strategy is the noise before defeat.

Sun Tzu

It all starts with the strategy. Strategy is about options and choices. But it's also about advantage. Two organizations may have the same business objectives but the route they choose to achieve those objectives may differ. They may adopt different strategies. The reason a competitive business develops a strategy is that it is trying to beat its competitors. And so it develops a strategy that it believes will provide an advantage over its competition. On the other hand, a public, governmental organization may not be out to beat a competitor and so its strategy may be more relevant to its effectiveness than its survival. It will be driven by different motivations and that will be reflected in its strategy.

We aren't going to discuss how to develop a good strategy. Rather, this chapter introduces a framework for deploying your strategy to the execution level, once you have it.

But why is executing to the strategy so difficult? Executive surveys consistently cite failure to execute strategy as a top reason for poor performance and even business failure. This continues to be a top challenge. But to say that we have failed at execution can be misleading.

First of all, strategies are never certain. There are many points of failure. Every strategy has an element of risk. Even when everything is done correctly, there is a possibility of failure that is beyond our control. Besides risk there are other points of failure that *are* under our control. We might fail to achieve the objective because the strategy itself is not the optimal one.

Secondly, you can't execute a strategy. It has to be translated down to the functional level, where it can then be executed. So the strategy, although sound, may fail to be properly translated into executable tactics. So even though we are executing flawlessly, what we are executing isn't what we should be executing. And of course we might have the proper tactics but we don't have the capability to properly execute them.

Quite often all of these are lumped together as execution failure. But each situation requires a different response and so we need to distinguish among them.

The strategy-function deployment approach will increase the likelihood of achieving the objectives through the strategy. Why is it called strategy-function deployment? The diagram below summarizes the concept.

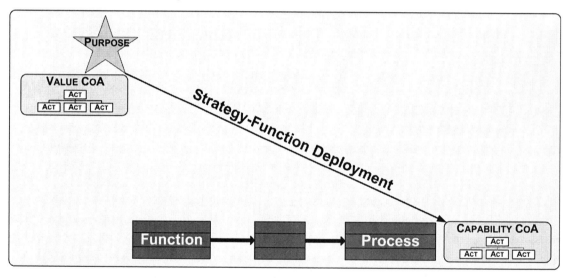

At the top left we have the purpose or intent of the organization, which is represented by the Stakeholder Value Chart of Accounts. At this tier we are defining the desired stakeholder outcomes in terms of accounts. Value measures are specific to a stakeholder group. For example, a "profit account," as represented by the economic dollar measure of "profit," is of interest to the shareholder, but not to the customer. It may be of relevance to an employee in that a company that doesn't turn a profit will shut down, but it isn't of direct interest.

But profit is rarely attached to a functional process. At the bottom we have execution of the functional processes. Function measures are not specific to a stakeholder but rather to a process. Here we measure process performance. We define performance in terms of a Process Capability Chart of Accounts. An example of a process measure might be capacity, which is a quantification of how many units of something that a process can produce. Or perhaps the process measure would be cost, which is a measure of financial resources consumed by the process.

STRATEGY-FUNCTION DEPLOYMENT FRAMEWORK

But how do we go from intent and the Stakeholder Value Chart of Accounts all the way to execution and the Process Capability Chart of Accounts? This is a significant challenge. First of all, we have to go from multiple intents by stakeholder all the way to a single execution. Not only do we have to traverse many different people but we also have to go across many functional silos and levels of organizational authority. Some organizations mistakenly believe that strategy execution failure is due to lack of communication. It might be the case that better communication is required. But communication alone is not sufficient. We need a stepwise, systematic engagement process that pulls in the right people in the right sequence. On a technical level, this process will produce an integrated and linked full Chart of Accounts from Value to Capability. The Value CoA will measure horizontal delivery of value to each stakeholder. The Capability CoA measures the vertical delivery capability of each process. But as important, at the socio level it can produce a level of commitment based on engaging everyone in an inclusive process to produce a persistent blueprint that can be used as the basis for execution and for management.

Strategy-function deployment is much more than a communication process. It is an organizational design and people engagement process. It is through strategy-function deployment that we design the organization components and it is through strategy-function deployment that we should define accountability through the Chart of Accounts. Regardless of how your organization deploys its strategy (your methodology), the framework will help you to capture the design that you have developed. This blueprint, as it were, can then be used to manage strategy execution.

One aspect of strategy-function deployment is to produce a linked Chart of Accounts from outcomes to capabilities. This is important because what is measured at the outcome tier is different from what is measured at the process function capability tier. A shareholder might measure profit, but to the person attaching the wheels to the car, profit has no meaning in relation to her work. We can communicate as much as we want the necessity of customer service and profitability to this person, but she can never connect customer service to the attachment of the wheel. On the other hand, we can define how much effort it should take to properly attach a wheel and how much cost should be related to the task. Connecting customer service (value

CoA measure) to cost of attaching the wheel (Capability CoA) is part of strategy-function deployment.

But there is quite a distance between the intent of an organization and functional process execution. We need a stepwise systematic framework for connecting intent to execution. Producing a great strategy and then failing to execute to the strategy will not produce success. And so we must be able to take the strategy and deploy it across the functional silos and across personal interests. This has been and remains one of the most challenging management tasks. Deploying a strategy requires more than good communication. It requires hard work, discipline, and total engagement. And it requires a strong framework.

In the movie *Batman Begins*, Bruce Wayne is speaking to Rachel and he says something to the effect of "inside I am a different man." Rachel's response is something to the effect of "It is our actions that define who we are—not our intentions." In the end, intentions are just mitigating circumstances. And so it is for an organization. It is not simply the strategy that determines the success of an organization. In the end, it is the actions (execution) that determine the results. In order to achieve the strategy we must have a systematic, transparent, measurable, and verifiable way to deploy the strategy that engages all levels and all silos in the organization. That's what strategy-function deployment is about.

Stop trying to *tie* current execution to strategy.
Execution must *flow* from the strategy.

Let's explore the elements of the framework, from intent to execution, by walking through each tier as depicted in the diagram.

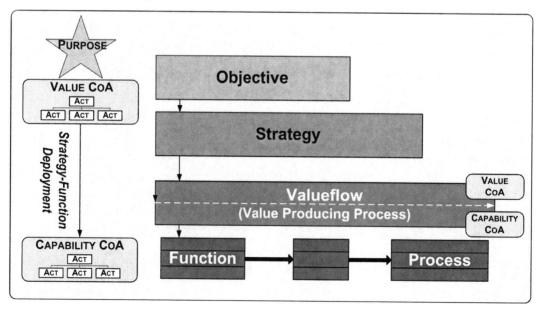

1. **Purpose**: At the top we have the purpose. It describes in broad terms the reason for the organization's existence. But purpose is directional. It rarely represents a specific end point, but rather a kind of North Star. It is a destination towards which we move but never expect to reach.

2. **Objectives**: Purpose needs to be translated into specific business objectives. An objective represents a specific destination or target that can be reached by a certain time. We interpret the purpose into measurable objectives that we will then attempt to achieve. Each objective would have one or more value accounts that can be measured and managed.

3. **Strategies**: But how will we achieve the objective? There may be many options, each with its own risks and required capabilities. An organization will need to choose among the alternatives. A strategy always involves choices. And, usually, the choices are relatively polar (far apart). What that means is that choosing one path means abandoning the others. Typically, it is difficult to switch from one strategy to another without significant penalty. An objective might require more than one strategy in order to achieve it. When we move from the objective tier to the strategy tier, we need to propagate the value accounts down to each strategy. So, if we think of an objective as a specific destination, then a strategy is a specific choice of paths. The strategy represents the path chosen from among the many available.

4. **Valueflows**: Objectives and Strategies have Value Accounts related to intended outcomes. But value is delivered through cross-functional (start-to-end or demand-to-fulfillment) value-delivering processes related to execution. So we need to begin making the link between intent and execution. A particular strategy will require one or more of these value-producing processes to perform in a certain way. But valueflows are not visible. They don't show up on the organization chart. So there is an entire tier that for most organizations remains unmanaged. Trying to go directly from strategy to functional processes is too large a jump to make. But that's exactly what happens in most organizations. The key distinguishing factor of a valueflow is that it will have both Value Accounts to link it to the strategy as well as Capability Accounts linking it to functional processes. And so the valueflow is truly the missing link between strategy and execution.

5. **Functional Processes**: Finally, the performance requirement for each valueflow must be translated into a specification for each functional process that makes it up. Actions are executed within the functional processes.

In order to progress from purpose to strategy and down to executable actions at the functional process level, we need to engage people using a common, systematic, and stepwise approach. We need to be able to verify, at each step, that we are true to purpose and to strategy.

We also need to build the mechanisms that will allow us to verify our decisions, manage the strategy, and adapt and adjust during execution.

At each tier we engage additional people. At each tier we must translate the requirements of that tier into terms that make sense for the next tier. In the top two tiers (objectives and strategy), the dialogue is around achievement. In the bottom two (valueflows, functions), the dialogue centres on actions and performance. Although it sounds simple, it remains difficult. Why is this? Among the many reasons, let's explore two:

1. Without the concept of the cross-functional valueflow, there is too big a leap required to go from strategy all the way to functional processes.
2. We often try to translate the entire strategy into functional process design. This is the same as the sequence problem presented earlier. When we try to take the whole strategy, we are trying to solve many problems all at once. And this exponentially increases the complexity.

To improve on the current process, therefore, we need to add the valueflow tier and reduce the leap. But we also need to simplify the problem by breaking it up into many smaller, more manageable, more understandable problems.

What we will do is create a deployment map in the form of a tree as depicted in the diagram.

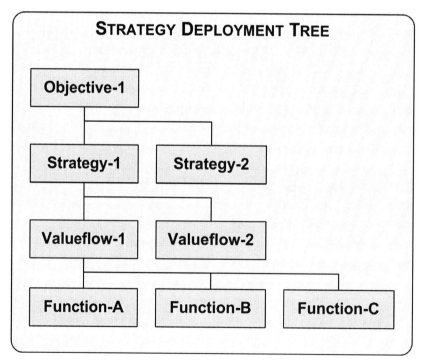

At the root of each deployment map is the business objective. Beginning with a single objective, we then determine the strategy or strategies we will adopt or have adopted in order to achieve that objective. Then, for each strategy within the objective, we determine which cross-functional valueflows contribute to achieving that strategy. Next, for each valueflow, we identify the functional processes that make it up. If we do that for every strategy and valueflow within a given objective, then we will produce a complete strategy deployment tree. But we aren't finished yet.

At each tier we will have alternatives from which to choose. So how do we select one alternative over another? To choose, we need to set performance standards at each level. Then we can use these to pick among alternatives and to verify achievement. There will be alternatives that may produce a desired output but won't achieve the desired performance. So we would rule these out.

STRATEGY-EXECUTION GAP

The strategy-function deployment framework defines the relationship among objectives, strategies, valueflow processes, and functional processes. And even though there is an implication that we should proceed from intent (purpose) towards execution (functional processes), every organization has its own approach and methodology. So what that means is that a good and useful framework can be populated in any order for an existing strategic plan.

But why do so many organizations end up with what is often referred to as the strategy-execution gap? There is a different dialogue happening at the strategy level versus what is happening at the functional levels. And so it shouldn't be surprising that the strategic intent doesn't always get properly translated into the correct functional actions. First of all, the inhabitants at the functional level (job holders) are already busy trying to keep up with their day-to-day work and challenges. So they are highly incented to make as few changes as possible because changes take time. That means that there is a bias towards interpreting the strategy in a way that is favourable to their current implementation. In other words, they will try to maintain the status quo—inertia. This is not malicious. It is simply a way to cope with task saturation. Task saturation means people are completely busy and, in order to avoid task overload, they will attempt to limit any additional effort.

In addition, the understanding gap between "achieving" and "executing" is huge. There is a lot of detail at the functional level that is simply not known or understood at the strategy level. And the people at the functional level may not fully understand the implications of the strategy for them and their unit. But functional processes aren't perfect. And it is the functional imperfections and problems that give functional units the headaches. Of course they will try to get rid of these problems through functional level changes. So the functional folks often try to sell or rationalize to the strategy folks the changes they want by framing their need as if it were a strategy need. After all, it can be difficult to evaluate whether what the functional folks are saying will deliver to the strategy. And so we make changes and then wait to see if those changes produce the right results. And that's why strategies are often the same from one year to the next—because either nothing was changed or what was changed didn't have the desired impact. The problem is that the process we use to justify our actions is usually the "rationalize" process and this process is often based on "**rational ….. LIES**." Yes, it does sound the same, but the latter is a more accurate representation of what actually takes place. And what do we mean by LIES? It is an acronym that stands for:

Looking
Intently for
Evidence to
Support.

Plans often include many LIES-based arguments, which present facts and statistics selectively to support an argument. Bottom-up reasoning virtually always follows this approach. The strategy-function deployment process works from purpose towards function, from intent towards execution, in order to avoid this significant and ever-present risk. In an organization, each of us is trying to convince others to do what we want to do. But in order to do what we want to do, we have to get someone else to decide to let us do it. This usually implies convincing someone to give us resources. And everyone in an organization is competing for these resources. That's why decision making is important in an organization. When there is no visible framework, people create their own. And of course they will architect a framework that will make it easier for them to convince us that the decision they have already made is a good one. In effect everyone in an organization is a *decision architect*. We are constantly organizing facts and assumptions not so much to allow management to reach the right decisions, but rather to nudge them over to our decision. When functional needs drive an organization's changes, a strategy-execution gap develops. The framework is designed to reduce the risks posed when people become decision architects. By following the connections from business objective down to functional processes, it allows us to see if the strategy is truly served. It allows us to see how the accounts are linked and to verify that each account measure has properly assigned accountability.

Let's return to the analogy of trying to get a customer from point A to point B, from the previous chapter. When management says we need to be faster, they mean the overall valueflow process needs to be faster. We need to get the customer from A to B faster. But the function folks don't see the whole process. So they can only understand in terms that make sense inside their function. They take it to mean that they must go faster. But since they are already operating at top speed, the only thing they can come up with is faster technology or more people or to blame someone else, like the customer, for presenting roadblocks. Both groups may be using the same words but a different language with different meanings. That's what leads to the strategy-execution gap. What currently happens inside that gap to translate strategy to execution is often nebulous. We need to make it transparent.

The strategy-execution gap is the place where strategic intent is translated directly into functional requirements. The gap is large, nebulous, and does not directly connect the two. What happens inside that gap is not well defined, transparent, or traceable. It is a source of much miscommunication. We need to be able to translate what we want to achieve into functional changes that we can make and be able to link those changes directly to the expected strategic impacts. That will give us traceability, which will allow us to understand results. But because there is such a large communication gap between strategy and functional execution, we need something to fill the strategy-execution gap. We need something that is equivalent to the trip in the example, or the outfit in the closet example. So what is that equivalent?

It is the **valueflow** process construct. The valueflow process is the equivalent of the start-to-end trip. At the functional level, it's all about the components. At the valueflow level, it's all about performance and the flow of stakeholder value through the system.

It is at the valueflow process level that we can begin translating the strategy into required changes. The systematic translation of objectives to strategy to valueflow performance and then to functional requirements followed by implementation is strategy-function deployment.

THE RELATIONAL PROCESS MODEL—A FRAMEWORK

A methodology should change, evolve, and progress at a rapid rate as we learn more. A framework should also evolve and progress, but at a slower rate. What's the difference between a methodology and a framework?

A framework is a blueprint model. It is used to represent the final output of the methodology, the design. The methodology, on the other hand, defines the actions required to develop the design. Of course, that means that a single framework can serve different methodology approaches. Our relational framework is *normalized* to ensure that all blueprints are divided in the same way and that all components are related in a defined manner. Normalization is a process of taking a design and separating components. Normalization was introduced in the field of database design by E. F. Codd and initially there were three normal forms. The result, of course, was the relational database. Essentially, normalization produced a data model, which was implementation independent.

The goal of the Relational Process Model is similar. We want to develop process models that are implementation independent, leaving implementation decisions to the last possible moment. Today, when processes are designed, implementation decisions are made at every step. Of course the problem is that with each implementation decision, we limit future implementation choices. One incorrect decision at the beginning can throw off the entire design. In addition, it becomes difficult to explore alternative implementation choices.

The **Relational Process Model** (RPM) is produced as part of strategy-function deployment. It is used to develop a normalized model for a valueflow. The model separates the true requirements from implementation choices and from personal preferences. So let's summarize the major *normal forms* (NF) of the RPM here. Later we will explore each in greater detail. To start, we will define the four normal forms of the Relational Process Model and introduce each briefly.

First Normal Form (1st NF)—Valueflow: A blueprint is in *first normal form* if it specifies a valueflow separated from other valueflows. We have introduced valueflows as being cross-functional value-centric processes. When all valueflows have been separated, we have the possibility of accounting for and measuring where value is coming from.

Second Normal Form (2nd NF)—Three Tiers: A process can be described from three different perspectives or tiers. The first tier is the Outcome Tier. This defines the intended outcome of the process in measurable value terms by stakeholder. Every process produces a primary output. An output can be evaluated for quality relative to a standard. The output tier is just below the outcome tier. Outputs describe an end state. The third tier is the task tier. Tasks describe the actions required to produce the output. As we progress from outcome to output to tasks, the blueprint becomes denser with more and different information. A blueprint is in *second normal form* if it is in first normal form and if the valueflow is separated into the three tiers.

Third Normal Form (3rd NF)—Three Streams: The work of a process can be segmented based on its purpose. There is the core work required to produce the output of the process from the inputs or raw materials; this is the transform stream. There is the work required to handle failures resulting from risks or capability weaknesses; this is the failure stream. And there is the work intended to prevent quality, risk, and optimization failures; this is the control stream. A blueprint is in *third normal form* if it is in second normal form and if the valueflow is segmented into the three streams.

Fourth Normal Form (4th NF)—Base Components: A process represents a real capability for producing some output. But the process has to be designed based on component parts. The major component parts of a process are input, output, method, people skills, technology function, and mental mindset. A blueprint is in *fourth normal form* if it is in third normal form and if each process is specified down to its base process components.

Process normalization produces true normalized requirements. They explicitly separate true requirements from implementation choices. They also clearly separate personal choices from what is really needed to achieve the outcomes. Normalization increases the likelihood that different people will arrive at the same correct model for a given scope. Normalization links task functionality to outputs and to outcome values, for a higher level of traceability. Normalization, with its systematic structure, permits massive parallelism in developing the requirements and blueprints. This can result in a significant, even enormous, reduction in the time it takes to deliver projects. A normalized model can greatly improve the success of any BPM (business process management) implementation as well.

Normalization leads to an implementation-independent model. Of course, we may have to change that model or denormalize it to achieve certain performance goals. But we should only denormalize when necessary.

Subsequent chapters will explore each normal form in greater detail.

SUMMARY

Strategy is about options and choices. If an organization is to have any chance at succeeding it must see the right options and make the right choices. That's what strategy development is about. And that's a key function of the senior management in any organization. But how do you get the rest of the organization to align and organize to the strategy? How do you get the operational body to heed and follow the strategic plan? That's strategy deployment and in some ways deploying the strategy is much more difficult and complex than developing it in the first place.

First of all, a strategy cannot be executed. A strategy represents intent and is not at the right level of detail to be executed. Many organizations *communicate* their strategy or intent with the hope that execution will follow automatically. But it doesn't. Developing the strategy into an operational blueprint is what's required. And that's what the framework helps us to specify. We cannot leave execution to chance. It has to be planned and it has to flow from the strategy.

All too often, organizations attempt to make the leap from strategy to functional processes. Because the gap between these two is so large, we introduced the concept of a valueflow as a tier between strategy and functional process. The valueflow allows us to produce a normalized process model—a model that separates requirements from implementation decisions. The valueflow represents the first normal form of a process. It brings together the value and cost components of a process so that we can see the net contribution of any process to stakeholder value. The second normal form of a process allows us to see a process from the three perspectives. Unlike traditional process models, which look primarily at tasks, the second normal form segments each process into three tiers: outcomes, outputs, and tasks. The third normal process segments a process according to the work being carried out. There is the core work of transforming raw material or work-in-process to produce the product—transform work. There is the work required to handle process failures and realized risks—failure work. And there is the work required to detect or prevent failures—control work. The ability to take a process and segment it into normal forms allows us to see how each component of a process contributes to a particular performance measure. This allows us to improve the designs and develop more perfect processes.

Strategy-function deployment gets us from objective to strategy to valueflow and to functional processes. The Relational Process Model produces a normalized valueflow blueprint.

Together, they comprise a systematic approach to developing the operational blueprint required to ensure correct execution. Together, they provide a stepwise process that ensures high quality designs, which help to improve execution and reduce the strategy-execution gap.

5

THE VALUEFLOW—MAKING VALUE VISIBLE (1ST NF)

If you can't translate strategic intent into functional requirements and maintain the link between the two, then you can't successfully deploy your strategy.

A strategy is about delivering specific outcomes to stakeholders. A functional process is about executing to produce an output. At the strategy level we measure value delivered. At the functional process level we measure capacity and ability to execute, i.e., execution capability. Value does not translate automatically into capability. So the gap between value thinking at the strategy level and capability thinking at the functional process level is large, often huge. Trying to jump from strategy to functional process is a leap that too often leads to poor execution and failure.

We need to turn the leap into a series of systematic steps. We need a tier between strategy and function. That tier should allow us to attach value measures to the strategy above and capability measures to the function processes below. It should help us to link and to align both the functional processes and the people to execute to the strategy. It should also allow us to generate accountability requirements.

The valueflow construct is that link. It is the first normal form in the process framework. The valueflow integrates the appropriate functional processes into a unit for which we can measure value and associate costs. Why is that important? Let's look at an example.

EXAMPLE: PIZZA SHOP—CONTEXT FOR OPTIMIZATION

Imagine you walk into a pizza shop. In front of you is a counter with a cash register and someone who takes your order. Behind the counter is a wall with a slit in it big enough to pass a pizza through. You can't see what's going on behind it. You place an order (demand) for a medium pizza with ham, olives, and onions. Ten minutes later your pizza arrives through the slit. You pay $12 and leave. That marks the end of the valueflow. Let's call it the Take-Out Pizza Customer Valueflow. Placing the order (demand) was the beginning of the valueflow. So the valueflow begins with the demand (order) and ends with the fulfillment of the order (receiving your pizza) and payment.

When you pay the $12, you are participating in a value exchange with the pizza shop. You measure value in terms of eating the pizza. The pizza shop probably measures value in terms of the revenue it earns and the profit it generates. Maximizing the value delivered for the participating stakeholders is a function of design. And design is about satisfying and optimizing. And both of these are about making choices. And choices require context. In a functionally organized enterprise, there is always the risk that a functional-level choice will lead to less value delivered overall (such as picking a beautiful green tie that was on sale for your blue suit). The valueflow construct provides a context within which functional choices can be made such that maximum value is delivered.

But why is it that functional-level improvements quite often don't lead to improvements higher up? If value and cost always happened together, then we could always be sure that a functional improvement would also lead to an improvement for the organization. But this is not the case.

Let's go a little deeper into the pizza example to see what we mean by this.

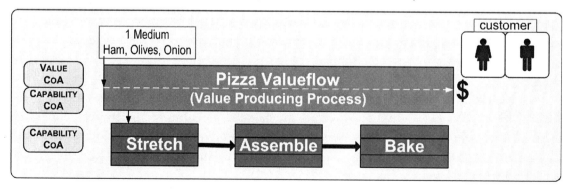

As the diagram illustrates, we have three functional processes:
- **Stretch**: This stretches the dough into the required shape and size and places it on the pizza screen.
- **Assemble**: This puts the sauce, cheese, and toppings on.
- **Bake**: This bakes the pizza to the desired doneness.

But where is value delivered and where is cost incurred? Let's look at things from the customer's point of view. The customer pays us only at the end, but is this where value is produced? Value is what's delivered to the external stakeholder. So let's do a mental exercise. Imagine that at the end of the Stretch functional process, we were to offer the product, in its current form, to the customer at a significantly reduced rate. Suppose we asked the customer, "How much would you pay for just the stretched dough?" Although it is possible that we might get an offer, we would expect that most customers would offer nothing. In other words, to most customers there would be no value in the stretched dough. Now suppose we did the same thing at the end of the Assemble process. Again, we are likely to get a response of "no thank you." In other words, the product in its current state still has *no value to the customer*. Suppose we make the offer one more time halfway through the Bake process. Again we are likely to get a negative response. The customer is unlikely to want a half-baked product, so to speak. So again, it has no value. Finally, the pizza comes out of the oven fully baked. Now it has a value of $12, which the customer gladly pays.

Even though to most methodologies stretching, assembling, and baking would be considered value-added tasks, no value can be assigned to the product until the customer is willing to pay for the product. What this means is that we can't imply or compute a true value associated with any particular functional process. Value happens suddenly (quantum). Value is a step function.

But what about the costs? Every step of the process will incur costs. So we can associate a cost with each functional process and each step of the process. So what if a functional process makes a change that reduces the cost for it. Should it make that change? From a functional perspective, the answer would be yes. But from an organization's perspective, the answer would be "it depends." And the thing that it depends on is the impact it would have on the valueflow as a whole. The thing about functional processes is that they only make sense within the context of delivering the end value. And so a functional process change always has to be evaluated inside some larger context. And that context is the valueflow. Again, the reason is that the value happens in discrete steps while costs are incurred continuously. And value is always about net value, which takes into account the final value and the costs incurred.

The diagram below plots value and cost at the end of each of the three functional processes. The value at the end of the Stretch step is $0. The value at the end of the Assemble step is $0. The value at the end of the Bake step is $12. So value, as represented by the triangles, is [$0, $0, $12].

Now let's look at the cumulative costs. The cost at the end of the Stretch step is $3. The cost at the end of the Assemble step is $7. The cost at the end of the Bake step is $10. So the cumulative costs, as represented by the circles, are approximately [$3, $7, $10]. Cost is a continuous function while value is a step function.

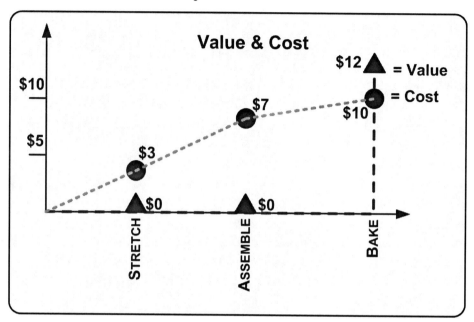

What a valueflow does is collect those functional processes that are *necessary* to the production of the value so that they can be designed and managed as a whole, because only as a whole do they create value. The diagram shows that value can only be attributed at the end of the Bake process. However, it does not mean that the value is created only by the Bake process. In order to determine that, we have to ask the following question for each process and each task within the process: "Is this necessary in order to produce the final value?" This is a better question than "What value does this process or task add?" Why is it a better question? Because individual processes don't add specific measurable value. They do, however, incur specific measurable costs. The valueflow construct groups under one umbrella all the functions that are necessary in order to produce the value. That way they can be managed as a whole. So we can treat a valueflow as a miniature business.

The valueflow construct can be used to evaluate the impact of local functional process changes against the valueflow's Chart of Accounts. If the valueflow CoA improves, then the change is desirable. If the CoA gets worse, then we don't want the change, no matter how good it may seem at the local level. If the green tie, no matter how attractive it may be, makes us look worse in the blue suit outfit, then we should not put on that tie. By providing the valueflow CoA to each functional process, we provide a standard against which we can evaluate any proposed changes. We can detect when a change that seems beneficial at a functional process level doesn't contribute to the valueflow performance. The valueflow provides the context within which we can make choices that are good for the functional process **AND** good for the organization. In other words, every functional choice must *simultaneously satisfy* multiple requirements, not just the functional requirement.

Just because we have incurred 70% of the cost by the end of the Assemble process doesn't mean we have created $8.40 of value (70% * $12 = $8.40). So if we ask how much value has been created so far, there is no meaningful or useful answer to that question. So don't ask it. Instead ask:

Is this necessary to produce the value?

If the answer is "yes", then ask: "Is there some better way to produce the value that results in more value for all?" Another way to look at a valueflow construct is to view the end as the place where the value is recognized by the customer and cost is at its maximum. The beginning is where the customer makes a request and where the value is zero and cost is at its minimum.

Costs and value are not co-located in the functional process. They are co-located in the valueflow. So the valueflow gives us several things:

- It has value accounts associated with it.
- It has capability associated with it through execution of its functional processes.
- It allows us to see the net result of a change in one process impacting other processes.

Since value ties to strategy and capability ties to functional process, we can connect strategy to functional process execution. A valueflow allows us to collect everything related to producing the value under one roof. That way we can evaluate what the net value is and whether it is worth the cost. Of course, each stakeholder will have a different equation for value measurement. If any of the stakeholders concludes that their net value is too low, then the risk is that they will pull out of the transaction. Of course, if the customer pulls out of the transaction, then this will eventually impact all other stakeholder values.

The importance of the valueflow is in its ability to associate both value and costs inside a persistent frame. If we change the entire way that we make the pizza, we can still determine if the new valueflow design represents progress or not. On the other hand, if we change just one of the functional processes and measure the before and after functional performance, without measuring the entire valueflow, then we might end up improving a function while doing the reverse to the valueflow.

This happens all the time in organizations. Someone improves their function, but the overall valueflow becomes worse. And if there is no one accountable for the valueflow, then it goes unnoticed until some aspect of performance has deteriorated so much that it finally becomes visible.

Let's slow down and do a little mental exercise. Take a few seconds to draw a line on the chart below that depicts the direction of desirable or increasing performance.

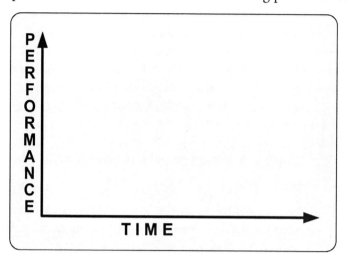

What does it look like? Does it go up or down? Remember that we specified "desirable performance."

-
-
-
-
-
-

Does it look a bit like the one below?

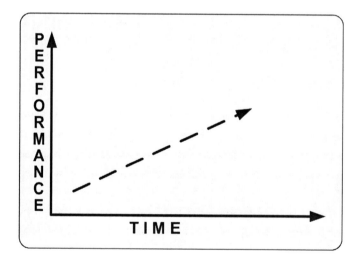

What do you notice about the chart? Did you notice that better performance requires an uphill climb? But deteriorating performance only requires a downhill slide. This is true for everything. But on top of that there is also the following observed principle:

People *will* freely make a local improvement change, even though it may have a negative impact elsewhere. But people *will not* freely make a local change that will have a negative local impact, even though it may lead to a much larger improvement elsewhere.

The consequence of functional bias is that an organization will have a tendency to get worse over time. If this bias is not countered, then organizations will continuously cycle from strong processes immediately following a redesign to inefficient processes as we get further from the redesign point. We can look at this as value leakage. We leak more and more value as time goes on. This is a source of both tremendous waste and great opportunity. If we can reduce or prevent this value leakage, then we get to keep the value that would otherwise have leaked. This would also prevent organizations from taking one step forward and two steps back. Organizations could confidently move forward or maintain the course, avoiding backsliding.

A local change might seem like an improvement. Imagine a local change that costs $100 and has a local return of $200. This seems like good value. But what if somewhere else in the system it causes a $200 loss? From a local perspective it looks fine. But from a system perspective we are spending $100 to get a local return of $200 and a loss somewhere else of $200. So the net result from the organization's point of view is that it is costing $300 to get back $200. Imagine if all functions behaved this way. Actually, they do. The framework through the Chart of Accounts and normalized processes allows us to make sure that a change at one tier (functional) is also evaluated at the next tier up (valueflow) so that we avoid this situation. A valueflow allows us to optimize functional processes across functional boundaries using the valueflow as context.

We can use the valueflow process to translate strategic intent into required function resources and actions. And we can do so in a way that effectively links the two in a manageable way. Let's begin with a general definition and then review some more examples to get a better feeling for what a valueflow is and how to begin to identify and see them.

TYPES OF VALUEFLOWS

Given the importance of the valueflow construct, it is important to understand how to identify a valueflow. Instead of a long technical definition, let's summarize the major characteristics of a valueflow.

1. It is made up of a chain of functional processes. So it is *cross-functional*.
2. It produces a specific and identifiable *output* that has a specification, so we can evaluate output quality.
3. The output goes either to an external *customer* or to another internal *valueflow*.

4. The output contributes to achieving one or more stakeholder *outcomes*. The outcomes have measurable value.
5. The *value* is determined by the relevant stakeholders.
6. The valueflow will also have *capability* attributes which measure its internal strength.

So now we can give the lengthy technical definition. A ***valueflow*** comprises a chain of functional processes that produce, for a customer, an output that is required to achieve or contribute to a stakeholder outcome of measurable value. The valueflow has a measurable level of capability performance.

A valueflow has both value performance as viewed from the outside and capability performance as viewed from the inside. This is why it can link a strategy, which is measured in terms of stakeholder value delivered, such as profit, to functional processes that have capability attributes, such as costs and capacity.

Every valueflow begins with a demand for its unique final output. Every valueflow ends when that output has been completed or delivered. There are two fundamental types of valueflows based on who or what is consuming that final and defining output. The distinction between the two is critical to measuring value.

1. **Customer Valueflow**: This is a chain of functional processes that begins with a demand and ends with the fulfillment of that demand. It responds to a customer request to produce an output (product or service) that the external customer wants and would be willing to pay for. An example might be a Car Loan valueflow for a bank. The process produces a Car Loan for a customer, which the customer is willing to repay with interest. Another example might be a Hernia Operation valueflow. It is delivered to a consumer or customer who would be willing to pay for it and is a response to an external customer demand. These are the valueflows that generate the primary and directly measurable value.

2. **Enabling Valueflow**: But an organization has many other processes that don't deliver anything directly to a customer. Nevertheless, no organization can do without these supporting processes. An enabling valueflow also begins with a demand. It also produces an output. But it is not a customer that needs to be willing to pay for it. It is the organization through one of its managers that must be willing to pay for it. An enabling valueflow delivers an output that will become a *component* part of another valueflow. The output is produced in order to close an actual or potential process performance gap. Imagine we have the bank Car Loan valueflow. An example of an enabling valueflow might be a Software Development process that produces software to be used by the Car Loan valueflow to improve how it produces the

Car Loan. The output—software—is a component that is used by another process. The purpose of enabling valueflows is to increase stakeholder value by improving another valueflow. We can't directly measure the value produced by an instance of an enabling valueflow. What we have to do is measure the change in value (value delta) in the valueflow that receives the output. So if the Software Development process produces software that is then used inside the Car Loan valueflow, we will have to measure the change in value produced by the Car Loan valueflow. The change delta for the Car Loan valueflow represents the value that can be attributed to the product of the enabling valueflow. That implies that for an enabling valueflow, it is crucial to establish what impact its output will have on the receiving valueflow before proceeding. If the output is unlikely to produce a change in the receiving valueflow, then no matter how well the enabling valueflow is executed, no value will be produced. People whose work is inside an enabling valueflow need to understand that their success will be partially at the mercy of others. So they need to ensure that accountability for the impact of their outputs rests in the right place, and that usually means someone outside the enabling process.

All valueflows deliver something of potential value to some stakeholder—hence the name. Each should be triggered by a demand that is outside of the valueflow. For a customer valueflow, it is the customer who generates the demand. For an enabling valueflow, it should be management that generates the demand based on performance gaps. Of course, if we don't detect a performance gap, or if we don't have a performance management framework, or if there is no clear accountability for performance, then there may not be much demand.

We would expect an organization to have at least one Customer valueflow regardless of whether that organization is for profit or not-for-profit. It is the Customer valueflows that reflect the product strategy of the organization—how they have decided to achieve their customer purpose. Different organizations may have similar purposes yet choose different strategies, and hence different products, to offer to their customers. For example, a gym and a manufacturer of exercise equipment may share a common vision and purpose in terms of improving the health of their customers. But they each take a different road with different products to achieve that customer-oriented purpose.

Whereas the output of a Customer valueflow process goes to a customer or consumer, the output of an Enabling valueflow would go to some other process that is part of a valueflow. Therefore, the output of an Enabling valueflow is not seen directly by a customer. This will be further explored later in this chapter. In order for any organization to excel, it must excel at both its Customer and Enabling valueflows. It is not a question of which is more important, but rather where attention would lead to greater value.

VALUEFLOW VARIANTS AND VARIATION

Imagine you are starting a new business. You have a single product. There are no variations. You know how to perform all the three major functional operations required and it's a simple cash business that doesn't require any accounting beyond the cash you have at the end of every transaction. You are able to handle all the demand by yourself. The total capacity needed and available is you and your time. Customers come to you and you don't need to advertise. So basically, a customer arrives asking for one or more of your products (demand). You perform all the steps required to make it, hand it over, and collect the cash—a simple business indeed. What we have just described is a simple customer valueflow. A customer valueflow is like a little business inside a bigger business. In this case it's the whole business. So it's easy to determine how you're doing at any time.

Now suppose that demand goes up and so you hire a second person. The two of you both handle the valueflow start-to-end, performing all operations. You've simply cloned the valueflow, so to speak. But then the business grows bigger still and you hire another person, so that now you are three. Coincidentally there are three major functions in your valueflow. And you're finding that not everyone is as talented as you are. Some are better at one function than another. So you reorganize by function, putting one person in charge of each function. Now you have three functions and three people, one person per function. You're probably thinking that this will be easier to work with because now you can hire for specific skills.

In this scenario, you might have gained functional proficiency. But you've also lost something. You and your first hire had a sense of the business because you each handled the transaction start-to-end, but now your functional people have lost that sense of wholeness. When you had one person performing all the functions in the valueflow, that person would not make a change to one function that hurt him in another. But since everyone is now only performing one function, you're beginning to run into the issue of one functional person creating an externality (negative impact) for another. In addition, you can't hire in increments of one person anymore. You will likely have to hire in increments of one person per function or three people.

The years pass. You're doing well and you add two other similar products, so that now you make *three similar products*. But each time you add a product, each function has to be modified to accommodate the new product. So now you have three variations of each function. But you are also selling much more, so that now you have five people working in each function. And of course, everyone performs each function a little differently. So you have functional variation due to the product and you have functional variation due to personal preferences. As you can imagine, complexity begins to rise quite sharply.

Many businesses and organizations have evolved in exactly this way. Each new product (good or service) introduces product functional variation. This is essential variation caused by real differences in delivering the product. In addition, each employee might also introduce preference functional variation. This is not essential. It's just different people doing the same thing in different ways based on their personal preferences. But that's not the end of it. People don't generally record exactly how they process a particular transaction. And since few people have perfect memories, they might process the exact same transaction a little differently from one time to another. We'll call this incidental functional variation. But even that isn't all. There are always options for implementation. And so, there can be implementation functional variation.

Eventually your process performance degrades and so you decide you need to take a hard look and perhaps re-engineer your processes. Of course, you have been told the importance of understanding your start-to-end process, not just each functional process. This is a typical situation organizations have to address. So you organize a "team" of subject matter experts, process engineers, and business analysts. But when the team tries to understand what's going on through the organization function lens, they are confronted with all the variations simultaneously:

1. *product* variation
2. *preference* variation
3. *incidental* variation, and
4. *implementation* variation.

The resulting complexity can be both overwhelming and divisive, especially as people tend to defend their personal variation, even if they don't know exactly why they have adopted a particular approach. In fact, people will even defend personal variation that has been handed down to them from previous job holders. So they are defending someone else's preference, someone who may not even be working there anymore. How much sense does that make? Well, it actually does makes sense because even though it may not have been our choice, we have nevertheless invested time and energy into becoming really good at executing that particular preference.

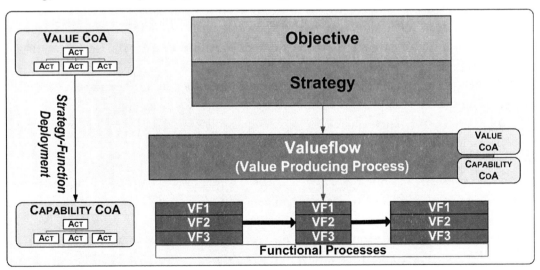

The business we have described is depicted in the diagram above. It shows the three functions and also shows that each function handles three valueflow variants (VF1, VF2, VF3) due to product differences. Since the three valueflows are similar, we show them as belonging to one valueflow group. When we try to understand processes cross-functionally, what often happens is that we try to understand all variations of each function in sequence. Then we try to connect that knowledge so that it makes sense. We try to understand all variations of the first function (three), then all variations of the second function (three), and then all variations of the third function (three). Then we try to piece it all together. So complete understanding doesn't take place until all individual functions are understood and we have been able to integrate them all together. This is what leads to the waterfall effect, where closure happens all at once, at the end.

Let's look at why this adds complexity to understanding. Essentially we have three functions with three variations each. If we think in terms of a kit, we have nine pieces (3 variations for 3 functions) which we can use to make the whole valueflow. The total number of combinations that the mind has to deal with is 3*3*3 = 27. There are 27 different combinations for the functions to be put together to make a valueflow. But there are actually only three different valueflows. And these are just the product function variations. That means there are 24 invalid combinations. This leads to errors and misunderstandings. Imagine adding personal variation on top of that and you can see why traditional process mapping can be an expensive, exhausting, and risky exercise.

When defining requirements for cross-functional processes, the requirements are often gathered serially by function. That is, we capture the current requirements of one function, then the next, then the next, and we try to piece it all together at the end. Basically, we lump a series of related functions and treat them as a whole. This is enormously complex because it leads to more potential valueflows than really exist. In addition, in order to identify the real valueflows, we also have to eliminate the false valueflows. Collecting requirements serially by function also leads to waterfall effects, where knowledge happens at the end of long segments, because only then do we have all the pieces we need to fully construct the understanding of a single valueflow.

The valueflow concept coupled with a normalized model can cut through all that complexity by segmenting the effort into meaningful well-defined chunks, by valueflow.

In the example, we stated that there were three similar products. A valueflow produces a specific, not a generic, output. And so, since we have three products, we can define three separate valueflows—one for each product. Of course each valueflow goes through the three functions. But we don't consider it as one valueflow. It is three valueflows. In capturing requirements by valueflow, we would select one of those valueflows and we would extract from each function only those operations required to produce the specific output of that valueflow. We would tell the entire team that we want to block out everything except what applies to the selected valueflow. By focusing on a single valueflow for a single product, we can cleanly capture a simpler set of requirements. Now, rather than identifying a larger team for the three functions, incorporating enough people to cover all three valueflows, we can form the team most suited for each valueflow by function. And because we will be producing a normalized process model, which is free of personal preferences, we don't need to load up the team. We would complete one whole valueflow before proceeding to the next. This significantly reduces the complexity related to understanding and gathering requirements. By gathering requirements one valueflow at a time, we remove much of the complexity.

Having understood one valueflow and developed its blueprint, we can move on to the next valueflow. In practice, the second and subsequent valueflows become much easier to understand because we already have a model blueprint from the first. We might even consider having three separate subject matter expert teams, one for each valueflow. We could have the first team present the requirements of the first valueflow to the second team before the second team tackles the second valueflow. This would serve to verify the blueprint produced by the first team. In addition, it would provide the second team with a verified framework as a starting point. We could repeat this and have the second valueflow team present to the third valueflow team. When the third valueflow is complete, we could have the first team validate it. That way we have one team producing a valueflow and a second team validating it. Of course, this only works if the valueflow specification doesn't contain personal preference variation. Fortunately, the normalized process model will remove preference function variation. We aren't suggesting that this should be your methodology, only that defining requirements by valueflow using the Relational Process Model will provide more options for team structure.

By tackling one valueflow at a time, we are also able to validate and approve the valueflows one at a time, rather than in a batch at the end, and we don't need as many people in the requirements process. That's where the normalized framework will come in handy. By producing a normalized model, which is implementation independent and personal preference independent, we are able to validate and approve each valueflow in an incremental manner. We eliminate the dreaded waterfall effect. We can even have separate teams working in parallel to each other to produce normalized models for independent valueflows, thereby potentially achieving massive parallelism in requirements discovery.

And how does the Capability Chart of Accounts fit into this picture? Well, the structure of the Chart of Accounts will likely be the same for each valueflow variant, but the content might be different. What we mean by structure is that each variant would have the same accounts. But each variant will have different targets and different measured values for each account.

EXAMPLE

A regulator for a particular jurisdiction in the health sector was responsible for registering health professionals. In order to practice in the jurisdiction, professionals had to apply and become registered to practice. Naturally, the regulator had a cross-functional registration process.

This process had been deteriorating for a number of years and the length of time required to complete a registration had grown over the years so that now many registrations took years to complete. Having been trained to think in terms of valueflows and a Relational Process Model, the regulator identified three separate valueflows. In this case, even though the end outputs, the registrations, were identical, they were each processed quite differently. The team identified three valueflows based on the source of the registrant. They identified Canadian, US, and International Registrations. When they reviewed the Chart of Accounts measures by valueflow, it was determined that it was the International Registrations that were the source of difficulty. Although the same things were being measured, the values were vastly different depending on the type of registration. So rather than trying to understand all variations of all functional processes, the team focused on International Registrations and redesigned it. A problem that had plagued them for years was more easily resolved after separating out each variant.

We can identify valueflows based on differences in the output. But we can also identify them by differences in the input, or the method used, or some other significant factor that impacts the Chart of Accounts. What the project allowed the team to realize is that each valueflow has to be first designed to be optimal by itself. Only then can we standardize, if it makes sense. The problem with standardizing functions as a whole is that we don't know how much value and performance we are giving up. But when we design one valueflow at a time and establish its best performance, we can then determine what performance is being given up through standardization.

We are not proposing that functional standardization is bad. We are simply bringing it back to its intended purpose. Standardization is about improving performance by removing unnecessary variation, especially preference variation. It is not about removing variation that is necessary due to product differences.

So, the question then is: out of the thousands of functional processes and thousands of cross-functional processes, how do we identify both customer and enabling processes in a consistent way? How do we do it so that different teams reach the same and correct conclusion every time? We need a method to help us do just that.

IDENTIFYING VALUEFLOW BOUNDARIES—CUSTOMER VALUEFLOW

Every organization has hundreds, thousands, or tens of thousands of functional processes. So how do we know where to draw the boundaries so that we can properly collect functional processes into valueflow processes? Identifying valueflows is like collecting individual dress components (tie, shirt, suit, shoes) into matching outfits and putting them together in a closet organizer by outfit, rather than by function. That way we can see what a whole outfit looks like. And if we are missing a component for an outfit, it will stand out. Let's look at customer valueflows first, since they are the easiest to identify.

1. **End**: Begin with a product, which can be a good, service, or combination. Identify the product and the customer to which it goes. The point at which the customer receives and pays for the product is the end of the valueflow. For now, let's assume there are no variants of the product.
2. **Start—Demand**: Next, identify the point at which we have an order for that product. That is the demand and it marks the start of the valueflow. That defines the boundaries for the valueflow. Everything between product demand and product delivery is part of the valueflow.
3. **Function Processes**: Then we can go inside and identify the functional processes that lie between the demand and the delivered product. That defines the scope of the valueflow.
4. **Chart of Accounts**: Lastly, we can attach a Chart of Accounts to the valueflow. And remember that a valueflow will contain both value accounts and capability accounts.

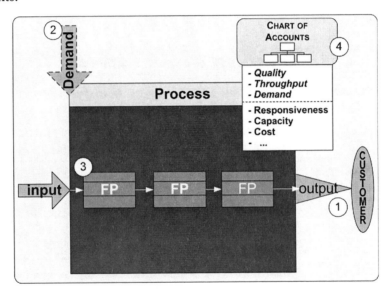

Let's summarize (refer to diagram):
1. **End**: Identify the product and its customer.
2. **Start**: Identify the demand.
3. **Functions**: Identify functional processes between demand and end.
4. **CoA**: Develop the Chart of Accounts.

An example of a customer valueflow might be a bank Car Loan valueflow. The product is a Car Loan, which goes to a customer. The valueflow begins when a customer requests a Car Loan. The functional processes that make up the valueflow might be:

- Car Loan Application Functional Process (FP)
- Credit Assessment FP
- Earnings Assessment FP
- Car Loan Assessment FP
- Car Loan Delivery FP (product delivery)
- Car Loan Repayment FP

And that's the customer valueflow.

IDENTIFYING VALUEFLOW BOUNDARIES—ENABLING VALUEFLOW

To understand enabling valueflows we have to understand the nature of the output of a process. The table below summarizes the types of outputs. For now we will focus on the first two. A customer valueflow can produce either of the first two. But an enabling valueflow produces a component type output.

Output	How it's used by receiving process
Transformed/Consumed input, raw material, work-in-process	This input is **used up** or **transformed** by the receiving process to make its output. E.g., flour for a cake, steel for a car, data for a decision, requirement for software…
Component input	This input becomes **part of** the receiving process. E.g., a mixer for a baking process, a robot for a welding process, an employee for a business process, software for a function.
Demand request	A demand is a request to produce an output. It is easily distinguished from the other two in that it will always contain a reference to or a specification of the desired output. This can take the form of a product description for a customer valueflow. Or it can describe a performance gap, in the case of an enabling valueflow.

When we examine the output of a process and we find that it is a component output, then we have the end of the enabling valueflow. Since an enabling valueflow should be initiated in response to a performance gap demand, we need to locate where the performance demand comes from. That's the beginning of the valueflow. As with a customer valueflow, we next identify the functional processes between the demand and the component output. The diagram below depicts an enabling valueflow process (on the left) producing a component output for a receiving process on the right.

Let's summarize (refer to diagram):

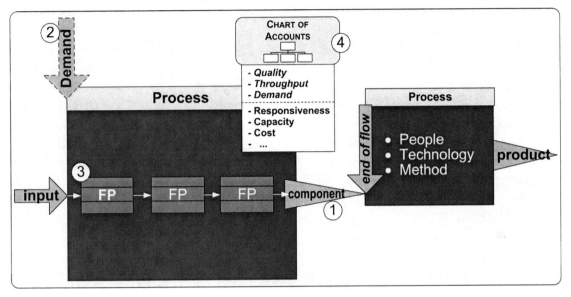

1. **End**: Identify the component output and the receiving process.
2. **Start**: Identify the performance gap demand.
3. **Functions**: Identify functional processes between demand and end.
4. **CoA**: Develop Chart of Accounts.

A software development process is an example of an enabling valueflow. It produces a software application system, which would be used as part of some other process. Perhaps it produces software for the previous bank Car Loan valueflow. The software becomes part of the customer valueflow. So the delivery of the software marks the end of the enabling valueflow. Next we need to identify the demand. An enabling valueflow should always be triggered by a gap in performance. That means that there would have been a performance gap as measured through the Chart of Accounts that was attached to the Car Loan valueflow. It is the performance gap that is the source of the demand for the enabling valueflow. But the demand must come from management. Then we identify the functional processes that make up the valueflow. A software development process might, for example, comprise the following major functions:

- Requirements Discovery
- Design
- Development

- Implementation

And, of course, we need to define a Chart of Accounts for the flow. But how would we measure value? This is where an enabling valueflow differs from a customer valueflow. We can measure value directly for a customer valueflow, but not for an enabling valueflow. Think about the intent of a software development process. Aren't we trying to improve the performance of some other process? Of course we are. So the only way to measure the actual value delivered is to measure the performance change in the receiving process. If the software is implemented and there is no performance change in the bank Car Loan valueflow, then we have invested but haven't received a return. It makes no difference if the software development valueflow was perfectly executed or not. This is where many organizations go astray. They might tie the failure to deliver value to the execution of the enabling valueflow, when the true problem is in the demand portion. If we think that software would boost productivity when the constraint is elsewhere, it won't matter what methodology we use to deliver the software.

When it comes to enabling valueflows, the first critical thing is to make sure that the product that is being requested has been verified to a high level of confidence to be what is needed to close the performance gap.

So a critical success factor in evaluating whether or not to execute an enabling valueflow is to determine the integrity of the demand. The demand should always be in the form of a performance gap whose closure has been quantified. What that means is that we know which performance accounts have a gap, how big the gap is, and what the value is in closing that gap. That gives us the success criteria. On the other hand, if the demand is in the form of a solution, without having first defined the performance gaps, then we are at risk of executing perfectly while delivering no additional value.

IDENTIFYING VALUEFLOW BOUNDARIES—FUNCTIONAL PROCESS

But how do we determine if a particular process is a valueflow or just a functional process that is part of a valueflow? Let's say we have a process and we have identified the output. Upon examining it, we find that it neither goes to a customer nor is it a component for another process. Instead it is an input which gets consumed or transformed by the next process in line. In this case what we have is a functional process. In order to find out what valueflow it is part of, we have to proceed to the next process and examine the output of that process. We continue this until we reach an output that goes to a customer, or a component that goes to another process. At that point we will have reached the end of the valueflow. Again, we look for the demand to get the boundaries of the valueflow. Then we identify all the functional processes in between and finally we develop a Chart of Accounts for the valueflow.

The diagram below illustrates this case.

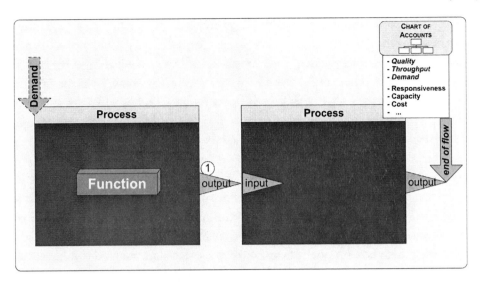

As we have seen, there are four key factors that help us to uniquely identify and scope a valueflow.

1. **Output**: What is the nature of the output produced by the process—component output or consumed output?
2. **Destination**: Where is the output going? Who is the receiver—external customer or internal process?
3. **Demand**: What triggers the requirement for the output?
4. **Chart of Accounts/Measurement framework**: How do we measure the output quality and the execution performance of the process?

If we can answer these four questions, then we can identify whether the process is a functional process or a valueflow process and what kind of valueflow. Let's explore each of the factors in a little more detail.

OUTPUT

Every process produces some sort of output. Processes that produce different outputs are different processes. The greater the difference in the output, the more likely it is that we are dealing with different processes. For example, take an apple pie versus a chair. These are completely different outputs and so will require different processes. On the other hand, take an apple pie versus a cherry pie. These have more in common than they have differences. So it's likely that the required processes will be similar but not identical. Therefore, we should consider these as variants of a valueflow. We would treat these separately while maintaining their relationship. Again, it pays to think of a valueflow as the smallest unit of business. Even if making an apple pie is identical to making a cherry pie, except for the filling, the apple pie market may be different from the cherry pie market. Demand may differ as well as profits. And that will make a difference to the decisions we make and to how we design the processes.

Since the output of one process is the input to another, we will consider outputs and inputs to be simply a matter of perspective. It depends on whether you look at a process from the upstream or from the downstream. Outputs connect different processes. For purposes of valueflow identification, we have defined three kinds of simple outputs according to how they are used by the next process in line. They are:

1. **Transform Input**: This is the simplest. If you produce flour and that flour is used to bake a cake, then that flour is a transform input because it will be transformed into something else—cake. A transform input basically becomes part of the output that is being produced. When you eat the cake, you are consuming the transformed flour along with other inputs. If your output is a decision, then you would transform facts and assumptions into a decision. If you are producing software, then the functional process of coding will transform requirements and business rules into computer code.

2. **Component Input**: Let's say that you make mixers, one of which goes to the bakery from above. Is the mixer a transformed input? No, it isn't. It will be used, as is, as a tool. We would hate to find mixer parts transformed into the cake. More likely the bakery will use the mixer as part of its cake making process. The mixer becomes a component of the process rather than a transformed input. So a component is something required by the process but not transformed by any one instance of the process. Components can be people, technology, methods, or other resources. Components normally persist across transactions. Transform inputs don't persist across transactions. You can't reuse the flour consumed in making one cake to make another cake.

3. **Demand request**: A bakery makes a birthday cake because someone has ordered the cake. The order is the demand. A demand is a request for the desired output. Some valueflows produce *to demand* while others produce *ahead of demand*. For example, the baker might make a few cakes with the expectation that someone will order one and want it right away. This is producing ahead of demand. We can tell when we have a demand because it will refer to some customer or enabling output. An internal person asking for a report is not a valueflow demand. A demand must come from an external customer or from another internal valueflow. A demand is a trigger that starts the process that produces the output.

That takes care of the first of the four factors.

DESTINATION

The destination, or receiver, of the output is the next factor. The output has two possible destinations.

1. **External Customer**: An output can go to a customer, which we define as an external, arm's length, receiver of the output. If the customer pays for the output, then we probably have a customer for-profit organization. If the customer simply receives the output but someone else essentially funds it, then we have a consumer/payer organization, which may also be a not-for-profit organization.

2. **Internal Process**: An output can go to another process inside the organization. Basically, if it doesn't go to a customer (which we refer to as external), then it must go to another process. Note that we don't say an internal customer. There is really no such thing. A customer provides something of value (usually money) to the organization in exchange for the output. Since internal employees don't provide anything in exchange for the outputs they receive, they aren't customers. They are part of, or participants of, the process. It is the needs of the process that should be satisfied, not the preferences of whoever is down the line. Process needs will be relatively stable and definable. On the other hand, personal preferences will be varied and ever changing.

So now we have enough information to identify the end boundary of a valueflow and to determine whether it is a Customer Valueflow or not.

The following table summarizes the four possibilities based on the factors of output and destination.

OUTPUT DESTINATION	OUTPUT TYPE	TYPE OF PROCESS
External Customer	Component	CUSTOMER Valueflow
	Transform Input	CUSTOMER Valueflow
Internal Process	Component	ENABLING Valueflow
	Transform Input (WIP)	Sub-process (connect to receiving process)

Let's review each case.

Customer Valueflow: If the output goes to an external customer, this is the end of a customer valueflow. It doesn't matter whether the output was a transform input (like flour) or a component input (like the mixer or software). The fact that it goes to an external customer makes it a Customer Valueflow.

Enabling Valueflow: If the output of the process goes to another internal process, then we need to identify what kind of output we have. If the output is a component, then this is the end of an enabling valueflow. For example, if the process produces a new employee (hiring process), then it's an enabling valueflow because an employee becomes part of some other process. Or, if the output is software, which is then used by some other process, then again we have a Software Development enabling valueflow. But if the output is a transform input, what we really have is work-in-process or WIP. That means we have a functional sub-process that needs to be connected to the receiving process because they are both part of the same valueflow. We would then move on to examine the output of the next process in line to see if we have identified the end of a valueflow. For example, let's say that the process produces a Software Design Specification and that the next process in line transforms that to produce actual software in the form of code. Then the two processes should be connected. Now we move on to the software and learn that the software goes to another process as a component. Then that marks the end of an enabling valueflow.

Function Process: When an internal process produces an output that is consumed or transformed by the next process in line, then we have a functional process that is part of some valueflow. In order to find the end of that valueflow, we must proceed to the next process until we reach a customer, or we have a component output or a demand. So, regardless of where we begin, whether we begin with an output or whether we begin at a specific functional process, we can always find the valueflows.

IDENTIFYING DEMAND—THE BEGINNING

So far we have identified the end of the valueflow. In order to understand the full scope, we need to understand where the beginning of the valueflow is. If we think in terms of the pizza example, it is only when we have delivered the pizza to the customer that they acknowledge value delivered and are willing to pay us. In essence, the output of the valueflow is providing the pizza eating experience to the customer. But where does the whole valueflow begin? Where is square one? To answer that, we need to find the demand.

Demand is different from input. Where an input is transformed somewhere inside the process, demand is a request to produce a specified output. The demand specifies the value to be delivered, not how it will be delivered. So an order is a demand to produce something. In a restaurant, it is your meal order. If you went online to buy books, then it is your book order. If you buy a car, then it's your purchase agreement. Basically, a demand request will describe the agreement for producing the output and the value that will be exchanged. A demand can be an actual demand or a forecast demand. So if you make things after they are ordered, you work to actual demand. If you make things before they are ordered, as in wine production, then you base your production valueflows on forecasts, ahead of demand. Demands are outputs that are themselves produced by a valueflow. For example, an individual order would be the output of a marketing-sales valueflow.

The importance of the demand request is that it marks the beginning of the fulfillment valueflow and the end of the previous demand valueflow. So once we have identified the output and the demand request, we know the scope of the valueflow process. A valueflow begins with the functional process that receives the demand and ends with the functional process that completes delivery of the output. We can think of a demand output as linking a customer demand valueflow to a customer fulfillment valueflow.

Why is it important to identify and scope a valueflow in this way? We need to be able to measure the effectiveness of the processes. If we measure functional processes without some higher context, then the risk is that the choices will be made based on achieving some local objective. Local objectives from a functional process will clash with those from another. Furthermore, achieving local objectives will rarely allow us to achieve the enterprise-level objectives that are part of the strategy. By identifying valueflows that begin with a demand and end with a value output, we will be able to attach performance measures to the valueflow and link them to the strategy. We will be able to attach the multiple sources of costs to the typically single source of value.

Another reason why the valueflow construct is useful is that a valueflow persists across organizational restructuring. That means that as long as the product is still produced, the valueflow is still in existence after a restructuring. Furthermore, it has the same boundaries or scope. Contrast that with functional processes, which tend to be aligned to the organization chart. When an organization restructures, the functional boundaries will change. That means that the content of a function can change dramatically every time there is a restructuring. What this does is invalidate the measurement framework for the function. We can't compare before and after because they are different, which means that we have to go back to zero and create a new baseline. Of course, this is sometimes deliberate. It releases everyone from accountability. Rather than demonstrate that the restructuring was progressive, they can simply argue that time is needed because there is no valid date for direct comparison. So we can't determine if a particular restructure was progressive by comparing performance at the functional level because the functions are different. Since we can't evaluate how progressive a particular restructure was, we can't learn from it. What is the end result? We cycle among competing organization structures. We don't improve. We simple swing from one to another. This is why companies are forever swinging between centralizing and decentralizing. Each model has strengths and weaknesses. Once we have had enough of the weaknesses of one model, we swing to the other model.

Valueflows can help us eliminate this cycling because a valueflow will persist across a restructuring. As long as we are still making the product, the valueflow is still there. What will change is the functional design and internal accountabilities of the valueflow. But we can still compare the performance of each valueflow before and after restructuring. That will tell us where we have made progress and where we have regressed. Then we can target the areas that have regressed rather than change the whole enterprise.

The valueflow construct persists across organizational restructuring and, therefore, allows us to maintain accountability across restructuring. No more free lunches by restructuring.

RELATIONSHIP OF VALUEFLOW PROCESSES TO FUNCTIONAL PROCESSES

How is a valueflow different from a cross-functional or end-to-end process that we so often hear about? First of all, a valueflow can be tied either directly or indirectly to a Chart of Accounts, which can be used to measure stakeholder value delivered. Secondly, although a valueflow is a cross-functional end-to-end process, not all cross-functional processes are valueflows. The only criterion for a cross-functional process is that it crosses functional boundaries. Thirdly, we have defined valueflow variants, which further distinguish a valueflow. A simple cross-functional process may contain several valueflow variants.

Whereas a cross-functional process is loosely defined, we have defined clear criteria for determining the boundaries of a valueflow. Most literature is not specific about how to separate one cross-functional valueflow from another nor does it acknowledge that a function may contain multiple variants. The same is true of the term "end-to-end process."

The valueflow construct is specific enough that two different people can independently reach the same conclusions and define the same scope in a given context. A customer valueflow, for example, is persistent across time and implementations. As long as we are still producing the customer product, then we have the valueflow and it has the same boundaries. We can measure the value it produces for each stakeholder. When we change the design and implementation of that valueflow, when we add or remove functional processes, the valueflow persists and we can measure whether the changes have resulted in progress, as defined by the Value CoA. The valueflow also helps us to step systematically from strategy to function, rather than leap to it.

Valueflows provide the context within which functional process performance should be measured in order to make sense. A valueflow ensures that we can measure in a way that allows us to determine progress, which is a more global perspective, rather than an improvement that could simply be a local improvement. There are many changes that can result in local improvements. We want changes that result in global progress as well. The valueflow and its associated Chart of Accounts can help make sure that people who are suggesting local changes also understand that these same changes must result in progress at the next tier, the valueflow tier. Their request must satisfy both the functional need and the valueflow need. This can ensure that management is not inundated with funding requests for changes that only serve functional silos.

Valueflows are start-to-end processes that deliver a specific output. A functional process performs a particular kind of function on some input. Functional processes will tend to have variations within them because each functional process may process variants of a valueflow. It is important to understand this distinction. Let's look at an Underwriting functional process in an insurance organization. People might buy a whole life or a term life or even a health insurance policy. Although each of these might go through the Underwriting functional process, we probably have more than one valueflow. Although there may be many similarities between a whole life and a term life, there are also differences. To the customer, they are different products. And so we should treat these as two different valueflows, both of which flow through the Underwriting function. Without the concept of a valueflow, a process-mapping exercise of the Underwriting function will produce a task description that would likely include both valueflows together. This creates unnecessary complexity. This is what makes some functional processes so difficult to understand—because we mix many different valueflows. A better approach is to be specific about which valueflow we are interested in and then understand only the portion of each functional process that applies to that specific valueflow. In virtually all cases this will simplify understanding and allow us to determine what the optimal design would be for each valueflow.

EXAMPLE: TELEPORTED CARS

Again, let's revert to an analogy to understand what the hidden complexities are in the functional view. Let's imagine that we live in a world where teleporting (the transfer of matter from one point to another) has become a technical reality. So we are able to teleport physical items almost instantly from point A to point B. This has many repercussions. One of these repercussions is that cars are no longer sold in the same way because we have found a better way. Statistically, most people only use their cars a small percentage of the time. So, in effect, cars are idle more than 95% of the time. This is a big waste and has led to a new approach and a new industry.

Here is how this new industry works. Basically, we no longer purchase a car. Rather, we buy a license for a particular model with particular features. We get a key for the car. When we need to use the car, we press a button on the key. This sends a message to the dealer. The dealer has the specification for the car and knows what parts are required to reconstitute the car model. The actual parts are manufactured and held separately by different companies because each one specializes in different parts. There are companies that specialize in engines, others in transmissions, etc.

When the signal is received, a computer looks up the customer information and sends a signal to all the participating suppliers. Sometimes there might be multiple suppliers for the same part. In that case, the first one to respond gets the business for that transaction. All the suppliers instantly transport the individual parts to the dealer. The dealer has a technology that puts all the parts together and then teleports the finished vehicle to us, all in a matter of a few seconds. If we press the key button while inside the house, the car will appear before the door closes behind us. One difference with the car, as compared to today, is that we never quite get the exact same car. Even though the parts list might be the same, there is no guarantee that we will receive the exact same engine, for example. So, in effect, we can never step into the same car twice. Processes are similar in that we don't quite execute the same process twice.

We hop in the car, drive to the destination, and get out of the car. Then we press another button on the key and the car is teleported back to the dealer, who then teleports the individual parts back to each company. Isn't this great? No more parking hassles and we don't even need a garage.

As with all great things technological, we have lost a few things. For one, because there are different companies making major parts, it's tough to improve the vehicle as a whole because there isn't really anyone in charge of the whole car. One result of such a system is that models may tend to change very little over time. Another issue is that a parts maker can only make new parts that don't impact any of the other parts. The parts may progress but the vehicle as a whole does not. Every once in a while the dealers might get together and begin a redesign project. Typically someone will be assigned to the project and she will follow the following general methodology:

1. She begins with one function, say the engine, and she visits the companies that make the engine. When she arrives, she tries to understand all the engines those companies make. They produce a single blueprint that documents all the engines. Let's say that there are 10 engine models. The blueprint is highly complex because it represents all 10 engines.
2. Then she moves on to another function, say the transmission, and she visit those companies. Again she produces a single blueprint representing all the transmission models. Let's say that there are 10 different transmissions.
3. Let's imagine she does the same thing for two other functional parts, each of which has 10 models.

What is the problem with this approach? We have four functional components, each with ten variants. So that means that there are 10 * 10 * 10 * 10 possible combinations or 10,000 possible combinations to make a car. But let's imagine that there are only 25 different car models. So that means only 25 of the potential 10,000 combinations actually occur. So if we wanted to improve, what could we improve using this approach? How could we conclude that there were only 25 actual models? Without gaining a clear understanding of the actual models first, we would likely only improve the parts, in the hope that this would improve the actual models. Add to that the fact that every part manufacturer has a stake in having their part continuing to be a component of the updated car.

This is the predominant approach to redesigning business processes. Functions are visited one at a time and treated as a single unit. Even when teams are employed, several functions are treated together. When we look at a process map and see a lot of "branching" logic or symbols, what we are seeing are different valueflows being documented as one.

Of course the reality is worse. In the car example, we expect that each actual engine for a particular model is the same as others of the same model. But in a process, each execution of a function for the same valueflow may differ for a variety of reasons. If we gave the exact same transaction to different people, would they execute it in exactly the same way? Probably not! So when a process is documented, whose version is being captured? The reality is that processes are often documented either at a high enough level that everything looks the same or they are documented based on what people can agree should be done, rather than what actually happens.

An alternative approach is to begin with the car models (valueflows). Then we select one model that we believe might have a higher payoff if improved. We might base this on how many people purchased that model compared to others, or some other factor. Once we select a model, we then proceed to understand only the specific variant of each part that makes up that particular model, as if no other model existed. We then produce a blueprint for that model, which contains a blueprint for each part. Now we understand a whole model and we understand the parts for that model. We can make a determination of whether that model has been designed optimally or not. The level of complexity of such a blueprint would be significantly less than in the previous approach. We don't have to wait to understand every component of every model to make an obvious improvement. We can proceed right away. We can also make a quick determination to see if a particular change might be applicable to other models as well. With one model complete, we could then move on to another.

The first strategy reflects how organizations largely approach process design. They try to design 25 models at once without even knowing that they have 25 models. No one can absorb that much complexity and so the process designs are really parts designs. This leads to poorly integrated processes.

A valueflow is like a model for the car. Just because all cars have virtually the same type of parts doesn't mean they should be designed as one car. After all, a Ferrari is quite a different design from a Corolla, even if the name of the parts may be the same. Different valueflow variations may flow through the same functional processes but each requires a variant of the function. The better way to understand and design is to tackle one valueflow at a time, then make any consolidations later. The idea that there are multiple valueflows going through a function is crucial. It is this concept that allows us to see that we must have someone who is *accountable for the valueflow* design in addition to and apart from each function. Otherwise, the processes will be stagnant and will not progress beyond what parts improvement can achieve.

By and large, we have passed the point where functional parts improvement yields the most significant gains. If you are still on that road, then you have missed the exit. That road was once a highway on which we sped along. Now it is no more than a single lane dirt road. If you doubt that, then compare the rate of progress today to that of 20 to 30 years ago. If you're too young, talk to someone with a little more experience.

The new highway is the valueflow integration highway. On this highway, we still need parts experts and parts excellence but we also need a Chief Valueflow Engineer (CVE), someone who will coordinate the parts to build the best car. In fact, real cars are designed just this way. Each car has a chief engineer who must understand customer requirements, design requirements, and execution requirements in order to build a better car. Excellence in parts is still necessary. It is just not sufficient. Excellence requires that we simultaneously satisfy multiple requirements.

More about the Valueflow

A valueflow is a capability that produces a value output. What if we produce a particular product or service called "Widget X" in a facility located in Canada and we also produce the exact same "Widget X" in a facility located in France? So we have two separate capabilities in two different geographic areas. Would this be one valueflow or two? The first choice should always be to treat it as two. Even if the method used by the two facilities were identical, there are enough other potential differences to warrant separate treatment. If we had two different people accountable for the two, then we would definitely want to know the performance of the two separately. But even if a single person were accountable, it would still be useful to treat him separately. So even though the design and description and specification of the two might be identical, we might want to separate the performance measurement or Chart of Accounts for the two. The customers could be different. The employees coming from two different countries might have different work habits. The regulations, taxes, and other factors might also be different. So we would treat these as two variants of the valueflow.

We would have

1. Widget X-Canada valueflow
2. Widget X-France valueflow

Even if the design of the two were identical and even if we measured exactly the same things, we might get quite different actual performance due to different factors. Even if the performance of the two were similar, if different people were accountable, then we might want to separate the performance. So geography might be one reason for us to create a variant of a valueflow. A different customer base would be another reason. We could always consolidate the metrics if we needed to but it would be difficult to go the other way. The point we are trying to make here is that we can identify valueflow variants based on requirement differences or design differences, or we can identify a valueflow variant for execution purposes or combinations of these.

Other reasons we might have for identifying a variant include:
1. When we have two different implementations where one or more components are different. Components include the method or the technology or the skill levels of the people. The idea is that we want to be as specific as possible when measuring performance.

2. We may have differences in how the process is executed. For example, imagine we are the College of Physicians and Surgeons of Ontario and we have a Registration valueflow that prospective doctors must use in order to register in the jurisdiction. We can imagine that the valueflow might require different amounts of effort and time if the doctor registering had graduated from a local university as compared to one that graduated in China. So even though both produce a registration, we might want to identify at least two variants of the Registration Valueflow. Perhaps we would have a Canadian Registration Valueflow and an International Registration Valueflow.

The purpose of identifying valueflows is that it allows us to connect strategic intent to functional execution through measurable performance. It is the functions that produce the outputs. But it is the valueflow that delivers the value because of the way that it links the functions so as to produce a certain quality and execution performance.

Examples

Let's look at a few examples of valueflows.

The first example is an Online-Books-Order valueflow. Imagine an online book retailer. The following might describe the Valueflow and its Functional processes.

Process Activities	Functional Process (FP)	Output
You go online, do searches & move your items to the cart and pay.	*Order Valueflow*	*Order (demand)*
The order is received (beginning of valueflow).	Order Receipt FP	
The order is scheduled for picking.	Scheduling FP	
The books are picked.	Pick FP	
The books are packed & readied for shipment.	Ship FP	
The order package is picked up and delivered.	Delivery FP	
You receive your order.	Receive FP	The Books Ordered

When online book services were initially started, it took many weeks to receive the order, often more than a month. Today, I receive the majority of my orders within a few days. Sometimes if I order early enough in the morning, I receive my order the next day. Such a dramatic change in responsiveness performance could not have been achieved without looking at the whole valueflow rather than just at the individual functional processes. Only by treating the valueflow as a whole and understanding the connections and inter-relationships could that kind of performance be achieved. Of course that implies that there is someone who is accountable for the valueflow level performance, apart from the functional performance. It is not enough to have people accountable for each function; we also need separate accountability for the valueflow performance. And accountability at the valueflow level is not about who owns the blame; it's about who owns the leadership to take action because, at the functional level, the problem may not even be noticed.

Let's look at another example. Let's call this the Patient Service Valueflow.

Process Activities	Functional Process (FP)	Output
Patient feeling somewhat poorly—calls doctor for appointment.		Order (demand)
1. Schedules appointment for 10 weeks ahead.	Doctor 1	
2. Gets examined and referred for tests—15 minutes.	Doctor 1	
3. Provide sample for test.	Clinic1	
4. Run the test.	Lab1	
5. Schedules appointment for results 3 weeks ahead.	Doctor 1	
6. Gets results from doctor—10 minutes, and gets referred to specialist.	Doctor 1	
7. Schedules with specialist 4 months ahead.	Doctor 2	
8. Gets examined and referred for tests—15 minutes.	Clinic2, Lab2	
9. Etc., etc., etc.		
10. Specialist advises an operation.	Doctor 2	
11. Specialist schedules surgery for 5 months ahead.	Hospital	
12. On his way to the hospital, the patient dies of old age.		Unsatisfied demand.

This valueflow can easily take many months. Depending on the tests being requested, it could even take a year or more. Each functional process may be quite simple and the total amount of time spent being treated by a function might be measured in minutes. And yet the valueflow is quite long and unresponsive, with many different and separate participants. The patient is the only one who truly knows and feels the length of this process. There is no one who is accountable for the valueflow, and so no one is going to pay attention to it except at the functional level. Everyone that participates in this valueflow may well be doing a great job. However, the patient didn't receive the value output that was desired and necessary. Of course, this valueflow crosses many different organizations as well as boundaries within organizations. A valueflow that crosses many organizations may be more difficult to improve than one that is under the control of a single organization. One problem here is that there may be many individual accountabilities defined but no master accountability for the valueflow. The assumption is that if each functional process works as specified then somehow we will get the proper result. This assumption is false in the real world.

In the patient example, the demand is caused by the "ill feeling" of the patient. The desired output is to be brought back to some baseline health that, in this case, doesn't happen. Even though every functional process may have worked to specification, the flow as a whole didn't deliver a successful result. Even though everyone worked hard to get the patient from one point to the next, it simply took too long to get him to point B. And if we asked anyone at any point in the process what more they could have done to make things better, it's a pretty safe bet to expect that they would have pointed elsewhere. And they won't do this because they are malicious or because they lack responsibility; it's just that they are going as fast as they can and so they assume that someone else must not be holding up their end. Of course, since everyone will likely feel the same way, we can see that this leads to inaction and maintenance of the status quo. We assume that people don't want to change. This is certainly true sometimes. But it is also true that people often can't see what would need to be changed to achieve better results for all, or that in order for one function to improve, another function might need to change. Also, they may not have the capacity (time) to think about it or the perspective to see a better way.

In order to connect strategic intent to functional requirements, regardless of the complexity or scope of the valueflow, what we must do is be able to determine which valueflows are required to deliver to a specific strategy and what the performance of those valueflows needs to be in order to maximize the likelihood of successfully achieving the objectives that the strategy is trying to deliver.

The implication here is that we need to start at the objective and strategy end rather than at the functional process end. Unless we start with the end in mind (the objective), we will have to accept whatever we happen to achieve based on the functional designs and actions.

Just like a person should accept accountability for their health and wellness, so an organization should develop an accountability framework that helps it to manage to deliver stakeholder value.

And, of course, to do so requires the capability to somehow measure and evaluate what the organization does. That's the purpose of the Chart of Accounts.

Now that we have a better understanding of what a valueflow is, the next chapter will explore how to use a Chart of Accounts to measure valueflow performance. Identifying a valueflow is the first step in producing a normalized process model blueprint. Subsequent chapter will explore how to fill in the blueprint.

SUMMARY

An organization is a mechanism for exchanging value among participants. So we need to be able to identify and quantify what that value is and where it occurs. But value is produced through work. One challenge that is common to all organizations is to determine what work is necessary in order to deliver the value and what work is not. A major factor is the fact that organizations are designed such that the work required to create the value is often in different organizational units from those where the value is delivered. So we need some way to bring together all the effort required to produce a particular value product. That way we can add it all up, so to speak, and compare it to the value produced to see the net effect. We need a framework that takes the functional organized work and reconfigures it according to value produced. The valueflow is that construct. It allows us to see all the work relevant to a particular product or service, while hiding all other work.

The valueflow gathers all the work that takes place starting from the external demand for the product all the way to the delivery of that product. It allows us to view the flow for a single product as if it were the whole business. That allows us to determine the health of that portion of the business. It allows us to temporarily take down the functional walls that often obscure what is truly happening. It allows us to see and measure any cross-functional impacts. It permits us to design a valueflow while putting functional constraints aside, to discover whether there is a more perfect design for the process.

The functional organization, like the functional closet organizer, is simple to understand. The pants go with the other pants. The shirts go with the other shirts. The shoes go together. The ties go together. And the suits go together. But let's not forget the socks and underwear. It's all very neat, very tidy, very organized. But we wear outfits, not individual items of clothing. We can make proper purchases for each individual item and we can easily defend each individual purchase. But the key question will be "Do the individual items come together to make an outfit?" Can you tell by looking into such a closet if everything matches or not? The only true way to tell is to put the pieces together into outfits and see what you get.

The functional organization is like the functional closet. It is neat and tidy but only with respect to people skills. It is a way to know where to put the people so we can pay them according to some simple scale. The valueflow is like the outfit. It is a way to determine if we have good outfits that are perfectly matched or not. It is a way to see if the functional components of a process are matched to deliver the maximum stakeholder value. In a functionally designed organization, value can often be obscured. Functional organizations separate the work from the value produced. That makes it difficult to determine what to change in order to create greater value. The valueflow brings value and work back together so that we can get a whole picture again.

The valueflow framework allows us to better see what work is necessary to create value and what work can be removed or modified. It also allows us to see where it might be more advantageous to reorganize by valueflow and where a functional organization is still better suited. The valueflow is based on the premise that although managing people is important, it is no longer enough. We must also manage the valueflow processes. That's AND thinking again.

6

THE CHART OF ACCOUNTS—
MEASURING EXCELLENCE

Account•ability is the ability to account for cause and effect relationships.

There is an expression "We manage what we measure." But how true is this? Organizations often measure significantly more than they manage. Consider this alternative: "We tend to measure what we have already done (managed)." Have you ever attended a presentation with a whole section dedicated to "Our Accomplishments"? I've seen this many times. Usually the accomplishments are presented as a list of positive or desirable things. Quite often the list refers to activities completed rather than outcomes achieved.

This is what happens when we look at the things that we *have* done and present them *as if* they were the things that *should* have been done and that we had planned to do. Can you identify which thinking process is being used? Of course it's our faithful friend the *rationalize* (rational lies) process. We are using it to validate rather than evaluate the past—specifically, our past.

Let's consider another, perhaps more useful, expression: "We manage what we account for." The Chart of Accounts is about specifying those things of interest that we need to account for and manage in order to achieve the objectives and purpose. So the idea of manageability

95

is directly tied to the idea of *account-ability*. And accountability requires verifiability, which requires measurement of some sort.

Let's explore an example of how accountability can help improve process management. This case is presented for illustration purposes only. The name of the jurisdiction has been changed to make it anonymous. Let's call the jurisdiction Canario.

In the Canario health care system, the wait times for MRI tests (magnetic resonance imaging) had become too long. To give an indication, in 2005 the MRI wait times had reached an average of approximately 120 days. This led to public outcries and complaints that wait times needed to be addressed. And so a project was undertaken to reduce the wait times, and a wait time target of 28 days was set (not sure how the target was set). Presumably, at some point the wait times were much shorter since there were no public outcries before that time. Now we might ask how a process could get that far from the target. The answer is quite simple. When the MRI functional processes were first set up, it was a new function with no demand since MRI testing didn't exist. So it's easy to understand that wait times might initially have been much closer to the 28 days. But the thing is there may not have been a specific wait time target set. There was no *wait time account* for which anyone was accountable. There may have been other measures set up, but wait time was either not one of them or no one was assigned to manage that account. And so, as the wait times increased slowly over time, no one noticed. Well, of course the patients noticed, but unfortunately the patients had no ability to respond to the situation. We could say that the patients lacked *response-ability*. Now we might go further and ask: "What about the doctors and technicians working with the patients?" They probably could have responded. But of course none of them had the *author*ity, individually, to address what was a valueflow issue. We might say that none of them could *author* a demand for change. None of them, individually, was accountable for the wait time account.

This brings us to an important specification for managing. We could conclude that in order to properly manage something, we need three key things:

1. *Account-ability*: Something of interest that we are able to account for (be aware of) in some measurable or verifiable way. It can be a condition, a state, or a performance factor. We must be able to detect when the thing of interest moves away from the desired state or value.
2. *Response-ability*: We must have the skills and knowledge required to take action. We must be able to respond to a situation when a gap has been detected. Responsibility is the *ability to respond* (response-ability).
3. *Author-ity*: We must have the authority to take the action required to close the gap. Authority is the power to *author* a demand for action.

Our formula for manage-*ability* is:

Manage*ability* = f(Accountability x Responsibility x Authority)

What this says is that the ability to manage something is a function of the product of the ability to *account* for an effect, the ability to *respond* to the effect, and the power to *author* a demand to take action to change the effect. We could assign a number to each factor, ranging from zero to one, where zero represents complete inability and one represents full ability.

Therefore, if there is full accountability (aware of and can detect a gap) and there is full responsibility (we have the ability to fix it) but there is no authority (authority = zero), then the likelihood of being able to properly manage a particular item of interest is close to zero (1 x 1 x 0 = 0).

What sometimes happens in an organization is that a valueflow is set up as a series of functional processes. Accountability, responsibility, and authority are defined for the functional processes. But no accountability or authority is defined for any of the valueflow level items of interest. What then happens is that the functions are "continuously improved" until the valueflow fails. This may sound like a contradiction, but it is what happens. Everyone improves their local functions, and in the process they create negative external effects for other functions in the valueflow or in other valueflows. Because there is no valueflow accountability, there is no response to these effects. For some reason, positive external effects are rarely created. The external effects often must be absorbed by the impacted functions. So while each function is taking one step forward with its local improvements, it is also taking two steps backward, absorbing negative impacts from other sources. What is happening is that although each function, individually, is making changes that appear to contribute to its own improvement, there are many functions creating negative external impacts. This continues until the performance gaps of the valueflows are so huge that they can no longer be ignored. Of course, by this time, we have allowed a lot of unrecoverable value to leak.

This may explain, in part, what has led to the higher MRI wait times. Let's further explore this example. Imagine that there are three functional processes in the chain:

1. MRI Request
2. MRI Test
3. MRI Evaluation

Below is a diagram of the MRI valueflow process chain, along with a few account measures.

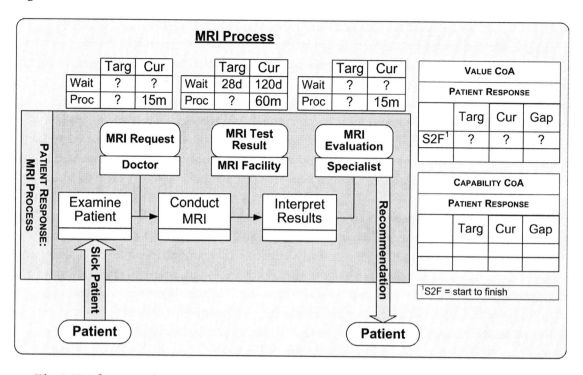

The MRI functional process is shown in the middle as MRI Test Result. The wait time in question is in front of that functional process. That is, it is the wait time from the request for the test to the time the test takes place. Before going further, we need to establish which valueflow it is a part of and where it sits in the valueflow. If we explore the output of that process, the MRI Test Result, we can determine that it doesn't go to the patient (customer). It goes to a specialist. Therefore, that's not the end of a customer valueflow. Also, the MRI Test Result is not a component that goes to another process, so it's not the end of an enabling valueflow either. What we have, then, is a transform input that goes to another process, which we have called MRI Evaluation. Let's imagine that the MRI Test Result is used as an input and interpreted by a specialist and that as a result the specialist produces a Treatment Recommendation that goes to the patient (consumer). So now we have the end of the valueflow. But where is the beginning? Well, the process starts when the patient arrives in an ill state at the doctor's office. The doctor examines the patient and requests the MRI Test, perhaps after other tests. So we can consider that to be the beginning, as depicted in the diagram.

In practice it's more complex because the results might go back to the original doctor who might request additional tests. But the simplification is enough for now. What it shows is that the MRI test is just one functional process in a valueflow that contains at least two other functions. Notice that the functional account measures are shown above the function. The target (Targ) is shown as 28 days while the current performance (Cur) is shown as 120 days. There is also another measure, "Proc," which we will discuss later.

To the patient, it is the valueflow level performance that is more important, not just the single functional process. If we look at the Chart of Accounts in the diagram, we can see that all we have is one account defined, the Wait Time (shown over the process function), and it's at the functional process level—the MRI Test. We don't have an account defined for the Start-to-Finish (S2F) time for the whole valueflow (shown on the right), something which might be of greater interest to the patient. If the purpose of the valueflow is to get the patient back to an acceptable level of health, then the time it takes to do that from start-to-finish should be an important account measure for the valueflow. For all we know, it may have taken many months for the patient to see the original doctor. It may also take many weeks or months to see the specialist to receive the recommendation. Yet we are only focusing on the wait time for a single functional process, possibly because it may be the longest. But it doesn't tell the whole story. What if we suddenly took some action to reduce the backlog for the actual MRI Test without doing anything about the next process in line, the MRI Evaluation? That would suddenly increase the rate at which test results are produced for specialists to review. When the specialists are suddenly inundated with a larger volume of test results to interpret, isn't it possible that we will just shift the wait time from one function to the next? That's creating an externality—moving an effect from one function to another—and thus shifting the problem around without solving it.

There is nothing wrong with focusing on one functional process, especially if it contributes the most to the performance we are seeking. But we need to define the whole valueflow to make sure we don't move the problem around. In this case, we don't even know what impacts the other surrounding processes may have on the total wait time. Notice all the question marks in the other Charts of Accounts. I remember having to wait more than four months to see a specialist who then scheduled me for a test for which I had to wait another four months. So the total wait time for the valueflow was eight months, not four. The problem with many complex processes is that things like wait times accumulate. Each on its own may seem imperfect but reasonable. But the total is unacceptable.

So what does this illustrate about the Chart of Accounts? Defining the valueflow first allows us to attach the Chart of Accounts to something that is more meaningful, something for which we can define and measure value. It is not the MRI Test that produces value. The value happens when the patient is back to good health. The valueflow CoA places functional performance in context. It highlights what we have and what is still missing. So in this example, we can see that we need some account measures for the valueflow and for the other two functional processes as well. We can also see that we have the process time (Proc = time actually spent on the patient) for all three processes. We can see that the patient is only attended to for about one and a half hours during the 120 days. It also shows us that we don't know the total time elapsed from when the patient first felt sick until the time he or she received the treatment options. And that doesn't even consider actual treatment. So we aren't even close to having the whole picture.

The other thing that the diagram points out is that there are at least three different participants in addition to the patient—the Doctor, the MRI facility, and the Specialist. If we were to draw an organization chart above these three and kept going up the organization chart until we found someone with authority over all three, we might not find a common authority. That tells us that this is going to be a difficult problem to solve, and not necessarily because of technical difficulties, but because of socio difficulties (lack of accountability and authority).

MEASUREMENT VERSUS EVALUATION

Why do we measure? Naturally there are many answers to this question. Sometimes we measure individual performance so we can decide who is going to get a 3% merit increase and who will only get a 2.5% increase. Sometimes we measure so that we can decide whether Mary gets the promotion or Jim. We often measure so we can decide whom to reward, whom to punish, and by how much. We do this because we believe that motivating people is important and this is one way to motivate people.

Of course we want and we need to have motivated people. Being motivated creates energy for movement, but not always movement in the right direction, and not always coordinated movement. There are two additional purposes for measuring that are equally important and necessary. To thrive we need these in addition to individual measurement and evaluation. Let's explore them.

1. **Focus Attention**: The first purpose is to help us to decide or choose where we need to focus our attention, what the nature of that attention should be, and what actions need to be taken, when and by whom. You could say that this is the navigation side of measurement. We want to navigate starting from purpose and ending with specific functional actions that we can take to achieve that purpose.

2. **Verify Principles**: The second purpose is to verify the principles. We rarely make a decision based solely on numbers because we rarely have all the necessary numbers at hand. Take driving, for example. Most of us, while driving in winter on a snow covered road, would slam on the brakes when we needed to come to an emergency stop. We believe or hold the principle that pressing hard on the brakes is the way to bring the car to a safe stop. But actually, slamming on the brakes only brings the wheels to a sudden stop (functional focus), which is not the same as bringing the car to a stop (valueflow focus). This is another example of what seems to make sense at the local functional level, but doesn't necessarily work at the higher, valueflow level. We now know that pumping the brakes is a much more effective way to bring a car to a safe and controlled stop on a slippery surface. So we held an incorrect principle. Automobile manufacturers now include a standard feature called ABS (anti-lock braking system) on their cars. What this does is prevent the wheels from locking even when we slam on the brakes. The ABS system was created to do this

because automobile manufacturers know that a driver is unlikely to pump the brakes under emergency conditions so the ABS provides the proper response. We manage a business according to principles we have been taught or that we have learned through experience. The problem is that when the conditions change and the principles no longer apply, we can easily miss seeing that the principles are now failing. Measurement through the Chart of Accounts helps us to monitor the success of the principles. That is perhaps the most important role of measurement. When we formulate a model of how something works and use that model to predict the results, we should use measurements to confirm or deny current principles. We should use measurements to ensure that the principles we are applying are indeed effective. If they are not, then we need to change those principles because to continue to follow principles that no longer apply is to reproduce waste, which will eventually kill the enterprise.

In this chapter it is in the context of these two objectives that we discuss measurement and the Chart of Accounts. We will not be exploring measures as a means to evaluate individual personal performance. We explore measurement as a means or tool that assists us in enterprise Process Performance Management, or managing to purpose *with accountability*. We want to use measurement to increase our knowledge of the processes, which in turn will improve what and how we measure, which will improve our understanding of the process, and so on, and so on. We can see that this will be a virtuous cycle.

The first distinction that we need to draw is between measuring and evaluating. When we evaluate we are making a judgment. When we measure we are trying to get to the truth about something without saying that it is good or bad. Of course, measuring without ever evaluating is of no benefit. But we want to distinguish between the two and make sure that we always separate the two. Why is it important to separate the two? It has to do with the emotional attitude required for each.

When we evaluate something, we are usually making an emotional decision with consequences based on what we believe is important. Of course, different people might evaluate differently based on the impact the evaluation might have on them personally. So the emotional attitude when we evaluate something will tend towards a desire to have what we would consider to be good news (for us). Let's call this attitude personal bias. Naturally this loads the dice. What we need, however, is a measurement that is as close to the truth as possible. This requires an emotional attitude of detachment (objectivity). If we measure and evaluate together, only one of these emotional attitudes can win, since personal bias and detachment are not compatible. Sometimes this is referred to as a conflict of interest. We can also call it a conflict of *emotional attitudes*. Separating the measurement from the evaluation allows us to determine if, in fact, the measuring and evaluating can even be done by the same person. In many cases it really cannot.

In essence we have two functional processes: the *measure* process and then the *evaluate* process. If a particular measure will be used to evaluate personal performance as well as process performance, there will be a lot of motivation for a person to measure in their favour. Furthermore, when we attach a process measure to a person, it implies that 100% of the process result is due to the person and none to other factors such as the method, input, or other conditions. Take a simple case of someone trying to lose weight. On the day that they weigh in, they want to show progress. So they are likely to do everything in their power to get the weight as low as possible by doing things such as wearing light clothes, no shoes, weighing in before supper, and then having a big meal afterwards, etc. They may even skip the weigh-in if they think they haven't lost any weight—bad news. They might even fail to weigh in when there is no one else involved. That's right—they will refuse to give themselves bad news. We are motivated to look as good as we can, even to ourselves. The lesson is that when we use a measure for both personal and process performance and we have the person impacted doing the measuring, then we absolutely should question the reliability and accuracy of the measurement. If the measurement is really important, we should consider getting a third party to take the measure, thus separating the evaluation.

Measurement is a task required in order to quantify the value for an account. Evaluation is about accountability, about accounting for why the value is what it is. Always separate the two.

CHART OF ACCOUNTS, STRUCTURE AND MEASUREMENT

Why is measurement such a challenge for so many organizations? We have already discussed one reason: personal bias. In addition to bias, there is the sheer volume of available things to measure. There may be tens of thousands of available measures or things we could measure. Also, measuring takes time and effort in addition to the time and effort it takes us to do the work.

Let's try to understand what measurements are. Think in terms of a noun—for example, a car. A car has certain characteristics, which can be measured. It has weight. It has wheel base width. It has fuel consumption. It has a price. It has interior room. Each of these things tells us something about the car itself or the performance when using the car. If we were to switch from a car to a sandwich (a different noun), we would want to measure different things. What we measure depends on what we need to know in order to achieve some purpose. So we need to think in terms of what it is that we want to manage, and then determine what measures would help us to manage. It is a mistake to think in terms of what we can measure. We should first think in terms of what we should measure.

In the case of an organization, we are trying to get better at achieving the purpose of that organization. That's measured in terms of stakeholder value, which is represented by the Stakeholder Value Chart of Accounts. But at the functional level where everyone works, the excellence of the process is measured in terms of capability performance, which is represented by the Capability Chart of Accounts. So one problem is that we measure different things depending on the context and level at which we are measuring.

If purpose is what we are trying to fulfill, then the measurement should be tied to that. As with all things, measurement needs to be properly structured in order to be effective. The **Chart of Accounts** is a construct for measurement and accountability. Its structure mirrors the strategy-function deployment structure. The Value Chart of Accounts should flow from stakeholder purpose. Since functional execution should flow from strategy, capability accounts should flow from value accounts. Whenever we address a particular account performance measure, we must always evaluate it within the context of the Chart of Accounts for the next higher tier. We always want to know if an "improvement" at one tier flows up to the next tier. If it doesn't, then we are introducing change without progress.

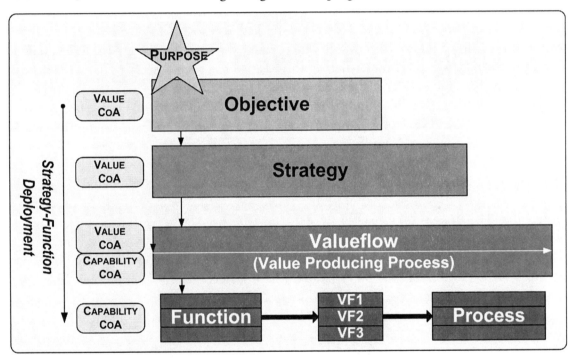

The diagram shows that we have two kinds of accounts: those that measure value as seen by the stakeholder (Value CoA) and those that measure capability as designed into and exhibited by the process (Capability CoA). A Chart of Accounts has a hierarchical structure to it. At the top of the structure are value measures associated with a business objective, and then the associated strategies. The diagram also shows that a valueflow has both a Value CoA and a Capability CoA. That means that it is at the valueflow tier that we convert strategic intent into functional capabilities. This is the crossover between value and capabilities. Therefore, valueflows link capability to value in a single construct.

Let's explore each tier in the diagram.

Purpose—Objective: We should begin with the purpose and then define business objectives. We should do this for each external stakeholder. It is natural to develop business objectives from the point of view of the shareholders, but what about the other stakeholders? Since the organization needs the cooperation of other stakeholders, isn't it a good idea to know how they are evaluating their participation? So we place ourselves in their shoes and develop business objectives that reflect the desires of other stakeholders. That way we can manage all the stakeholder relationships.

Objective—CoA: For each business objective, we need to establish a Value Chart of Accounts. Quite often, organizations will have objective statements, but they may not have thought through how they will determine whether an objective has been achieved. The CoA defines what will be measured and how. The CoA will need to tell us how we will know. It provides a structure for both accountability and for measurement. Each account will need to be managed. We will also need to evaluate the status of an account through measures. And someone needs to be accountable for the account.

Strategy—Identification: For each business objective, we need to explore and choose one or more strategies to achieve that objective. There are usually multiple ways to accomplish something. The strategy specifies the chosen way. We may even require multiple ways or strategies to achieve a particular objective.

Strategy—CoA: We need to develop a Value Chart of Accounts for each strategy. This links into the CoA for the associated objective. As with the objective, we need to know if a particular strategy has succeeded. We need to think through how we will validate the relative success through measures. The CoA for a strategy contains measures that are the same or compatible with those for the associated objective as well as measures specific to the strategy.

Valueflow—Identification: For each strategy, we identify the valueflow processes, which, when executed, will fill the accounts. After all, something has to produce the value to fill the accounts. It is the valueflows that are the source of individual value production. There may be a single valueflow or multiple valueflows required to achieve a particular strategy.

Valueflow—COA: For each valueflow, we first develop a valueflow Value Chart of Accounts. The Value CoA for each valueflow will contain measures that are the same or compatible with those for the associated strategy as well as measures specific to the valueflow. This is the last tier where we can measure value.

As we progress from one tier to the next, we expand the Chart of Accounts. As we identify each account, we also determine how the account would get measured and evaluated. For example, we might have an account related to business growth. But how would we measure that? Should we measure market share? Or should we measure revenue growth? Or should we measure profit growth? Or, perhaps, we should measure all three. Of course we have to be careful, because it is possible to increase market share while the other two fall. So perhaps we designate one of the three as being primary. That way we can focus on one, while ensuring that we don't abandon the other two. The point is that we must think through how we will measure and evaluate because there are almost always multiple options.

We have already covered the concept of stakeholders. There are certain basic stakeholder groups that are virtually always present regardless of whether we are talking about a for-profit organization or a not-for-profit organization. Let's review these role groups:

Consumer: This refers to the primary external recipient of the product (good or service). The consumer consumes or is the recipient of the product. It is the consumer who determines the gross value of the product (without reference to price). The consumer is the one who generates the demand for the consumption of the product. The key is that he or she is the external target for the product.

Payer: This refers to the person or entity that pays for the product (good or service) consumed or received. The payer sees the price of the product. She may or may not experience the value the product delivers, depending on the type of transaction. If the payer is different from the consumer, then that will generate a different set of behaviours as compared to when the consumer and payer are the same entity.

Customer: When the consumer and the payer are the same, we will refer to them as the customer. A customer may exhibit very different behaviour from a consumer/payer pair. The key difference is that a customer can make an emotional evaluation of value received versus price paid. Because of this, a customer will always have a more direct and immediate impact on the demand for the product (good or service). This has strong implications for not-for-profit organizations that have separate consumers and payers.

Employee: These are the people the organization employs in one capacity or another to make the products or deliver the services. This includes people at all levels of the organization. Even the president falls into this category. Employees care about compensation, career, challenge, security, etc. "Employees" is not a single group with a single set of objectives. Several Value Chart of Accounts may be required to represent them.

Supplier: These are external people or organizations from whom we purchase products, raw materials, or services required to make the products or deliver the services.

Shareholder: This refers to those who have some level of ownership stake and who normally share in the profits or the value of the organization. Shareholders normally seed the start-up of a company and may also seed a specific expansion.

Sharefunder: Not all organizations have shareholders, especially when they are not-for-profit. Nevertheless, these organizations also need initial funding and operational funding. For lack of a name, we will refer to them as sharefunders because they share the funding rather than the profits. Going forward, when we refer to shareholders we will also be implying sharefunders.

Organization: This refers to the organization as an entity on its own, apart from all other stakeholders. The shareholders may own the business but the organization includes all the stakeholders. So no one can own the organization. It is a mechanism apart from all the components. We will treat it as if it were a separate stakeholder because there are organization behaviours and objectives quite apart from all the others. The simplest objective to imagine is the objective of survival. An organization needs to survive quite apart from any of its stakeholders.

We can, of course, add other stakeholders, such as the community, depending on circumstances. Since an organization is a mechanism for exchanging value among participants, it is good to understand what value outcomes each stakeholder is looking to achieve and how they will measure it. Each value account is a representation of something a particular stakeholder would consider as important to him—something he would value. We need to put ourselves in the shoes of each stakeholder and imagine they are asking the question "What Is of Value for Me (WIVM)?" so that we can understand what the interests of that shareholder are and what their position and behaviour is likely to be. Will they be aligned or opposed? The attitude should be one of trying to understand the various needs and interests rather than focusing only on the shareholder. This will help us move away from conflict and towards mutually beneficial solutions, where such solutions exist. Of particular benefit is to understand how each value account is impacted when a change is made. Does the account change in absolute value or does it change relative to some other account? For example, when an organization changes a process in order to increase its profit, employees may not be that motivated if none of their accounts change. We might think that as long as we aren't negatively impacting the employee accounts, we should have no problem. But a socio view of the change should tell us that if there is a significant gain on the part of one shareholder group compared to another, then the other group may perceive their value as having dropped, even if in absolute terms it remains unchanged. A change in the relative balance of accounts is likely to get a reaction from those whose absolute or relative balance has changed.

We also distinguish between the organization's needs and the shareholders' wants. We liken the organization to a ship. The ship may have an owner, a crew (employees), suppliers, and customers (as passengers or for freight). Each of these groups has a stake in keeping the ship afloat, but each has a different interest. Even though the ship is owned by the shareholders, it cannot achieve its purpose without the cooperation, assistance, and contribution of the others. Therefore, we don't want any of the stakeholders to be motivated to sink the ship, so to speak, because then everybody loses something of value.

At the level of enterprise objectives and strategy, we would want the chart to be a Stakeholder Chart of Accounts. This means that the chart should always have a section for the four major groups—customer, employee, supplier, shareholder—and also one for the organization as an entity separate from the other stakeholders. That way we can easily see which stakeholders are represented by each objective and which are not. In addition, this will help us to detect when someone may be trying to *sink the ship*. If all the objectives relate only to the shareholder, then we know that the focus may be one-sided and that we don't have a sufficient understanding of the needs and interests of the others. We may or may not care about the needs of the other stakeholders, but we should understand what they are because they will impact us.

EXAMPLE—THE PIZZA SHOP (CONTINUED)

A Chart of Accounts has a structure. To better understand that, let's expand the pizza example from the previous chapter. Assume that we have a business objective of growing the business. Tied to that objective are a set of strategies. One of these is to increase the "pizza pickup" volume of business using the current pizza products. In order to do that, we have identified two main valueflows that we must engage to achieve that goal. The valueflows are:

1. The Marketing-Communications-Sales Valueflow: This is a customer demand valueflow whose purpose is to generate the sales volume required. If we want to make more money, then we have to sell more pizzas.
2. The Pizza Production Valueflow: If we sell more pizzas, then we must make more pizzas.

The Chart of Accounts (yearly) for this might look like the following based on:
- Unit price per pizza: $12.00
- Unit cost per pizza: $10.00

STRATEGY: PICKUP			
	NEW TARGET ($000)	**CURRENT TARGET ($000)**	**GAP ($000)**
Revenue	960	720	(240)
PICKUP MARK-COM-SALES VALUEFLOW			
Revenue	960	720	(240)
Units	80	60	(20)
PICKUP PRODUCTION VALUEFLOW			
Units	80	60	(20)
Cost	800	600	(200)

The table shows the shareholder CoA for the Pickup strategy. It shows the two valueflows that are impacted and their corresponding CoA. The Mark-Com-Sales (marketing, communications, and sales) chart shows two accounts: revenue and units expressed in thousands (000). The Production valueflow shows units and cost. The units are identical because clearly we need to make as many pizzas as we sell. Both show the target required to meet the business objective (grow business) as well as the current situation. Since we are trying to grow the company, the gap is a negative one. The simple act of changing the target from the current state creates a gap. A gap should generate management demand to close the gap. If these were only metrics, then no demand would likely get generated. However, if we have assigned the accounts to someone to manage, then the appearance of a gap means that whoever is managing that particular account needs to be engaged, and she needs to take action to determine how to close the gap.

In this case we have two valueflows that have gaps, and both valueflows need to be addressed in order to achieve the business objective. If the Mark-Com-Sales valueflow does its job but we don't upgrade the production valueflow, then we will likely not fulfill the new sales demand. On the other hand, if we upgrade the production valueflow capability but the sales don't materialize, then the production valueflow costs are likely to rise as a percentage of sales. This is why a properly structured Chart of Accounts is important. By having both valueflows related to a single strategy, then the manager of that strategy can make sure that the two valueflows are aligned. They can make certain that the proper valueflow managers are engaged.

VALUE VERSUS CAPABILITY

What's the difference? Value goes to the heart of why a stakeholder is participating in a transaction. An organization is a socio-technical-economic mechanism, and it is the socio part that relates to value. Yes, that's right; it isn't just the economic part, although in many cases we will use an economic measure in order to gauge the socio. For example, take profit. It's an account measure that has importance for the shareholder. But shareholders, if you look deeply enough, are people. And every person has his or her own reasons for investing. Some are investing for retirement security while others are saving for college. These are the socio reasons. But it's tough to measure security and so we might use an economic measure, such as return on investment, which relates to profit.

Value measures are always evaluated by the stakeholder. Each stakeholder makes his own decision about whether to continue to participate in the organization. The customer does this by continuing to be a customer, thus providing revenue in exchange for something of value. An employee does this by continuing to be an employee with a certain level of engagement and enthusiasm. A Value Chart of Accounts is a construct or tool used by the organization to gauge how a particular stakeholder feels about her participation. In a sense, the Chart of Accounts represents the organization's view of how a stakeholder is evaluating. At any point in time, this stakeholder evaluation will be more or less accurate. It is never 100% accurate because the stakeholders themselves might not have an accurate way to measure or they may not use a consistent method for evaluation. That's why it might sometimes be useful for the organization to help the stakeholders clarify how they evaluate or at least understand how the stakeholders reach their conclusions.

Value measures represent result measures that are of value to a stakeholder. And so, we have to ask "What Is of Value to Me (WIVM)?" for each stakeholder. Naturally, different stakeholders will value different things. That's what makes organizations work. Because an employee might have something in greater abundance than he needs, such as time, he is willing to exchange it for something he wants more of but that someone else has an abundance of, such as money. Since stakeholders are exchanging different objects, their value must necessarily be negotiated. Of course, everyone's perception of value may change depending on circumstances. This is what makes value measurement somewhat uncertain (risky). Let's explore some typical measures used for Value Accounts:

- **Profit**: This is a shareholder value measure. Every business will have at least one Profit account. It is important, especially as it relates to the investment required to generate the profit. Some people associate this account with for-profit organizations and believe it isn't important to not-for-profit organizations. However, this isn't quite true. Profit is also important to not-for-profit organizations. The difference is that a business will have profit as a primary account that they would want to increase. A not-for-profit organization, on the other hand, might have profit as a control account with a value of zero. In other words, they aren't out to create huge profits but they may want to operate without losses. Another way to look at profit is simply as the difference between what you took in and what you spent. Even a not-for-profit must take in revenue to run its programs.

- **Responsiveness**: This is the speed at which a transaction is completed. Next to price, speed tends to be one of the more important things to a customer. We may not be able to place a dollar value on speed, but we know that if we make a transaction faster, then that will have greater value to the customer.

- **Price**: This is both a shareholder and a customer measure. The difference is that for a shareholder, higher is better, but for the customer, lower is better. That means price has to be negotiated.
- **Quality**: This is a family of measures. Quality can measure how closely the product comes to its specification. So, in a sense, the specification is the value measure. Quality is an indication of how close we are to it.
- **Demand**: This is a measure of how desirable a product is. Naturally, many things can impact demand, such as quality, price, etc.

Value level measures are not standard. They will depend on the business and the stakeholder, and can be anything the stakeholders decide. Value measures must often be evaluated as a group because they tend not to be independent. For example, when price moves, so might demand.

Value measures are useful for objectives, for strategies, and for valueflows, but not for functional processes or for components of a functional process.

CAPABILITY CHART OF ACCOUNTS

As we move from strategy to valueflows and then to functional processes, we need to begin thinking in terms of how to design the processes. We need to think in terms of what capabilities are important in the process to achieve the strategy and objectives. Capability, however, does not relate directly to stakeholder value. It relates to the design of the processes and the components of the processes. Let's highlight some typical capability measures:

- Quality: Degree to which the primary output meets the specification
- Throughput: Quantity of output actually delivered
- Demand: Measure of the external demand for the output of the valueflow
- Responsiveness: Speed in filling a demand request—Start-to-Finish time
- Capacity: Potential throughput under specified conditions
- Availability: Measure of the time the process is available to produce its output
- Cost: Measure of the resources consumed/used
- Productivity: A measure of throughput relative to capacity, for example
- DPMO: Defects per million opportunities—measure of process ability

Unlike Value Accounts, which can vary depending on the purpose of the organization and the stakeholders, capability accounts will tend to be more standard across processes. The account measures above, for example, apply to virtually all valueflows and functional processes, regardless of organization type and regardless of the product or service being delivered by the process. That implies that valueflows and functional processes can be managed in much the same way regardless of organization.

Capability measures tell us how well a process needs to operate with regard to a particular measure. By measuring actual performance, we can determine if there is a capability performance gap. Capability measures don't tell us what value is being produced. That's because value only has meaning when an output touches a customer/consumer. For example, we can make a perfect pizza cheaper, better, faster, but if there is no customer who wants to buy one, then there is no primary value flowing into the organization. If there is no value coming in, then there can't be any profit for the shareholders. Eventually the organization fails and there are no more jobs and so employees lose their value as well. Customer value is important because like the sun, it represents new energy entering the organizational system. Without it we can't generate value for the other stakeholders.

When we identified the valueflows, we created a valueflow Value Chart of Accounts that flowed from the strategy. Next, it's time to translate the valueflow Value Chart of Accounts into a valueflow Capability Chart of Accounts. In order to do that, we need a deeper understanding of the potential capability measures and what they tell us about the process. Once we propagate the strategy level measures to the valueflow level, we are able to measure and monitor the value accounts up to the valueflow level. But in order to truly understand the processes, we must get into the detail and propagate the stakeholder measures even further to the inside of each valueflow, down to the functional tier, and even to the component tier. The question is how do we do this? The measures that the stakeholders care about tend to be result measures. These are things we can only measure at the end. And we do need these because they represent the ultimate proof that we are "on purpose." But these may not be the measures that will mean something to someone inside the functional process being executed. For example, someone inside the Production valueflow isn't necessarily going to relate to a revenue dollar number. They may understand what it means but they can't use that number day to day, hour by hour, to ensure that the goal will ultimately be met. So we need to translate Stakeholder Value Account measures into something different, something that correlates well but is more meaningful to the function.

Stakeholders measure value. But a process possesses capabilities. A valueflow should produce its designated output perfectly, with no defects whatsoever, consuming only those resources absolutely required and creating no external risks to other processes. Of course that's the ideal, the true north, but no valueflow will ever perform to such an ideal. So how can we measure how close we are to that ideal at any time? We have to measure the capabilities of the process.

The Capability Chart of Accounts performs this job and is shown below with some typical account measures. Notice that the measures are under the label "attributes." That's because a measure is really telling us something about the process and what it can do. Therefore, it represents an attribute of that process.

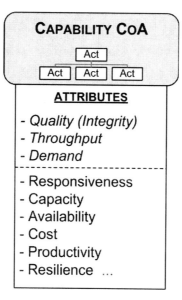

Let's discuss a few key attributes in more detail. The first three are absolutely essential to any valueflow because they measure the quality of what we are producing and how many or how much is being produced and the rate at which we are being asked to produce.

Quality: Every valueflow must produce some sort of primary output. The output of a valueflow needs to be specified so that we know if we have produced the right output and if it is a good one. Valueflow Product Quality is a measure of how much of the output meets the specification. The typical metric (the thing we measure) may be defectives and/or defects.

Throughput: This measures how much quality output is produced by the process over a given period of time. This is not how much can be or should be produced, but how much is produced. There are many different potential metrics for throughput depending on what it is that is being produced. We can virtually always measure it in several different ways. For example, if we are producing cars, then we can count cars or calculate the price value of the cars or the contribution margin for the cars. We can measure throughput based on the value to the customer or the effort and cost that goes into it. There are many different ways to measure it, and so great care needs to go into designing throughput measures. Let's look at another example. Imagine we have a plant or factory that produces motor oil products. We might have different formulations that come in different sized containers. The cost to produce each might vary and the mark-up on each might be different. So how do we measure throughput? We could measure units, but then we have different sized units. We could measure volume, but then we can produce more volume when producing larger sized containers. We could measure retail value. We could measure contribution margin. Hopefully you get the point that some measures can be obtained in so many ways. One of the problems is that the production line produces multiple product variations. That means that we may have multiple valueflows and certainly multiple variants of a valueflow using the same production resources. How we decide to measure throughput will depend on the particular process and on what needs to be managed.

Demand: This is a measure of how much output is being requested and the frequency with which we are being asked to deliver. At the valueflow level this refers to external product demand from the customer. The demand and its shape are important because they can have a strong impact on design. Imagine we have a valueflow that receives one customer order per hour for every hour of a 40-hour week. Compare that to the same valueflow receiving 40 orders during the first minute of a 40-hour week and nothing until the next week. Yes, the weekly demand is the same, but the shape of the demand is different. A valueflow with a particular design will exhibit different costs and responsiveness under each of the two demand scenarios. In this case knowing the average isn't enough. We also need to know the shape of the demand.

Responsiveness: This is a measure of the speed of the process. So it's a time measure. It measures how long it takes the process from start to finish. It is not a measure of the effort time but rather the elapsed time. If we order a pizza and start our watch when we finish dialling and we stop the watch when the pizza arrives at the door, then that's a measure of responsiveness. If it takes 45 minutes, that's the responsiveness. The handling time required to make the pizza might be only 2 to 3 minutes plus an additional 5 minutes or so to bake it. As with every measure, we have to be precise in defining it. When does the clock start? Does it start when I pick up the phone to order the pizza? Or does it start when the order is handed to the pizza maker? Perhaps it starts when the pizza has begun cooking. There can be numerous responsiveness type measures. It is not unusual to have more than one.

Let's return to the MRI test example where the wait time was the measure in question. The wait time is interesting because it is time during which no one is doing anything. There is no response-ability attached to wait time. There is probably someone who books the appointment, and there is a different person who carries out the MRI test. The booking person can't do anything about the fact that there is a queue for the test, so he can't help you to get an earlier time. The MRI test person is not involved in booking so she can't do anything either. And there is no one in between. Effectively, there is no one to account for the wait time. There is no one accountable for the valueflow and that's where the responsiveness would be visible. So it increases until it becomes intolerable. Lack of valueflow accountability is one reason that wait times tend to increase, whether it's getting a doctor's appointment or trying to get through to a call centre.

Capacity: This represents the ideal theoretical throughput, assuming nothing goes wrong, and we have full availability and continuous demand. Capacity should always be more than throughput. There are many ways to measure it, and the same metrics that can be used for throughput could be used for capacity at the valueflow level. Capacity will almost always have multiple factors, of which one may be the current constraint. For example, we may have sufficient machines to produce 100 widgets per hour but only enough manpower to produce 50. In that case it's the manpower that is the constraint on the valueflow. As with throughput, capacity can have many values because functional processes, whether they are manufacturing or services, have multiple valueflows going through a fixed set of resources. In the service sector, this issue may be further compounded by the fact that transactions may vary in terms of the quantity of resources required to complete them. So if we measure transactions completed for throughput, we might nudge people into handling the easier transactions first, the ones that require less capacity.

Availability: This is a measure of the percentage of the time (or some other metric) that the process is available to produce the output. This can sometimes be difficult to measure but is still useful. Suppose the pizza guy is by himself assembling the pizzas. When he goes to the washroom, no pizzas can be made. So, at least part of the process is unavailable. Or let's say that the power goes out for 30 minutes and there is no backup power; then the oven is not available to complete pizzas during those 30 minutes. Because the people are still available, there will be some functional processes that are still available to do work. Availability is a simple concept to understand in an environment where equipment is being used, but it applies to all processes. Let's say you work for a bank and the boss calls a staff meeting for one hour. Whatever process you are part of is potentially not available while you aren't there. At the least, it will only be partially unavailable. One reason that throughput is less than capacity is due to lack of 100% availability for most real processes. As a personal example, I worked with an organization that was unhappy with the throughput of one of its customer processes. The claim was that there was more than sufficient capacity to handle the transactions. In this case, the capacity was all about people. When we looked at the start-to-end valueflow together, we discovered that about 50% of staff time went towards meetings, answering phones and queries, and other activities that were not directed at processing the customer transactions. Even though the organization had a certain number of people, half of the time was unavailable to process transactions. That was an eye-opener that generated management demand for change. Knowing how much of the nominal capacity is available to produce output can be enlightening.

Productivity: This is a measure of how close the process comes to its maximum throughput. There are different ways to measure this. For example, we can measure throughput versus capacity. We can measure the number of defects at every step of the process as an indicator. Capability is another reason the throughput is below capacity. If we have defects then these have to be reworked. That takes time, effort, and resources but doesn't add to the throughput. In other words, correcting defects consumes capacity but doesn't contribute to throughput. Productivity is a measure that takes into consideration all the things that get in the way of producing throughput. This can include availability, defects, realized risks, and other factors.

Cost: Cost refers to how much it takes to produce the output of the process. Cost can be subdivided into raw material (for physical products), direct labour, indirect labour, and other items. Cost is often difficult to calculate for an item. Also, cost will vary depending on the throughput because there are variable costs and there are fixed costs.

There are other measures that may be of interest depending on the process, organization, and industry. Every valueflow has its own unique *Capability Profile*. For one process, availability might need to be 95% while for another 80% is sufficient. It is useless to talk in terms of which measure is more important. We need to define, for each valueflow, what the profile needs to look like and what it is. Then we must move to make changes to close any gaps and achieve that profile so that we can meet the performance needs.

Capability measures can be more difficult with regards to setting targets and getting actual measures. A great deal of thinking and practice needs to go into the development of a truly good Capability Chart of Accounts.

PRIMARY VERSUS CONTROL ACCOUNTS

Our Pizza Chart of Accounts example includes only primary account measures. But there can also be control measures. At each tier, from business objective down to functional process, a Chart of Accounts will always contain primary measures but can also contain control measures or accounts.

Primary measure: Represents the account measure that we want to change and the target we want to achieve. These are usually the measures we most want to improve.

Control measure: Represents an account measure for which we want to set a floor below which we don't want to go. Sometimes we can get more of one thing by giving up something else. For example, we might determine that we want to reduce the cost (primary) of a certain help desk transaction. But what if we have an option that would accomplish that but would also lead to an increase in the customer wait time? If we don't want such an option to be selected, then we can specify a control account—wait time (control)—and specify a target that we don't want to violate.

In the pizza example we want to grow the business and so we have set a primary measure for revenue. But we may not want to grow at the expense of profits. So we might also want to include profit as a control account measure (shown as italic-underlined). But rather than setting a target for profit, we set a floor, a value we don't want to go below. The updated Chart of Accounts is shown here. It says we have a target for Revenue, but we have a floor for Profit. Here the floor is expressed as an absolute number. It could also be expressed as a relative number or formula.

STRATEGY: PICKUP			
	NEW TARGET ($000)	CURRENT TARGET ($000)	GAP ($000)
Revenue	960	720	(240)
Profit	*>= 35*	*30*	*(5)*
PICKUP MARK-COM-SALES VALUEFLOW			
Revenue	960	720	(240)
Units	80	60	(20)
PICKUP PRODUCTION VALUEFLOW			
Units	80	60	(20)
Cost	800	600	(200)

Control measures are important to specify when it's possible to increase one account at the expense of another. Of course, in order to specify control measures we would need to understand the relationship among the various accounts and how they impact each other.

It should be a matter of policy that when changing one process, the Chart of Accounts for other processes always represents a set of control measures. In other words, it should not be acceptable to improve one process at the expense of another, without a deliberate decision to do so.

BALANCE SHEET AND PROFIT & LOSS STATEMENT

As part of financial management, organizations produce Profit & Loss Statements and Balance Sheets. But what are these? A P&L statement summarizes the revenue, costs, and expenses incurred during a specific period of time. It provides information that shows the ability of an organization to generate profit. A P&L statement is based on some financial Chart of Accounts.

Similarly, we should produce P&L statements for a valueflow, based on its Value Chart of Accounts. That would indicate the organization's ability to achieve the business objectives through its processes.

A balance sheet is a statement of financial position. It is a summary of the financial balances of an organization and is based on the financial Chart of Accounts. Similarly, we can produce a balance sheet for a valueflow, based on its Value Chart of Accounts.

Let's look at a potential application of this. Let's say that we have a Software Development valueflow for software projects. Every project represents an individual execution of the Software Development valueflow, even though it is a long valueflow. For every project, we can produce a P&L statement. Rather than covering a specific period of time, the P&L covers the project. We might record such things as the total benefits realized over a period of time—this is the equivalent of revenue. We might also record the investment required to produce the software—this is the equivalent of cost. The net of the two could go into the Software Development projects Balance Sheet. This would provide a running summary of the contribution being made by Software Development projects.

Why would we want to do this? We use financial reports to manage the financial health of the organization. We can also use P&L statements and Balance Sheets to manage the health of the processes. And the Value Charts of Accounts would be the backbone for this. So if someone asks the question "What value is being added by the Software Development Group?" we should be able to answer that question by looking at the relevant Balance Sheet. Of course this doesn't exist in most organizations, so when the question is asked, it is answered with an argument rather than with relevant facts. Later we will explore the concept of an Office *For* Strategy Achievement as an organization unit, which could provide a home for this information.

The Valueflow P&L and the Valueflow Balance Sheet are two tools that can be used to verify that any changes we make are indeed leading to progress. Like the financial counterpart, the valueflow Balance Sheet adds long-term memory to our process performance management.

THE DASHBOARD

Is a dashboard different from a Chart of Accounts? A dashboard contains metrics; so does a Chart of Accounts. If you want to consider them as the same because they both contain measures and metrics, we have no objection. However, I believe that there is a big difference. That difference is in how each is developed and in *how each leads us to think*. The Chart of Accounts is focused on accountability. The Chart of Accounts is a framework for linking intent to execution through the tiers of objective, strategy, valueflow, and functional process. The Chart of Accounts is meant to be an integral part of the Process Management System, in the same way that the Financial Chart of Accounts is an integral part of the organization's Financial Management System. In fact, the Process Management System is in support of the Financial Management System.

Dashboards come and go. Metrics come and go. Sometimes dashboards are used to manage but other times they are nothing more than collections of things we can measure. Rarely do the measures directly relate execution to strategy to objectives. That's because dashboard measures are "brain stormed" in, rather than designed in.

A discussion of dashboard measures centres around leading measures, lagging measures, results measures, and indicators. The discussion is around whether a measure is qualitative or quantitative. All of these things are good and they apply to CoA measures as well. But the point is that the dashboard seems to focus people on the technical aspect of the measure, rather than its purpose and its target—the entity the measure is trying to describe and manage.

On the other hand, the discussion of the Chart of Accounts centres on business objectives, strategy, valueflows, and functional processes. We have been talking about stakeholder value and about process capability. These are the things we need to understand and debate. It may be fun to have a discussion on whether a measure is an indicator or a lagging measure, but first we have to decide what that measure helps us to manage and whether or not it needs to be managed. Then, someone must be accountable to manage each account measure.

The distinction between a dashboard and a Chart of Accounts can be small if you think about them just in terms of measures. But if you think about them in terms of their socio impact—how they make us think—then the difference between the two can be significant. The Chart of Accounts is an extension of the dashboard concept with a focus on accountability and linkage from intent through to execution. Like the financial Chart of Accounts, it is meant to be an organization-wide tool to help manage business processes to achieve strategic objectives. It is meant to provide a direct and continuous link from business objectives and strategy through to functional processes.

SUMMARY

Manageability is about being able to produce the outcomes that we want. And accountability is at the heart of manageability. So how do we implement accountability in an organization? First of all, we need to distinguish between personal accountability and process accountability. Personal accountability can be all about who gets the credit and who gets the blame—carrot and stick. Process accountability is different. It is about being able to tie effects to causes. It is about understanding how things work.

We manage what we account for. Process accountability is at a higher, more encompassing level than personal accountability. Therefore, it should be defined first. What we are saying is that it is useless to try to establish personal performance inside a poorly designed process. The Chart of Accounts (CoA) is a framework for specifying those things of interest that we need to account for and manage in order to achieve the objectives and purpose. The CoA is an enterprise management tool for specifying process accountability first and personal accountability next. The CoA is a linked set of measurements that start with an objective and proceed all the way down to functional process measures. It comprises all the things of interest that we need to measure in order to monitor process performance and detect gaps that need our attention.

At the objective and strategy levels, the Stakeholder Value Chart of Accounts measures value delivered to the stakeholders. At the functional process level, the Capability Chart of Accounts measures process capability, such as capacity, defects, responsiveness, etc. At the valueflow level, it measures both value and capability, and so the valueflow is the connection between value and capability.

The Stakeholder Value Chart of Accounts measures not just value for the shareholders, but for all the stakeholders. If we want to design more perfect processes, then we have to understand which measure is a carrot and which is a stick for every stakeholder group. The major stakeholder groups include consumer, payer, customer, employee, supplier, sharefunder, and shareholder.

We introduced the concept of a Capability Chart of Accounts because individual functional processes don't necessarily deliver something to which value can be attributed. Functional processes, however, need to have certain capabilities in order to be able to deliver to the value. These capabilities can be measured in terms of quality, throughput, demand, responsiveness, capacity, availability, cost, and others. A functional process needs to be designed based on its functional requirements *and* based on the capability required for that process.

It is not uncommon to improve one performance measure at the expense of another. And so the idea of primary and control accounts was introduced. A primary measure represents the account measure that we want to change and the target we want to achieve. A control account measure represents an account measure for which we want to set a floor below which we don't want to go. This helps ensure that any proposed changes actually lead to a more perfect process rather than just a trade-off. We are after global progress, not local progress at the expense of others.

A dashboard contains measures. So does a Chart of Accounts. Dashboards are not typically developed by objective. In addition, they also don't normally contain fully linked measures from objective to functional process. The Chart of Accounts expands on the dashboard, and is a management tool to ensure accountability and manageability. It links objectives to strategy to valueflow to functional process. It also helps us to think of measures as representing things that need to be managed and not just measured. If you love dashboards, then you can think of the Chart of Accounts as viewing measures from a more structured point of view. You can look at a horse from the back and you get a certain picture. You can look at a horse from the front and you get a different picture. It may be the same horse but the view affects what you see and how you think about the horse.

7

Propagating Performance—A Case Study

The beauty of cause and effect is that when we understand how they are related we can focus on creating the right causes.

It's time for a break from acquiring new knowledge. Let's explore how to apply some of the concepts discussed so far. We will take each concept in turn and apply it to a realistic yet fictitious organization called Widgets 4 All.

A useful framework should allow us to build the model one step at a time. It should also keep step complexity to a minimum. We will follow the strategy-function deployment approach already presented and step through each tier. To refresh our memory, the strategy deployment diagram is repeated below. Feel free to take a minute to review it.

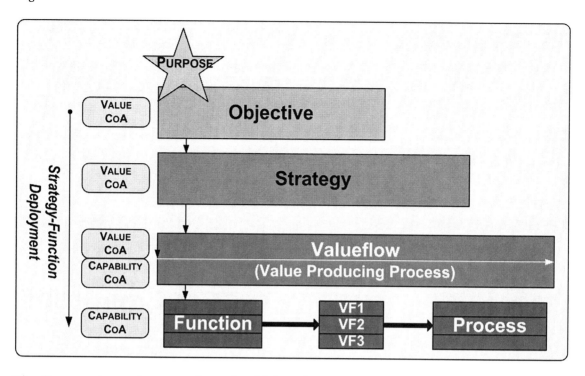

The diagram shows that everything should flow from purpose through each tier and down to the functional processes.

> **Step 1**: We begin with one stakeholder and develop one or more objectives that reflect the purpose for that stakeholder. Often we begin with the shareholders. But we should not forget the others.
>
> **Step 2**: Then we take one objective at a time. For each objective, we develop one or more strategies, which, together, will achieve that objective.
>
> **Step 3**: Then we take each strategy in turn. Each strategy is going to need one or more valueflows in order to achieve it. And so we first identify those primary valueflows. Then we identify any secondary or dependent valueflows.
>
> **Step 4**: Each valueflow comprises several functional processes and we identify those, paying particular attention to those we think will need to be changed.

We will follow these simple steps to develop a strategy-function deployment map. It will clearly show how a business objective is linked to execution, which happens at the functional tier. When we have completed a deployment map for each objective, we will begin to see if there are any cross-impacts. For example, a number of strategies may require the same valueflow. Or several strategies may impact the same objective. Knowing these cross-impacts will help us to prioritize or sequence changes to achieve the greatest positive impact. When we are done, we will have a set of Charts of Accounts for each objective. The charts will link in a tree-like structure, as shown in the following diagram.

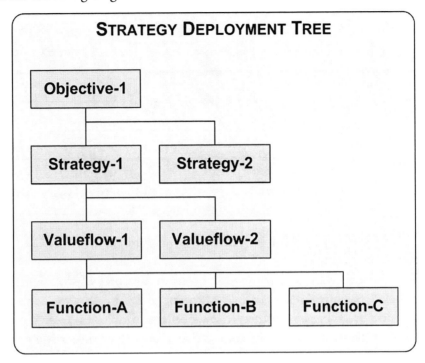

The tree will allow us to manage performance from the objective, rather than simply managing changes at the functional level with no real assurance of which objectives are impacted by specific functional changes. If someone asks for resources and funds to make a functional change that seems to make sense yet is not attached to any objective gap, then we should question who or what the change is serving since it isn't connected to any of the objectives.

A strategy-deployment map makes the connections visible and allows us to generate the proper change projects rather than being forced to select from among a list of initiatives that may not even be related to any organizational objective. The purpose of strategy-function deployment is to have each tier flow from the previous, verified, agreed-to, accountable tier. That way we maintain a kind of chain of accountability, which ensures that we remain on purpose.

So let's explore an example.

FROM PURPOSE TO OBJECTIVES

Imagine a fictional organization called Widgets 4 All Corporation, which is updating its strategic plan. Management has determined that the organization needs to grow in order to remain competitive. They are following the strategy-function deployment approach and have developed an objective related to growth, as captured in the table below.

WIDGETS 4 ALL: BUSINESS OBJECTIVE		
STAKEHOLDER	MEASURE – PRIMARY	MEASURE – CONTROL
Customer		
Employee		
Supplier		
Shareholder	Increase revenue from $50M to $100M by Jan 20xx.	Maintain profitability at no less than 6% of sales—current is 8%.

Here we have a financial objective that is of interest only to the shareholder. So there is nothing yet for the other stakeholders to get excited about. It shows that we have a primary measure, which reflects the goal we want to achieve, and a control measure, which is a measure that we don't want to violate. Control measures are important to ensure that we don't inadvertently achieve one measure by giving up another. In essence, the primary measure specifies a ceiling that we are reaching for, while the control measure specifies a floor that we don't want to break through. The control measure should be a different measure from the primary measure. Notice that the control measure is specified at a lower target than it is currently. Sometimes we know that there is a risk of a particular account measure worsening, and we are willing to accept that, but only to a point.

The importance of showing all stakeholder groups is that we want to make sure that we aren't creating any additional risks. In the above example, we are only showing the objective that is changing. Even though there isn't anything for the other stakeholders to get excited about yet, there is nothing evident that should scare them in any way. Of course, a full Chart of Accounts would show all other account measures as well. That way we can see what's changing and what's not.

Now let's look at a different objective.

WIDGETS 4 ALL: BUSINESS OBJECTIVE		
STAKEHOLDER	MEASURE – PRIMARY	MEASURE – CONTROL
Customer		
Employee		
Supplier		
Shareholder	Improve profitability by reducing costs by 5% of sales.	Maintain sales at least at current level of $50M.

In this particular case, we again have a financial shareholder objective. But here there is something for the employees to potentially be concerned about. How will costs be reduced? Will people be laid off? Will compensation be reduced somehow? If we try to implement this objective with those unspoken threats left open, then we need to be prepared for resistance and other hidden risks. Certainly we aren't going to get everyone willingly aligned behind this objective. Let's say that the organization's intent is to maintain the current workforce intact, that the intent is to keep all employees.

We might reformulate the objective so that it is more specific, as follows:

WIDGETS 4 ALL: BUSINESS OBJECTIVE		
STAKEHOLDER	MEASURE – PRIMARY	MEASURE – CONTROL
Customer		
Employee		Maintain current levels of workforce and compensation.
Supplier		
Shareholder	Improve profitability by reducing costs by 5% of sales.	Maintain sales at least at current level of $50M.

This is better in that it makes it clear what we don't want touched and it makes it clear that we are thinking about the other stakeholders. If all the objectives are associated with a single stakeholder group and none of the other stakeholders are mentioned, we might want to ensure that we aren't creating any stakeholder-related risks. Of course, if we had not made the empty space visible, we might never be concerned about the other stakeholders. By making all stakeholders visible, we make sure that we don't forget them. In the North American culture we would probably rather not see the empty space, but it is important to make visible both what is there and what is not, in order to get a fuller picture. The concept of always showing the picture of the whole puzzle along with the pieces we have filled in will recur many times in this book. Useful frameworks should help us to see what we have and what we are missing.

FROM OBJECTIVE TO STRATEGIES

OK, so we can imagine developing a number of different objectives during planning. For each objective we need to develop a corresponding set of strategies. Our set might include a single strategy or several. Let's continue with the revenue objective reproduced below.

WIDGETS 4 ALL: BUSINESS OBJECTIVE		
STAKEHOLDER	MEASURE – PRIMARY	MEASURE – CONTROL
Customer		
Employee		
Supplier		
Shareholder	Increase revenue from $50M to $100M by Jan 20xx.	Maintain profitability at no less than 6% of sales—current is 8%.

Based on the above objective, imagine the following potential strategies:

Strategy 1: Increase sales, using current "Widget A" product, in the Canadian market, by Jan 20xx.

Strategy 2: Increase sales by developing and selling one new product, to the existing Canadian market, by Jan 20xx.

Let's express the Chart of Accounts in the form of a Strategy Deployment Map.

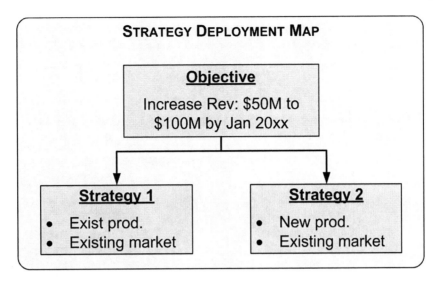

Let's also update the table to include the strategy statements. We are going to drop the control measure from the table for now, and focus on specifying and linking to the primary measures.

WIDGETS 4 ALL: STRATEGY DEPLOYMENT		
STAKEHOLDER	OBJECTIVE	STRATEGY
Customer		
Employee		
Supplier		
Shareholder	Increase revenue from $50M to $100M by Jan 20xx.	Increase sales using current "Widget A" product in current Canadian market. by $25M from $50M to $75M by Jan 20xx.
		Increase sales by developing and selling one new product to the existing Canadian market. by $25M from $0 to $25M by Jan 20xx.

Here is the corresponding map. The advantage of the map presentation is that it is visually stronger, showing how a tier flows from the previous one.

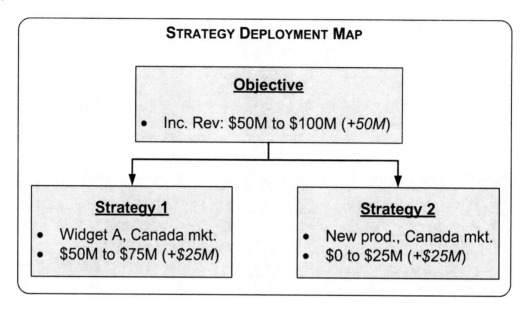

So we have one objective, which we are planning to achieve using two separate strategies. Neither strategy on its own is expected to achieve the objective. It will take both strategies. The key here is that we have tied the two strategies directly to a specific objective. And we have tied the strategy account measures to the account measure of the objective. We have created a direct link between the two.

FROM STRATEGY TO VALUEFLOWS

So what's next? Let's consult the strategy-function deployment diagram again.

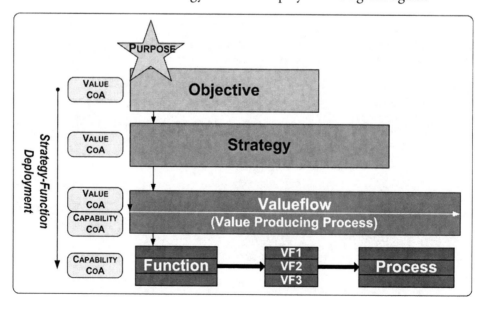

It seems that we now need to tie each strategy to one or more valueflow processes. So now we need to first identify which valueflow processes need to be engaged and then link them to the strategies through performance measures. To help us identify the valueflows, let's quickly review the valueflow definitions and the categories.

A valueflow comprises a chain of functional processes. It produces an output for an external customer or for an internal process. The output is required to achieve or contribute to a stakeholder outcome of measurable value. The valueflow exhibits capability performance.

The two major types of valueflows are:

1. **Customer Valueflow**: A start-to-finish chain of functional processes that delivers an output (product or service) that an external customer wants and is willing to pay for. A valueflow responds to a customer demand. An example might be a Passport valueflow. The process produces a Passport for a customer.
2. **Enabling Valueflow**: A start-to-finish chain of functional processes that delivers a component output that will become part of some valueflow. The component is produced in order to close an actual or potential process performance gap. An example might be a Workflow Design process that produces a new workflow that might be used to improve how passports are issued. The output (a new method) is a component that is used by the receiving process.

Having identified and selected strategies for the objective, we now need to connect each objective to a valueflow. We do this because value is delivered through individual valueflows. Therefore, if we can measure the value throughput at the valueflow level and if we connect each valueflow to the strategy account, then we should be able to predict the likelihood of achieving each enterprise objective.

Let's continue with the example and explore Strategy 1, repeated below:

- Increase sales by $25M
- using current "Widget A" product
- in current Canadian market
- from $50M to $75M
- by Jan 20xx.

Sales Revenue is a measure of Demand for a specific individual product. Today, the company only makes a single product called "Widget A," as specified in the strategy. If the company made several products, then we would want to identify each product as being potentially produced by a different valueflow, with a different demand. But for now we have only one Demand Valueflow. Let's call it "Widget A Individual Demand." In the next chapter we will introduce a general valueflow map, which will help us identify valueflows.

So, let's update the Strategy Deployment map to include the first valueflow tied to Strategy 1.

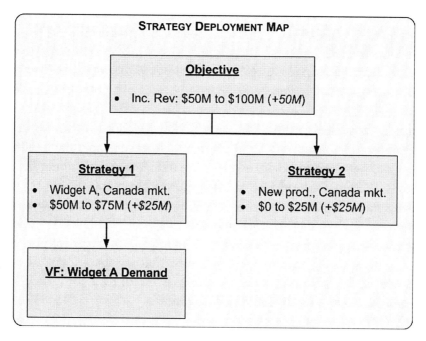

But, of course, we need to propagate the performance measures from the strategy tier down to the valueflow tier. In this case we have a single valueflow corresponding to the strategy, so propagating is simple. Let's develop the Chart of Accounts for the Individual Demand valueflow. It looks like this:

WIDGET A INDIVIDUAL DEMAND (STRATEGY 1)			
SHAREHOLDER VALUE COA			
	CURRENT TARGET	STRATEGY TARGET	GAP
Revenue	$50M	$75M	($25M)
Units	50k	75k	(25k)

What the diagram and CoA say is:

1. Strategy 1 impacts the Widget A Individual Demand valueflow. We called it the Widget A Individual Demand based on the name of the product that is currently sold by this valueflow. If there were two products there would be two valueflows, each with its own targets.

2. The strategy is intended on getting us from a current sales target (current strategy) of $50M to $75M (breakthrough strategy).
3. We have two accounts/measures: revenue and units. Why did we do this? We could have decided to use a pricing strategy where some of the increase in sales comes from an increase in price. So this demonstrates that the strategy as stated is not specific enough. In this example, let's assume that the price is a standard $1,000 per unit and that we have decided to keep the price at the current level. Therefore, we will need to sell 25,000 additional units to make an extra $25M. There are many instances where we will want to express a certain account using more than one measure just to make sure that we have a fuller understanding of the objective.

But are we finished yet? Actually, we don't yet know. We have to look upstream and downstream from this valueflow to determine whether other valueflows might be impacted as well. So far we know that the Widget A Individual Demand valueflow (sales) is impacted because the strategy measure is in terms of sales, which is what this valueflow produces. Let's assume that we have determined that there is enough market demand to support the strategy, that it's a question of how we are selling the product and, therefore, no upstream (prior) valueflows are impacted.

But what about downstream? Clearly if we sell more of Widget A, we will have to produce and deliver more of Widget A as well. Therefore, we should add the customer delivery or fulfillment valueflow as well. Since we are only making Widget A, let's call it the Widget A Production Valueflow.

Here is the updated Strategy Deployment map for the demand and production valueflow.

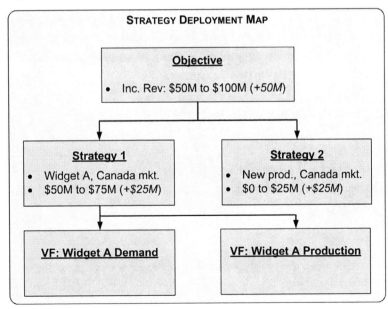

131

Here is the Chart of Accounts for the demand and production valueflows.

WIDGET A INDIVIDUAL DEMAND (STRATEGY 1)			
SHAREHOLDER VALUE COA			
	CURRENT TARGET	STRATEGY TARGET	GAP
Revenue	$50M	$75M	($25M)
Units	50k	75k	(25k)

WIDGET A PRODUCTION (STRATEGY 1)			
SHAREHOLDER VALUE COA			
	CURRENT TARGET	STRATEGY TARGET	GAP
Revenue	$50M	$75M	($25M)
Units	50k	75k	(25k)

The numbers look identical and that makes sense because we have to deliver as many units as we sell. We called the measure "Production Revenue" here and it refers to the value of units delivered and is measured in dollars. However, to people working in a production valueflow, a measure of revenue may not make as much sense as units, since all units are the same price. So we have Production Units. We can imagine a different scenario where a single product has different prices due to options. In such a scenario the revenue measure might be more meaningful.

We can see that the current strategy target is $50M and that the new breakthrough target is $75M. So let's say we are done for now. We have linked an objective to two strategies and we have linked one of those strategies to two valueflows.

Now let's look at the second strategy, repeated below:

- Increase sales by $25M
- by developing and selling one new product
- to the existing Canadian market
- from $0 to $25M
- by Jan 20xx.

Again we can see that the Individual Demand valueflow is the primary one involved. But it's not the Widget A Individual Demand. We have called it the "Widget X Individual Demand" valueflow and it shows that we will be going from a target of $0—because it is new and we don't yet have any sales—to a target of $25M. Let's update the Chart of Accounts to include the new product.

SHAREHOLDER VALUE COA			
WIDGET A INDIVIDUAL DEMAND (STRATEGY 1)			
	CURRENT TARGET	STRATEGY TARGET	GAP
Revenue	$50M	$75M	($25M)
Units	50k	75k	(25k)
WIDGET X INDIVIDUAL DEMAND (STRATEGY 2)			
	CURRENT TARGET	STRATEGY TARGET	GAP
Revenue	$0	$25M	($25M)
Units	0k	25k	(25k)
Total Rev	$50M	$100M	($50M)
Total Units	50k	100k	(50k)

As before, if we sell more, then we must deliver more. So again there is a production valueflow that is impacted. Let's call it the "Widget X Production" valueflow. Since it is the same family of production valueflows, let's update the CoA, showing them together along with a total. The bottom of the dashboard shows the total throughput change in Revenue and Units for the two strategies combined.

SHAREHOLDER VALUE COA			
WIDGET A PRODUCTION (STRATEGY 1)			
	CURRENT TARGET	STRATEGY TARGET	GAP
Revenue	$50M	$75M	($25M)
Units	50k	75k	(25k)
WIDGET X PRODUCTION (STRATEGY 2)			
	CURRENT TARGET	STRATEGY TARGET	GAP
Revenue	$0	$25M	($25M)
Units	0k	25k	(25k)
Total Rev	$50M	$100M	($50M)
Total Units	50k	100k	(50k)

But are we finished? Since we have created a new Individual Demand valueflow— "Widget X Individual Demand"—we should also look upstream for impacts. If we are to sell units of a currently non-existing product, then there must be some valueflow that creates new products and develops a market for them. Let's call it the Market Demand valueflow, which is upstream (prior) from the Individual Demand valueflow. Its purpose is to innovate, produce a new product, and develop the market demand for it.

So, we need to add a Market Demand valueflow to the list of valueflows that must be engaged. The CoA for that valueflow might look like this:

SHAREHOLDER COA			
WIDGET A MARKET DEMAND (STRATEGY 2)			
	CURRENT TARGET	STRATEGY TARGET	GAP
Market	$?	$?	$?
# of Models	0	1	(1)

There is no current or strategy target value because we haven't yet engaged anyone from the Market Demand valueflow. So we have no measures for Market Demand. We only need one new product according to the strategy, so that's why we have indicated [1] for number of models (this is the number of new product models). Naturally, none of these Charts of Accounts can get completed without the active engagement of the appropriate subject matter experts. We don't yet know what numbers to put into this chart. But part of strategy deployment is to identify where more work is necessary in order to proceed. Developing the chart and identifying measures is a crucial step that serves to align everyone that needs to be aligned to the particular objective and strategy. It ensures that people are communicating about the right things and that they are doing so in both a qualitative and a quantitative way. The process should be highly interactive. The whole point is to make sure that the objective is thought through and that we have in place a set of account measures that can be used to measure success and to determine if we are on the right path.

Below is a summary of the Chart of Accounts for the first strategy, beginning at the valueflow tier. It shows the measures we have so far.

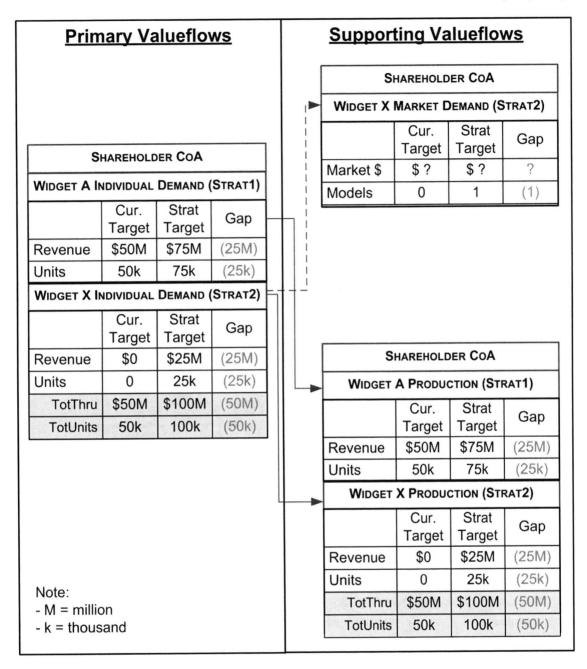

SHAREHOLDER CoA		
WIDGET X MARKET DEMAND (STRAT2)		
	Cur. Target	Strat Target	Gap
Market $	$?	$?	?
Models	0	1	(1)

Primary Valueflows

SHAREHOLDER CoA		
WIDGET A INDIVIDUAL DEMAND (STRAT1)		
	Cur. Target	Strat Target	Gap
Revenue	$50M	$75M	(25M)
Units	50k	75k	(25k)
WIDGET X INDIVIDUAL DEMAND (STRAT2)		
	Cur. Target	Strat Target	Gap
Revenue	$0	$25M	(25M)
Units	0	25k	(25k)
TotThru	$50M	$100M	(50M)
TotUnits	50k	100k	(50k)

Supporting Valueflows

SHAREHOLDER CoA		
WIDGET A PRODUCTION (STRAT1)		
	Cur. Target	Strat Target	Gap
Revenue	$50M	$75M	(25M)
Units	50k	75k	(25k)
WIDGET X PRODUCTION (STRAT2)		
	Cur. Target	Strat Target	Gap
Revenue	$0	$25M	(25M)
Units	0	25k	(25k)
TotThru	$50M	$100M	(50M)
TotUnits	50k	100k	(50k)

Note:
- M = million
- k = thousand

This summary Chart of Accounts diagram depicts the primary valueflows that are affected on the left and the supporting valueflows on the right. It also shows the upstream valueflow higher up and the downstream valueflows lower down. This way we can get a visual sense of the valueflows involved. Naturally these Charts of Accounts are not yet complete. We would want to add dates and it would make sense to develop the targets into scheduled targets. We wouldn't, for example, want to meet the target for the Widget Market Demand so closely to the Jan 20xx deadline that we have no time to sell the product. The exact presentation that you use is not critical as long as it is quantifiable and visible.

But remember that we had a second objective related to profitability. Let's say that we developed the strategy deployment map for that objective and obtained the following result:

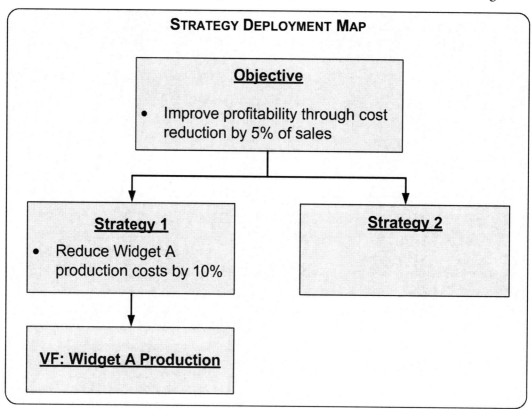

We're not going to go into detail on how we arrived at this. You can study it at your leisure. The key thing to notice is that the Widget A Production valueflow also supports the profitability objective. So we have one valueflow that supports two different objectives. When trying to prioritize where we should invest, it's good to know when a single valueflow is in support of multiple objectives.

FROM VALUE TO CAPABILITY

So far we have developed the Value Chart of Accounts down to the valueflows. But we have only defined the Value accounts. So how do we go from Value to Capability?

Let's focus on the Widget A Production Valueflow. At the Stakeholder level we have two measures:

1. Revenue, and
2. Units.

SHAREHOLDER COA			
WIDGET A PRODUCTION (STRATEGY 1)			
	CURRENT TARGET	STRATEGY TARGET	GAP
Revenue	$50M	$75M	($25M)
Units	50k	75k	(25k)

These are throughput measures. They measure the quantity of value that flows through the valueflow. This is where we begin to need actual knowledge of the inside of the valueflow. We know that capacity, availability, and productivity all work to affect the throughput. In general we can imagine the following relationship:

Throughput = f ([Capacity] X [Availability] X [Productivity])

This defines throughput as a function of capacity, availability, and productivity. Basically what this says is that we start with an initial capacity. Then we multiply by the percentage of time during which the process is available and then multiply by the productivity. So let's say the capacity is 100,000 units and the availability is 70% and the productivity is 75%. That means that:

- due to availability, we can make [100,000 * 0.70] or 70,000 units, and
- because of defects and such, only 75% of the total effort is productive so we only get [70,000 * 0.75] or 52,500 good finished units.

This is a simple example, just so we get the idea. In reality these numbers might be difficult to obtain precisely. The key thing to understand is that we have options. If we truly understand the factors that impact each of the measures, then we can take action to improve the process, even if we can't get nice precise numbers.

In the Widgets 4 All case, we need to go from a Throughput of 50,000 units to 75,000 units for Widget A. In order to determine what the options are, we need to engage those people who have accountability and who understand that particular valueflow and leave others alone for now. Let's imagine that we have the Capability metrics as depicted in the dashboard below (yearly). We need to understand what kind of results we could get if we focused on each account measure in turn.

CAPABILITY COA			
WIDGET A PRODUCTION (STRATEGY 1)			
	ACTUAL	CURRENT TARGET	GAP
Capacity	100k	-	-
Availability	70%	-	-
Productivity	75%	-	-

Given the above, we see that we can make 100,000 * 0.70 * 0.75 = 52,500 units, which is close to what the company produces today. So we can increase the capacity or we can improve availability or we can improve productivity. Let's look at the options:

1. **Capacity**: By how much would we need to increase capacity to make 75,000 units if we left the other capability measures as is? If we increased capacity to 145,000, then we would get *145,000* * 0.70 *.75 = 76,125. So if we increased capacity by 45% to 145,000 units and left the other two alone, then we could expect to produce approximately 76,000 units. Of course, increasing capacity by approximately 50% means we would need to increase some resources by that amount as well. This is the typical first response —build a bigger factory, so to speak.
2. **Availability**: By how much would we need to increase availability to make 75,000 units? 100,000 X *1.00* X 0.75 = 75,000. If we focus on availability alone we would need to get it to 100% to be able to get 75,000 units. We can see that this alone won't do the trick since we know from experience that 100% availability is not an achievable target.
3. **Productivity**: How much more productive would the process need to be to get to 75,000 units? 1000,000 X .70 X 1.0 = 70,000. If we focus on the process productivity alone and got it to 100% we could only produce 70,000 units. Again we can see that this is neither achievable, nor is it sufficient even if it were achievable.

We used the "ideal" strategy in the above scenarios. We set each attribute to its ideal setting of 100%. This shows us the best that can be achieved by focusing on that particular attribute alone. By doing that with each attribute in turn, we get a good sense of which factors should initially be explored. It also prevents us from making the mistake of focusing on an attribute that is less likely to achieve the objective. Every valueflow has its capabilities and these will need to be well understood in order to know what to do to improve the performance of the process. That's why we need the proper people engaged in strategy-function deployment. We want to generate ideas for improvement based on a good understanding of which capabilities need to be improved. We need ideas that directly impact the valueflow under consideration. Without having any measures available, the first option, to increase capacity, is the likely option that will be taken. Give me more money, more people, more technology. This is the option that has led many organizations to failure. This option works well if you can charge whatever you like to absorb the additional costs.

Of course, when we increase capacity we have to have more of everything we need. On the other hand, if we use one of the other two options, then we can change the cost-profit structure in a positive way. And, in addition, when we focus on reducing waste we also create awareness for waste that spills over into other areas.

So can we decide on a course of action based solely on these numbers? The answer is probably not. We need to begin to go inside the valueflow. We need to begin to connect to the functional processes so that we can understand how we reached the current process capability. In the end we may need some combination of the options to achieve optimal results.

Let's review what we have so far.

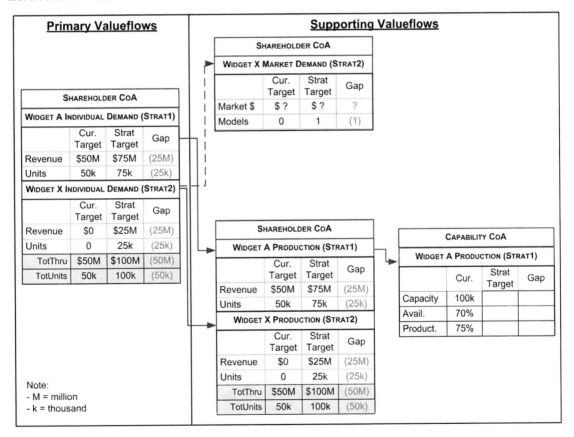

We should be starting to get the sense that it really isn't enough to simply communicate the objectives and strategy at large. We have to engage, quantify, and propagate. We should also be getting the sense that we need to see how each individual objective translates to strategy, valueflows, and then functions. If we batch all the objectives together, and then batch all the strategy statements together, and then all the functional objectives together, we lose the connectedness and we run the risk of ignoring critical components that must be addressed. We run the risk of tackling challenges that are comfortable for us rather than those that must be solved. We also run the risk of creating challenges that are too big and beyond our ability to clearly understand. By breaking up the larger problem into smaller, more manageable problems, we improve our ability to achieve the objectives, as long as we maintain the connections among the smaller problems.

SUMMARY

What we have explored in this chapter is an example of how we move from an objective to strategies and then to valueflows. We showed how the Chart of Accounts is developed and how the accounts are propagated from one tier to the next to maintain linkage. It is crucial that the measures be quantifiable; otherwise, it will be difficult or impossible to propagate them down to the valueflows. If we start with non-quantified objectives, then we can't get to quantified strategies or valueflows. This will inhibit our ability to check to see if we are on track or not. The most important aspect of progressing from an objective to a strategy and then to the valueflow is the level and extent to which we engage people and demand that they truly think through what is trying to be achieved. It is the thinking through and the dialogue that ensues that is the greatest benefit of strategy-function deployment. The framework helps us to blueprint our understanding.

PART III

THE RELATIONAL PROCESS MODEL

8

THE THREE-TIER PERSPECTIVE (2ND NF)

All models are wrong, but some are useful.

George E.P. Box

So far we have discussed how to reach the valueflow, the cross-functional unit to which we can attach value. We have discussed how to travel from an objective down to the valueflow. We have not yet discussed how to model the valueflow process so that we can design more perfect processes.

The Relational Process Model (RPM) begins at the valueflow level. It is a framework for developing a blueprint for a valueflow and all its components. For those who don't participate in strategy development or deployment, the valueflow level may be their starting point. The RPM framework comprises four normal forms:

- First Normal Form (1st NF): The Valueflow Perspective
- Second Normal Form (2nd NF): The Three-Tier Perspective
- Third Normal Form (3rd NF): The Three-Stream Perspective
- Fourth Normal Form (4th NF): The Component Perspective

The purpose of the RPM framework is to take complex processes and normalize (segment) them to reduce their complexity. Normalization divides a process into smaller, more cohesive, low-coupled segments. It allows us to understand and design processes using a systematic, stepwise, and verifiable approach that reduces personal and incidental variation.

Identifying valueflows and developing their Chart of Accounts represents the first normal form for an enterprise process model. In many ways, getting to the first normal form is the most important and difficult step because it represents a departure from the typical functional view. It is the single step that will change our *field of vision* and allow us to see all the other normal forms. Along with the Chart of Accounts, it also sets the foundation for managing the processes to the strategy. Once we propagate the strategy level measures to the valueflow level, we are able to measure and monitor the value accounts up to the valueflow level. For many organizations, to be able to manage performance to strategy up to the valueflow level would be an important step forward. It would open up their field of vision and begin to create a more performance-aware organization.

The performance gaps at this level are what should be the primary drivers behind populating the pools of value-creating projects. This would replace the traditional functional gaps as the drivers behind project creation. That doesn't mean that functional needs would be ignored. Instead, the valueflow performance gaps would filter out those functional needs that are unlikely to lead to organizational progress. In other words, the valueflow performance gaps would filter out *false* needs. They would highlight those situations where closing a functional gap would lead to more business success rather than just local success.

Of course, once we identify a performance gap we will have to identify the functional processes that may need to be changed to close the gap. In order to more deeply understand the functional processes and in order to know what to change with confidence, we need to go inside each valueflow to the functional tier and we have to translate the value measures into capability measures. The question is how do we do that?

The measures that the stakeholders care about tend to be result or value measures. These are things we can only measure at the end of the valueflow. And we do need these because they represent the ultimate proof that we are "on purpose." But to someone who is executing inside a function, there are likely other measures that will have more meaning—that will resonate more with the work he is doing. For example, someone inside the Production valueflow may understand the idea of the sales value of what he produces. But units produced may be more meaningful to him. So we may need to translate Stakeholder Value Account measures into something different, something that correlates well but is more meaningful to the local functional inhabitants, so to speak. Nevertheless, we must never lose the connection between the two. In order to do that, we need to go inside the valueflow to look at the functional processes. And how do we depict or describe the inside of a valueflow?

A process map, depicted below, is a common way to present the inside of a process. The diagram is presented for illustration purpose only. There is no need to understand its content.

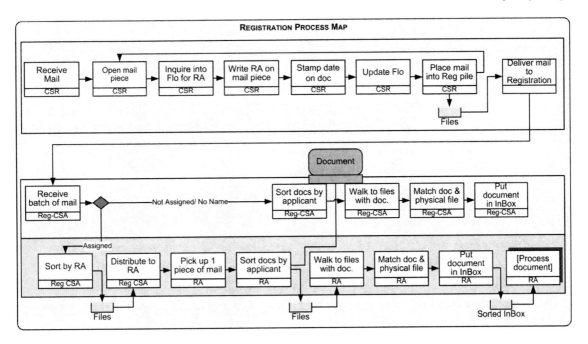

A process map is basically a diagram that depicts the steps (tasks, operations, activities) that make up the functional process. No doubt we have all seen such diagrams, which can take many forms. Sometimes these process maps can be seen adorning entire walls of conference rooms or project rooms. Process maps can take a significant amount of time and effort to develop. They are useful to functional and process improvement experts when trying to understand how a particular part of a process is performed. But they are of less value in understanding the capability attributes of a process, such as quality or throughput or availability, and they aren't the best tools to understand the flow of work or value inside the process. It is especially difficult to tie performance measures to the task level of a process. Even when we can do it, we can't compare different implementations when measures are at the task level because tasks appearing in one version may not appear in the other. In addition, it is difficult to go directly from a strategy to a functional process at the task level. Process maps are **rarely** maintained up to date and, in the end, cannot accurately represent what is truly happening in the real process. For these reasons and others, we introduce the Relational Process Model, which allows us to represent the valueflow from additional and distinct perspectives. We are not getting rid of task level models; we are adding additional perspectives to create a more complete picture and that allows us to create a blueprint incrementally.

THE THREE-TIER VALUEFLOW MODEL

The Three-Tier Valueflow model, as the name implies, is applicable to valueflows. It is a structured way to segment (normalize) each valueflow and expand it to the functional tier. It expands and builds on process mapping to tie functional processes to valueflows, which link to strategy. The three tiers of the model are the outcome tier, the output tier, and the task tier. The diagram below shows the symbols we will use to represent objects at each tier of the model. Please read the diagram from the bottom up starting with the task tier.

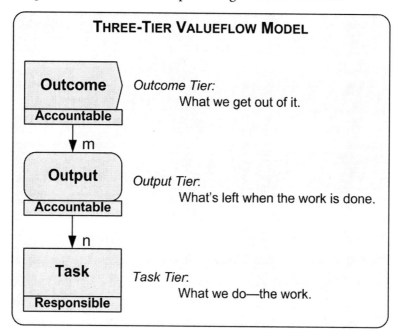

To understand a valueflow we need to know:
- *firstly,* the outcomes that it is supposed to contribute to achieving;
- *secondly,* the outputs it needs to produce; and,
- *thirdly,* the tasks required to produce those outputs.

Each of these three represents a distinct yet complementary view of the valueflow. Any of the three on their own will not completely describe the valueflow, but the three together provide a more perfect view. Notice that each tier describes essentially different things. This is in contrast with typical process maps, which have different levels of detail but describe the same kinds of things (tasks, operations, activities) at each level. Of course, for a given tier of the Three-Tier model, we can also have levels of detail. Let's summarize each tier of the model before exploring each in greater detail.

The first tier, the outcome tier, specifies the measurable/verifiable results that we wish to produce and that are consistent with the linked objectives of the organization. The outcomes are defined via the Stakeholder Value Chart of Accounts for the valueflow. The outcome represents the purpose of the valueflow. The outcome measures need to be in the same form as the objectives and strategy measures to which the valueflow is linked. Someone in the organization needs to be accountable for and manage the achievement of the outcomes of the valueflow. Accountable doesn't mean that this person is fully "responsible" for achieving these outcomes. There may be multiple responsibilities involved and the manager of the outcomes may not have authority over all the participating parties. Nevertheless, if no one is accountable for the outcomes, then it is unlikely that they will be achieved with any consistency. The CoA will be used as part of modelling the valueflow. Measurability is an important characteristic in order to continuously verify that we are on the right track. If an outcome can't be verified, then learning can't take place.

The next tier, the output tier, describes what outputs the process must produce in order to contribute to achieving the outcome and fulfilling the linked strategy. The output tier contains outputs, things that are produced. Outputs are culminating deliverables that can be used as a base upon which to build the next output, without having to understand the steps used to create the starting output. For example, a software development valueflow ultimately produces software. But there are also intermediate outputs such as the Requirements Specification and the Database Design, both of which are part of the valueflow. We can build on the Requirements Specification without understanding all the work that was required to produce it. Someone needs to be *accountable* for each output of a process, regardless of who is contributing to its production. And the accountability for each output can differ from the accountability for the valueflow as a whole.

For most, but not all, outputs we can verify the quality against a specification without any reference to the conditions and method used to produce the outputs. For example, we can evaluate the quality of a pizza without knowing how it was produced. For some outputs, such as decision outputs, we cannot evaluate quality by examining the decision. We have to review the inputs, conditions, and even the method used to reach the decision. And even that doesn't tell us the quality. It only tells us the likelihood of quality. A verdict is an example of a decision output for a Trial process. But we can't directly validate the verdict itself. All we can do is refer to the conditions and method used and make an evaluation as to the likelihood that the verdict was the correct one based on what happened during the trial. This is not a direct validation of the quality of the output. It is an evaluation of the process as a whole used to produce the verdict. Quality is a necessary measure for an output but in some instances it can only be evaluated long after it has been produced. Planning outputs fall into this category. When quality can't be evaluated directly, the risk is that other more measurable but less relevant interests will take over as time progresses, leading to process corruption. Some may argue that the justice system and the educational system are slowly deteriorating because output quality is difficult to measure and validate.

The last tier, the task tier, describes the tasks, operations, activities, or steps required in order to transform the inputs to produce the output. The task tier describes the functional work. Operators need to be identified so people know who is responsible (response-able) for executing each task. When we produce a process map, it tends to be largely a representation of the task tier. This is what we are most familiar with. The process map answers the question, "What do you do?" The task tier requires the most effort to describe and is the most distant from the strategy and objectives.

The outcome tier is the closest to the strategy. The task tier is the closest to execution. As we proceed from the outcome to the output to the task tier within a valueflow, we add distinct information and more detail. There is a geometric growth of information as we move towards the task tier. So it is important that we only progress to a particular lower tier if we must. One drawback of traditional process mapping is that it goes directly to the task tier, which contains the most amount of detail and is the most expensive to produce and maintain. If we could learn everything about a process by going to this level, it might be worth it. But we can't.

Let's look at an analogy. Suppose your car won't start. So you have it towed and your garage immediately begins to produce diagrams of all the functional components of your car. After completing all the design and wiring diagrams, the workers shake their heads at their inability to figure out what's wrong. Then someone decides to check the fuel gauge and realizes that you are out of gas.

Did you need to understand all the intricate details of how all the components function in order to determine that the gas tank was empty? No; if you had looked at the gas gauge (measurement device) you would have known right away.

Of course a process is not a car. But the analogy applies. We use measurements to tell us how well the car is *running*. They don't help us to understand why the performance is what it is but they do help us to understand where we should place our attention if we want to achieve a different level of performance, or if we are trying to find the source of a problem or performance gap (car won't start). Without measures, we can only evaluate whether a particular functional component conforms to what we believe the design should be.

The Three-Tier model helps us to connect execution performance to design to strategic objectives. Now let's explore each of the three tiers in greater detail.

OUTCOME TIER

The outcomes for a valueflow are defined through the Chart of Accounts for the valueflow. The diagram below is an example of a Car Loan valueflow at the outcome tier level.

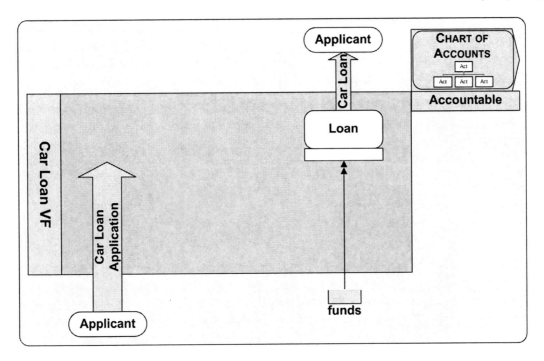

At this stage we have the final or defining output of the valueflow, which is the Loan output. We also have the demand input, which is the Car Loan Application. Finally, we have a symbol that represents the Chart of Accounts for the valueflow. So we know the boundaries or scope of the valueflow and we know there is a Value CoA.

Notice that the outcome symbol contains the Chart of Accounts. Basically, the outcome tier presents the defining output, the boundaries of the valueflow, and the Value Chart of Accounts. We will explore this in greater detail later in the chapter.

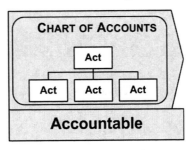

In an earlier chapter we introduced the concept of a normalized process model with four normal forms. When we have identified a valueflow, specified the boundaries, and attached a Chart of Accounts, then we have a valueflow in first normal form. To get it to its second normal form, we have to expand the inside of the valueflow to the other tiers. The outcome level is all about the Chart of Accounts, which we have already covered in previous chapters.

OUTPUT TIER

Processes produce outputs, which we hope will lead to outcomes. An Automotive Assembly valueflow may produce a car as its output. But this is not an outcome. When the customer pays for the car and we make a profit on the car, then the valueflow has produced an outcome for the shareholder. At the same time, when the customer receives the car and it solves her transportation problem (assuming that was why she bought it), then the customer has achieved her desired outcome as well. One difference between an output and an outcome is that the output is the same to everyone, but the outcome depends on the individual stakeholder. In other words, an outcome is measured from the point of view of the stakeholder. The output can be measured against a fixed specification.

The final output of a process is what distinguishes one process from another. A process that produces a car is significantly different from one that produces a Car Loan, which is different again from a process that produces a pie. On the other hand, a process that produces a Car Loan may be more similar than different from one that produces a Vacation Loan.

Processes produce intermediate work-in-process (WIP) outputs in addition to the final or defining output. The output tier of a valueflow is basically a representation of all the intermediate and final outputs produced by the process. In essence, it shows the various stages the product or service goes through in terms of the work-in-progress. When we move from the outcome layer to the output layer, we are moving from just outside the valueflow to the inside of the valueflow.

Why is this tier important? It represents another layer of segmentation. It is yet another way to *chunk* the valueflow into smaller pieces, but not quite as small as at the task level. A given valueflow may contain a single digit number of transform outputs (1 to 9). Outputs often require different skills to produce them and so might be associated with different functional units. When we produce an output tier model we can begin by slowly engaging additional people without trying to get everyone fully involved. If we are trying to improve a process or fix a problem, the output tier allows us to propagate the CoA measures at the valueflow level down to each output. That can help us to better pinpoint where the initial focus should be. Before we invest in task level process maps, let's make sure we aren't just "out of gas."

Let's look at the Car Loan valueflow expanded to show the output tier. It shows all the outputs (final and WIP) for the Car Loan valueflow.

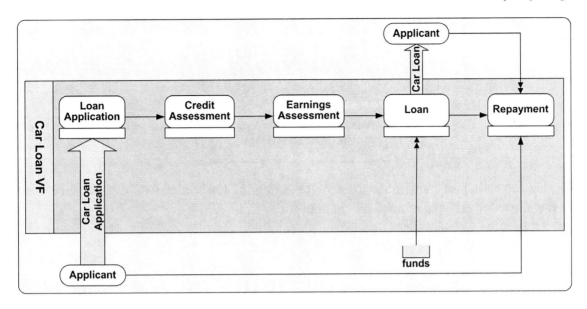

Notice that there are no tasks showing, only outputs, so it's definitely not the typical process map. Although tasks will need to be defined to produce the outputs, no tasks are shown here. Outputs, like tasks, have a precedence relationship to each other. So some outputs will be sequential, as in the diagram above. Others may require two or more outputs to come together before the next one begins.

This diagram shows the outputs that are produced along the valueflow and shows a simple sequential structure. It looks similar in structure to a task process map. That's because what is being shown is the precedence relationship among the outputs—what comes first, next, and last. Of course, a process map also shows a precedence relationship but among tasks. In this example, the precedence relationship is a simple finish-start pattern. But it can get more complex. An output tier model will be much more compact with far fewer entities than a task level model. That's because an output is the culmination of many—perhaps hundreds or thousands of—tasks.

The "Car Loan" output, which goes to the "Applicant," a customer, defines what this valueflow is—a Car Loan valueflow. We make no claim as to the accuracy of this valueflow. It is just an example.

The diagram contains the output symbol, shown below.

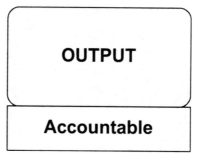

The top main part contains the name of the "Output." The bottom would contain the name of the party that is "Accountable" for that output.

Our Car Loan valueflow contains five named outputs:
1. Car Loan Application
2. Credit Assessment
3. Earnings Assessment
4. Car Loan (goes to customer and is the defining output for the Valueflow)
5. Repayment (comes from customer)

The ultimate customer output that this process produces is the "Car Loan."

Notice that by developing an output tier model, we are producing a framework for organizing any future process maps into reasonable-sized chunks. Process maps can be produced and organized by output. An output model is compact as compared with a task level model, typically by at least one order of magnitude (factor of 10). That means it takes far less time to develop.

But what else do outputs really represent? An output is a point of convergence that produces something tangible whose quality can be assessed before moving on. An output is a point where we can forget what came before and proceed forward. It can represent a potential handover point in a process. Of course, outputs have to be first identified and then specified. The specification of an output is important because without an explicit formal specification, it will be open to anyone's and everyone's interpretation. But until we have assigned someone to be accountable for each output, there is no sense in adding detail because there is no one to be accountable for the specification of that detail. Once we have someone assigned and the output has been specified, then that person can lead in the expansion of the output to the task level detail.

It is possible to have a different person accountable for each of the outputs. When that's the case, then it's important that both the receiver and the producer have a common specification for the output. What that means is that once the specification for each output is agreed to, we could, if we wanted to, have separate teams defining the task level detail for each output concurrently.

The ability to reliably discover and produce requirements in parallel has the potential of dramatically reducing the length of technology and process improvement projects.

An output may seem like it's a single output, as shown by the picture on the left. But when the producer and receiver of an output have different ideas about what that output is, then we get the picture to the right.

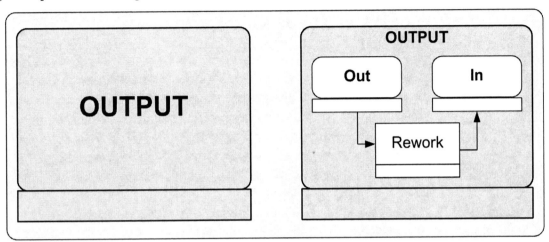

It shows that an output called Out is reworked by the receiving process into an output called In before the next segment of the process starts. Of course, this is a waste and can lead to errors. It is not uncommon, especially for knowledge-based valueflows, for the outputs from one functional process to be reworked by the next functional process before work continues. This causes additional effort that does not add value and can and does create errors. To avoid this, it's important to standardize the specifications of the outputs of a process so that the outputs from one process are immediately useable by the next process in the valueflow.

Once we have standardized the outputs, we can eliminate these wasteful efforts and then move on to defining how the outputs will be produced. We can even explore different implementation options.

In the Three-Tier Valueflow model, we define accountability separately for each of the three tiers. Firstly, someone needs to be given *accountability* for the outcome. Secondly, each output needs to have someone *accountable* for its specification and its production.

TASK TIER

Once we have completed the output tier and assigned accountabilities, we are ready to proceed to the task tier. The task symbol is represented here.

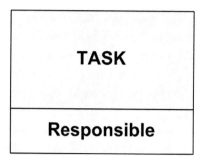

The top contains the name of the Task.. The bottom names the party "Responsible" for executing the task. What is the difference between accountable and responsible? Account-ability is about looking after something and accounting for it. Response-ability is about the ability to respond to or act. When you are responsible, it means that you are the one who executes the tasks for which you are deemed responsible. When you are accountable, you are monitoring or managing. You have to engage someone else who can respond in order to actually execute.

The first step in going from an output level model to the task tier is to create a functional task process box corresponding to each output and to give it a name. The name can reflect the function being performed or the output being produced. In the example, the task process names reflect the output. This is a matter of your local standards for naming. The example below shows an output tier model expanded to the functional process task level.

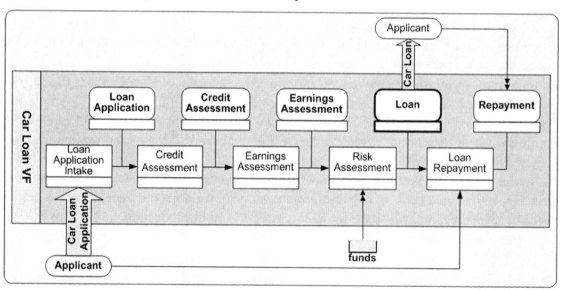

At this point we have only added a single high level task (the function) required to produce each output. Of course, we will need to expand that by adding the detailed operations. That will look much like a task level process map because that's essentially what it is. One nice thing about the Three-Tier model is that we don't need to produce a large, complex process map. We can produce a master map like the one above and then produce a task level map for each high level task shown but only as it is required. That way we segment the complexity. We may produce more individual maps but they will be simpler maps.

We can use whatever method we want to produce the detailed task level model for a function. The Three-Tier model doesn't replace process mapping. It adds to it. By adding an outcome tier and an output tier, we provide more structure and greater segmentation. This helps to break down the complexity of larger processes, especially whole valueflows. Once the output specifications have been produced and agreed upon, we can proceed to expand the functional task processes in parallel. We can dispatch separate teams to work in parallel knowing that they will meet up at the outputs. This is kind of like digging a tunnel from both ends except it goes even further. It digs the tunnel from one output to the next. Of course it is crucially important that the outputs be precisely defined because that defines where the teams meet up. If they are poorly defined then the risk is that when the separate parts of the blueprint are put together they may not match up quite right.

EXAMPLE: WIDGETS 4 ALL

Let's apply some of what we have just learned to the previous example of Widgets 4 All. Let's explore the Widget A Production valueflow and see what we might find inside. Together with subject matter experts, we have produced this diagram. It is basically at the output level with task function placeholders.

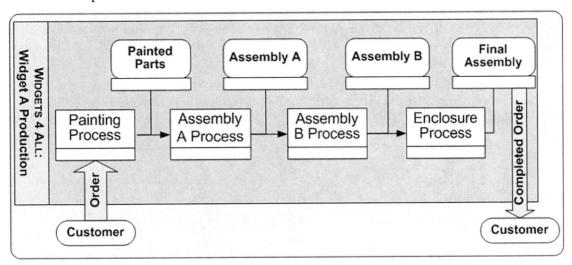

Remember that this particular valueflow was identified as instrumental in achieving two different strategies for Widgets 4 All: higher product throughput and lower costs. Right now the diagram is mainly focused on the outputs. But at some later point we will want to expand each functional task level model into a more detailed task process blueprint. So every tier can have levels of detail.

Let's review the diagram to see what it is telling us:

1. **Scope**: We receive an order from a customer. This is an individual demand. We send a completed order of widgets back to the customer. This is the defining output. Since we have a defining output and a demand and it goes to a customer, this is a Customer valueflow.
2. **Outputs**: We also have intermediate outputs:
   a. Painted Raw Material: Our first output in the valueflow is basically a set of painted parts. The corresponding task function process is Painting Process.
   b. Assembly A: Even though we don't know what the widgets look like, we know there is some sort of an assembly of components. The corresponding task function process is Assembly A Process.
   c. Assembly B: This is another assembly of components, which is produced by adding to or transforming Assembly A. The corresponding task function process is Assembly B Process.
   d. Final Assembly: This is the final product with all assemblies put together. The corresponding task function process is Enclosure Process.

We don't need to have an understanding of the actual product to understand the flow of an output tier model. Of course, only a knowledgeable participant working inside the valueflow process can verify its correctness. But once verified, we can use it to understand capability and flow.

So the first thing we need to do is to take the valueflow level Capability Chart of Accounts and see if we can propagate the measures down to each output. Let's imagine that the following diagram does just that.

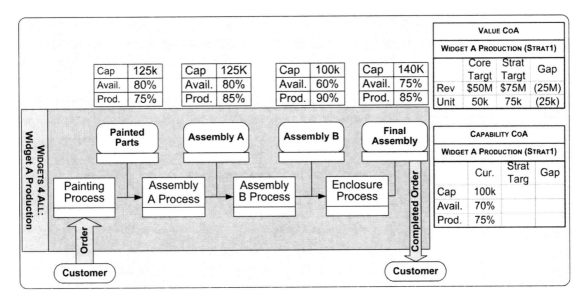

This diagram shows how the capability measures apply to each of the outputs separately. The valueflow level capabilities are defined on the right side of the diagram under the label "Capability CoA." These were measured, so simply assume that they are correct. The diagram also contains the Value CoA, which is shown in the top right corner.

What does this diagram tell us?

1. The capacity of the valueflow is 100k (right side of diagram) If we look at the raw capacity above each output, we see that we have greater capacity in three of the four processes than the valueflow does as a whole (125k, 125k, 100k, 140k versus 100k for the valueflow). Only the Assembly B Process has a capacity that equals that of the valueflow—100k.

2. From a capacity perspective, it appears that the limiting factor is related to the making of Assembly B. We calculate throughput as being capacity times availability times productivity. So we see here that the potential throughput is 100,000 units X 0.60 X 0.90 = 54,000 units. This is close to the current production levels. It seems that the Assembly B Process may be what is limiting the throughput.

3. The next limiting factor seems to be with the Painting Process at 125,000 X 0.8 X 0.75 = 75,000 units. This would satisfy our new production target as it relates to strategy 1. The others are all capable of producing greater than 75,000 units without any further changes.

So what would we conclude from this? Should we simply increase the capacity of the whole valueflow? Of course we shouldn't. What we should do is take a closer look at the sub-process for Assembly B and determine what the options are there. Can we increase the local throughput for that process and would that increase the throughput at the valueflow level? Notice that we are now at the task tier for a specific functional process. But we didn't get here by documenting and examining the tasks. We didn't need to create large diagrams and wallpaper boardrooms. We worked our way from objective, to strategy, to valueflow, to valueflow outputs. And by understanding the source of the performance we were able to pinpoint where our attention needed to go. We should point out here that individual valueflow outputs tend to align to specific functional processes.

If we had simply convened a cross-functional team and examined all the functional processes, we would most certainly have gotten requirements from every one of the functional process participants. The problem is that we would likely get a whole lot of pent-up demand for local changes that weren't related to the problem we were trying to solve. If you ask people "What do you need?" they will tell you *what they need*. But what they need functionally versus what the process needs may be and usually are two different things. Actually, if you ask five people, then there may be six different things—one need for each person plus one for the process. Also note that a process map would not have told us where the capacity constraints were. That's because a process map presents a static task picture whereas availability, for example, is a dynamic execution attribute. It can't be determined by looking at a task picture alone.

When we model a process we have to model both the static and the dynamic behaviour. A task process map represents the more static elements in the sense that it is telling us what we are constantly doing or executing. The dynamic behaviour captures the results based not only on what we are doing but includes the effects of all other conditions, stated or otherwise.

So what would the next step be? We probably want to take the model to the task tier for the functional process that is limiting the throughput. But before we do that, let's define another aspect of the model—Streams. That's the topic of the next chapter.

SUMMARY

The Three-Tier Valueflow model is built incrementally with accountability and alignment happening at each tier for each output before proceeding to the next. The model has the objective of increasing people engagement and **account**ability in an organization. It chunks the process into three tiers for increased visibility. It ensures that we address accountability for all three tiers. It allows us to build incremental alignment among people and also facilitates aligning a process to the overall goals of the organization. It permits us to model and document a process to the optimal level of detail to support progressive understanding. We can begin by modelling at the outcome tier for key valueflows to understand what the performance needs to be. Then we proceed toward the output tier and then to the task tier as we gain experience and as we acquire discipline. The level of effort required to model and document a process using the Three-Tier model can be a fraction of the effort typically taken to model at the task level.

More importantly, the Three-Tier model leads to a more accurate and precise blueprint that can be used as an operational tool and as a knowledge framework and repository for process knowledge. This is rarely the case with a task level process map.

Our approach is to produce a **normalized Relational Process Model**, a blueprint that significantly reduces the effort and difficulty of understanding complexity. However, the outcome that we are looking for is to gain the commitment of the participants through total engagement. The blueprint model is a tool in a journey. It is not the journey. We use the blueprint to explore opportunities, make changes, and validate improvement. The production of the model and the improvement in performance go hand-in-hand. We don't do one and then the other.

The Three-Tier model starts with propagating the relevant objectives and strategies to the valueflow level in the form of outcomes. The implication is that we need to gain process alignment from top tier to bottom tier and that we need to keep the three tiers connected and aligned. First we need to agree on which outcome(s) a valueflow process is supposed to achieve and why that outcome is important to achieving the goal of the organization. In other words, we need to tie the outcome of the process to some higher level outcome in order to maintain connectedness between strategy and execution. If there is disagreement at this level then obtaining consensus at the task level will be difficult. Alignment can take longer than model building. Alignment also changes the process itself. So there isn't much point in building the whole model first. It might make more sense to act on key issues along the way, change the process, and then continue the modelling. In this way, the model becomes a living instrument rather than just documentation.

Once we agree on the outcome, how the outcome will be evaluated, and which higher outcome it relates to, we then move to the identification and definition of the defining output and the intermediate outputs of the process. For many knowledge processes, the outputs may never have been defined or synchronized. If different people have different ideas about what the outputs look like and their content, then we can be assured that the tasks they execute will differ as well.

From outputs we proceed to tasks and identify the operators *responsible* for executing the tasks that produce the output in conformance with the standards set for the process. If the process is not executed in conformance to the blueprint, then we won't be able to spot patterns that lead to improvements. In essence, we can create an accountability tree that shows accountability for an outcome at the highest level and also shows how that accountability is propagated and shared as we move towards execution. Accountability must be shared and expanded as we move towards execution. Accountability cannot be delegated.

If we clearly define task responsibilities but no one is in charge of the desired outcome, then normal drift will eventually lead to a situation where everyone is faithfully executing their tasks but the outcomes are not being achieved. Have you ever experienced this?

The Three-Tier model is a systematic and stepwise approach to creating a process blueprint. Unlike process maps and other diagrams, the model is used to manage process performance in addition to helping to understand process behaviour. The blueprint is a persistent output rather than a temporary output that gets thrown away once a project is complete. Think of all the process maps your organization has created over the years. How many still exist and are used for managing the organization?

The Three-Tier model expands on the task level process map. It builds an intelligent structure on top of task level models, making them more useful and even easier to produce. The Three-Tier model blueprint should be a living representation of the current state of a valueflow and its functional processes.

9

The Three-Stream Perspective (3rd NF)

We only see what our mental models (paradigms) allow us to see.

We have identified a valueflow. That gives us the first normal form. We have defined the outcome tier, the output tier, and the task tier. That gives us the second normal form. The first two normal forms help us to connect functional processes to the business objectives and strategy. But what about the functional processes themselves? We need some way to analyze and evaluate the work done in a process so we can determine its level of excellence.

A valueflow comprises work that produces results in the form of outputs that should lead to the desired outcomes. But how do we know which work to leave alone, which work to remove, and which work to change? How do we know what work to focus on first? Is there some existing concept that can help us analyze the work of a process?

It turns out that there is already a concept. It is the concept of value-add work. Let's quickly review the concept of value-add and non-value-add by starting with the definition.

Work is considered to be *value-adding* (VA) if it changes the fit, form, or function of a product in a way that the customer is willing to pay for. Otherwise, it is non-value-adding (NVA), or waste.

This concept divides all work into two piles. One pile contains work called "value-added work." The other pile contains "waste." As useful as this concept may be, there are a few limitations with the concept. It was originally developed and used in manufacturing environments and primarily to assess and evaluate processes that produced physical customer products. And it worked quite well. Its purpose was to bring people's attention to all the effort that didn't contribute to customer *value-add*. It has served well in that environment. But some difficulties arise when we try to export the concept to processes that don't produce a customer product. Such processes are technically 100% waste. So applying the concept to these processes does not yield any further distinctions. Furthermore, from a socio perspective it is counterproductive to try to tell someone that all of their work is waste. Somehow that's a hard pill to swallow. Nor is it true.

Of course there are attempts to define additional terms such as business-value-add, but this hasn't made things all that much clearer. It is an attempt to solve the solution rather than the original problem. Our approach is to go back to basics.

A valueflow produces an output in accordance with a specification. The output is produced in order to achieve some outcome. Outputs can be objectively measured because they are objectively specified. So we can measure the amount or quantity of output produced by a process. We will call this the *throughput*.

The throughput is a measure of the amount or quantity of a particular specified output.

But an output is intended to achieve some outcome and outcomes can be measured in terms of value. So an output can lead to value for one or more stakeholders. Because value is stakeholder sensitive, it cannot be objectively or singly measured. Value depends on who is doing the measuring and when the measurement is being done. If the output increases the value to some stakeholder, then we can say that our output has led to more value for that stakeholder.

Value is measured through the stakeholders' Charts of Accounts.

So we have split the original value-add concept into two concepts: throughput-add and value-add. Furthermore, value-add requires an adjective to define the stakeholder perspective. We can have customer value-add, shareholder value-add, employee value-add, supplier value-add, etc. Defining the value-add impact of a proposed change is more difficult than defining the throughput-add impact because the value-add depends on the perspective from which it is measured. That means that a change can increase value for one stakeholder while reducing value for another. Since an organization exists to exchange value, is it not important to understand how the balance of value might be impacted as a result of a proposed change? Is it not possible to make a process more efficient without adding any additional value?

Let's look at how the two concepts might apply to an organization. Let's return to the Car Loan valueflow. Let's say that we determined that some custom software would really make the valueflow better. So we start up a software development project to produce the software. Our project is executing an enabling valueflow. Let's call it the Custom Software Development valueflow. The valueflow produces software, which we implement into the Car Loan valueflow. Following implementation, we look at the Value Chart of Accounts for the Car Loan valueflow and discover that there is no change in value. In other words, the new software has had no measurable impact on any of the value measures. It is not unusual for new software to have no measurable impact on the receiving process. So we have basically invested money for which there is no return.

Does that mean that we have not properly executed our project? The Custom Software Development valueflow did produce throughput. It did produce an output. It's just that the output didn't make a value difference. On some other occasion we might produce the same throughput (quantity of software) and it can have a massive and positive impact on value. In fact, it is the nature of enabling valueflows that the same level of throughput can produce widely varying amounts of value.

In an enabling valueflow it doesn't make sense to ask, "Does this task add value?" But it *does* make sense to ask, "Does this task add throughput?" The two questions are totally different. Sometimes an organization will attempt to improve the value-add of an enabling process through cost-cutting or process improvement methods. But process improvement, in this case, may increase throughput without affecting value. Going back to the previous example, would we have delivered greater value if the software would have cost us less? If the software cost less to produce, it would still not deliver any value. We could argue that we didn't waste as much, but we still didn't add value. By separating the concepts into two, we have greater insight into the valueflow. If the outputs are not increasing value for anyone, then we don't have a process productivity problem. We have a problem of focusing on the wrong issues. On the other hand, if the output does increase value but most of that value is consumed in delivering the solution, then we might have a throughput problem that could be addressed through process improvement.

So in summary, work produces throughput, not value. Value is attached to outcomes, not work. Throughput can be objectively measured and should be independent of the person doing the measuring. Value is subjective and measurement will be affected by the stakeholder doing the measuring and the circumstances present when the measurement takes place.

Because not all processes produce a customer product, we need a way to determine the excellence of a process regardless of whether it is a customer process or an enabling process. For that, we need to measure throughput independently of value.

Chunking by Streams

That brings us to the third normal form, which segments the work done in the valueflow into three separate streams, because not all work has the same purpose. There is work effort that directly impacts the production of the intended output (*throughput*) and there is effort that does not. All processes contain both kinds of effort and, therefore, it can be difficult to tell the difference. But our ability to distinguish among the different kinds of work goes to the heart of producing excellent processes and reducing non-opportunity risks.

The Three-Stream model examines the work being done to determine its impact on throughput. Although it builds on the concept of *value-add* versus *non-value-add* work, it also makes further distinctions among the different types of work effort.

The central purpose of a valueflow is to transform some input into its defining output. The output can be tangible, like a cake, or it can be conceptual, such as a blueprint or a business strategy.

While executing operations intended to produce that output, an error or failure can occur. And so we must expend effort to handle or fix the failure or to remedy the product or service. Such work does not add to the overall throughput but is still necessary in a real process. Failure can be considered pure waste because it adds value to no one.

In order to reduce the volume or severity of failures in a process, we tend to add controls, which attempt to reduce or detect specific failures or risks. Controls add a burden of work to the process and don't directly add to throughput. But we might be worse off without them.

Therefore, all effort or work in a process can be categorized as being:
1. transform work,
2. failure work, or
3. control work.

We can visualize a valueflow as a coaxial cable that delivers output intended to create some sort of value along its core. So if we draw a cross-section of such a valueflow with a circle denoting total effort, then that total effort can be divided into three parts, or *streams,* as described below and illustrated by the diagram.

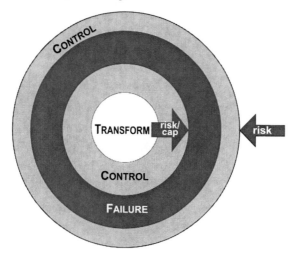

1. Transform Stream (white core): Every valueflow has a primary output. At the centre or core of every valueflow is the process required to produce that primary defining output. It comprises the essential effort and resources that directly work to produce the product or defining output of the process. Only this effort can produce measurable throughput. If we reduce this capacity then throughput will decrease. If we increase the transform capacity then throughput will increase. Throughput flows only along the core. All other work is in support of that central, core effort. Only the transform effort has the potential to directly increase the throughput of the process.

2. Failure stream (dark grey band): Unless the transform stream is perfect and there are zero risks, we will encounter failures as we execute the core. When that happens we need to expend effort to handle or correct them. The failure stream comprises the effort and resources required to correct or deal with any errors, deviations, or failures that have occurred and to deal with any risk events that have materialized. Failures may be caused by an internal condition or event or an external condition or event. Failure effort will cause a reduction in the throughput of a process. Failures reduce throughput by consuming capacity that could have been used to increase transform effort.

3. Control Stream (two light grey bands): Failures are not desirable. Therefore, we put into place controls to try to prevent either the severity or frequency of failure. So controls represent the effort and resources required to get the process performance as close as possible to the ideal, in a non-ideal world. Since controls also use capacity, they also reduce the amount of transform effort that is available. However, individual controls *may* reduce the amount of failure effort, which indirectly adds to the transform effort. So, a control consumes capacity, thus reducing available transform effort, but it can also reduce failure, which can increase the amount of transform effort available. Therefore, a control must be individually evaluated to determine if we are better off with it or without it. In addition, since controls are implemented as processes, they too can fail. So controls can increase throughput and eventual value in an indirect way by subtracting failure waste. But they can also subtract value if they cost more than they save. What this means is that the value of a control can range from negative to positive depending on the particular process. There are three basic categories of controls: quality controls, optimization controls, and risk controls, as described below.

   a. ***Quality Controls:*** These are intended to prevent or detect failures and reduce potential waste caused by defects in quality (deviation from the specification of an output or component) anywhere along the flow. By quality we don't just mean quality of inputs or material; we also mean quality of any component that is part of the process. For example, imagine that we have not been able to hire to the correct level of skill for a particular job. As a result, we have resorted to adding some additional quality assurance for the work produced by this hire. That would constitute a control because it is implemented as a result of a specification (quality) gap with regard to skills. Quality controls are aimed primarily at reducing specific internal causes of failure. In terms of Six Sigma, quality controls primarily address common cause.

b. **Optimization Controls**: There is also the waste associated with sub-optimal processes. Such waste is not always directly visible. For example, if the process is less responsive than it could be, then that will cause indirect waste. Our customer may have to wait longer for her product than is necessary. If we have periods of idle time, then that is a waste of resources, but not a product-related defect. If we organize transactions in a way that causes greater costs, then that is optimization failure. Although we don't usually think of these things in terms of failure, they are failure to manage optimally. We may not easily see that waste but it does have a negative impact on throughput. Controls to reduce this kind of resource waste we will call *optimization controls*.

c. **Risk Controls**: There are also events that are outside the control of the process that can cause failure. And so we can have controls whose purpose is to manage these events. A risk control might simply monitor the conditions that make the risk more or less likely, for example. In terms of Six Sigma, risk controls primarily address special cause. In fact, some Six Sigma tools provide a good way to determine whether a particular defect is the result of common cause (built into the design) or special cause (external or special event). An uninterrupted power supply unit (UPS) is an example of a physical control designed to reduce the impact of a power failure to a computer or other electrically powered device. Note that we specified "outside the control of the process." Sometimes we can convert a risk to a quality or optimization issue by expanding the context until the risk is no longer "outside the control of the expanded process."

Controls work together to get us as close as possible to perfect performance. In other words, they allow us to achieve *near perfect* performance. Therefore, the control stream is made up of three sub-streams: quality, optimization, and risk.

THROUGHPUT-ADD (TA) VERSUS THROUGHPUT-SUBTRACT (TS)

The Three-Stream model helps us to evaluate work or tasks by assessing whether a task is going to increase the throughput or decrease the throughput of a process. A task or operation is *throughput-add* if it adds to the throughput of the process, whatever that may be. Since all tasks consume capacity, a task that doesn't add to the throughput must necessarily be subtracting from the potential throughput. Let's say we have a process with a transform core that requires one hour of TA effort to produce the output. And we have seven effort hours of capacity available in a day. So in a seven-hour day we should be able to produce seven units, since each takes one hour. Our throughput should be seven units. Now let's say that we have a failure that takes one hour of effort to handle. That means we are left with only six hours for producing throughput. Therefore, at the end of the day the throughput will be six units. The one hour of failure effort has cost us one unit. We have produced one unit of throughput less than we should have produced—potential throughput. It is in that sense that we refer to it as *throughput-subtract*, rather than the more neutral non-throughput-add. We want to make sure that it is understood that effort that does not add to the throughput has a negative (subtracting) impact on what could have been produced.

We want to nudge people into making good decisions. That's another reason for referring to work that doesn't directly add to throughput as throughput-subtract. Let's say that a particularly embarrassing error occurs in a process. An immediate reaction might be to implement a control to catch such an error before it becomes visible to anyone else, without bothering to determine whether this is really the best decision. Controls don't add to throughput. By referring to them as throughput-subtracting, we want to remind people that whenever they implement a new control, they are automatically reducing the throughput of the process. That should trigger the question "Who and how will we pay for this control?" If it can be shown that the control will reduce failures by more than the cost of the control, then we can go ahead and implement it, because the control is paying for itself. But if we can't and we still want to implement the control, then we have to change the Chart of Accounts for that valueflow to reflect reduced throughput. Then we have to quantify what that reduced throughput means in value. By referring to the control as TS (throughput-subtract), we are trying to nudge people away from having an automatic reaction that simply increases the size, or burden, of the control stream. Many organizations become control-heavy precisely because they may implement controls as a response to a particularly embarrassing incident, which may or may not happen again. This is especially true in organizations where politics play a leading role.

An important part of process design is making choices about what work to add, what to change, and what to take away. One of the drawbacks with the simpler concept of value-add and non-value-add is that it sometimes creates the illusion that we can simply remove the non-value-added tasks from a process. But life is not that easy. No real process can be designed to contain only throughput-add tasks. That means that all real designs will contain many throughput-subtracting tasks as well. The TA-TS concept helps us determine where to focus our attention, in order to minimize TS effort. The question of what to keep, what to change, and what to throw out depends on the impact on throughput and how that translates into changes in stakeholder value. When a change has a negative impact on throughput and subsequent value, then the change may need to be reversed.

The concepts of Throughput-Add (TA) and Throughput-Subtract (TS), along with the Three-Stream model, are summarized in the diagram below.

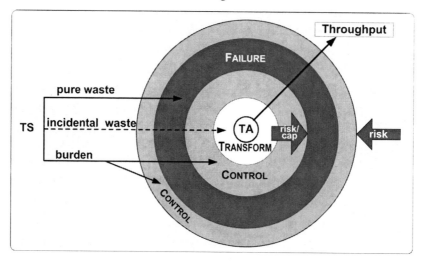

The three streams help us to locate where the throughput-add (TA) work is in a process and where the throughput-subtract (TS) work is. Since the purpose of the process is to produce the defining output, the only stream that can produce direct throughput is the *transform* stream. Why? Because it contains the transformations that directly produce the desired output (throughput).

Let's review what this diagram tells us.

1. Transform: This stream contains the effort that can increase the throughput of the valueflow. But it also contains operations that may be necessary to producing the output but that don't add to the throughput. As shown in the diagram, only a small portion of the Transform circle (stream) actually contains throughput-add effort. The rest we will call incidental *waste*. The throughput of a process is a consequence of the amount of TA effort available in the transform stream (the TA core). If this effort is not increased, then the throughput (a measure of the quantity produced) cannot increase. As an example, if we are making a physical product, then shaping, cutting, and joining would all be throughput-add because they work on the product at some state of progress and they transform the product, bringing it closer to its final form. But picking up pieces, rotating them, or moving them from one work station to another does not add to the throughput. Nevertheless, such work may be necessary in order to permit the next operation. That's why they are part of the transform stream. If the state of a product is the same after an operation as it was before, then it was not changed. If an operation does not change or transform a

product such that it is closer to its final form, then it is not a throughput-add task, no matter how necessary. Such a task is throughput-subtract (TS) even though it is in the transform stream. Again, a task may be necessary yet not be a TA task. TS tasks in the transform stream are considered incidental waste. The objective of design, for a given paradigm, is to maximize the amount of TA effort available and to minimize the amount of TS work required.

2. Failure: Failure handling and recovery is a necessary part of every process. Failure effort is throughput-subtract (TS) and pure *waste*. There is no value attached to handling a failure. We might be tempted to say that an activity that fixes something that is broken has value. We need to be careful because of the many meanings that can be attached to the word value. In this context, what we mean is that it makes sense to fix something that is broken. But in the context of a process, throughput should have been increased when we first produced the output. Failure handling is often unavoidable due to the current level of process *capability*. It is pure waste because it cannot increase throughput. It only consumes capacity and resources (cost). Making corrections and doing rework are examples of failure effort. We spend failure handling effort in order to restore throughput that should have been initially created in the transform stream. For example, defectives returned by the customer may need to be reworked or replaced, which is waste but necessary. If you order a steak cooked rare in a restaurant and receive it well done, then that's an example of a failure. A good restaurant will want to replace your steak with one cooked rare. That's failure handling. It doesn't produce more throughput than if the steak had been properly done the first time. We should always try to eliminate failure effort by eliminating the cause of the failure first. All failures are *pure waste*. The first response should be to improve the transform portion of the process, making it more capable. The second is to reduce or eliminate through countermeasures (controls). The last response is to optimize the failure handling. We should note that operational risks in a process will eventually show up as some sort of failure in some process or multiple processes. Therefore, whenever we have a failure, we should look to the list of process risks and determine whether it needs to be updated. Transform effort is the primary cause of failure. A weak or risky transform stream will present a high potential failure rate, which may require a high control effort. Note that control effort itself can also cause failure. Finally, in the process of dealing with a failure, we may also cause additional failures. So we can see that failure will tend to lead to negative compound consequences and, therefore, it is always prudent to aim for the most reliable transform stream that we can implement.

3. Controls: Any checks, quality controls, scheduling, monitoring, and other activities fall under controls. Basically, if it isn't transform and it's not failure, then it must be a control. The benefit of a control is essentially the difference (delta) in throughput

between having it and not having it. The key questions with a control are "Is it effective—does it work?" and "Is it productive—is it worth it?" We should try to optimize control effort and resources in conjunction with failure. Controls impose a *burden* on the process. Controls must be managed carefully because sometimes the cure can be worse than the disease. So we must always evaluate whether a particular control should be implemented or if we should change the transform stream or if we should live with the failure instead. In general, most organizations seem to have an automatic response to failures, which results in a control burden that is ever increasing. Collecting all the effort related to a particular process and showing it separately as streams allows us to make visible each control separately and allows us to evaluate the total control burden on the processes. A control is intended to produce a certain performance outcome and so we can have a Chart of Accounts for each and every control. A control is not de-facto waste. It depends on its effectiveness and productivity. If a control is not effective—doesn't work—then it's pure waste. Otherwise, its value will depend on its impact on value for each stakeholder. Controls have to be evaluated from the perspective of throughput to see if they are technically designed properly. But they also have to be evaluated based on their impact on the total delivered value for the valueflow. So controls can range from really productive to total waste.

STAKEHOLDER-VALUE-ADD VERSUS THROUGHPUT-ADD

There is a fundamental difference between throughput and value. Let's take the simple example of an automobile company. Throughput is about measuring the output, which can be described using a specification. So if the automobile company makes a single model car, then we can measure throughput in terms of the number of automobiles. Value, on the other hand, is measured through the eyes of the beholder. So customer value can be measured in terms of how much the customer is willing to pay for that car.

When times are economically tough, customers may be willing to pay less for the car, thus reducing shareholder value. But throughput has not changed. So the process has not deteriorated even though there is less shareholder value coming in. This distinction is important in that it provides us with more information about an organization's processes.

When we want to know the excellence of a process with respect to delivering its defined output, we should use the throughput as a measure. Sometimes organizations will profess to have improved a particular process when all they've done is changed the value balance. For example, if we nudge (squeeze) the suppliers to arbitrarily lower their prices, we will see higher shareholder value, at least in the short term. But have we improved the process? Fundamentally, we have not. We haven't changed the throughput structure of the process, just the value structure. When we change the value structure we might be creating future risks, especially when the structure is changed through some sort of coercion.

Using the concepts of Throughput-Add and Throughput-Subtract is a more objective way to evaluate the excellence of a process. The Three-Stream model helps us to categorize and evaluate the work taking place inside a process so we can assess and evaluate that work, to produce a more perfect process. The concepts apply equally well to customer and enabling valueflows.

The current Value-Add (VA) concept refers to stakeholder value-add, specifically customer value-add. For some organizations the total amount of customer VA work can be as low as 5%. That means that the bulk of work—95%—is non-value-add or waste. Putting 95% of an organization's work into a single bucket isn't all that helpful. Referring to all that work as waste isn't helpful either because it doesn't create the right attitude among employees. It can create a defensive attitude rather than a desire to design more-perfect processes.

That's where the Three-Stream model comes in handy. It helps us to separate the work that adds to the throughput of a process from the work that does not. That means the concept applies to all valueflows. By definition, only work done in the transform stream can contain work that is throughput-add. The TA-TS concept accepts that value and waste is partially subjective depending on the stakeholder. Here is the formal definition:

A task is Throughput-Add (TA) if it transforms an intermediate output into a form that is closer to the final form of the defining output for the valueflow. Otherwise, it is Throughput-Subtract (TS).

The classic use of value-add is to assess the work of a process from the customer's perspective. So how do we connect value-add with the concepts of throughput and burden? The concept originated on the manufacturing floor with regards to customer processes so that's where it has the clearest applicability. Throughput-add can be related to the classical value-add. If a task is throughput-add and if the final output goes to a customer and if the customer is willing to provide value in exchange for that output, then we have a TA task that leads to Customer Value-Add (CVA).

A task is Customer Value-Add (CVA) if it is *throughput-add* and if the output goes to a customer in exchange for something of value to the organization.

For purposes of clarification, an input into a process is considered an intermediate output for that same process. For example, if the valueflow produces software, then the activity of "coding" is taking a requirement specification and bringing it closer to the final form, which is software. Therefore, the activity of coding is a TA activity. On the other hand, inspecting the code for errors does not change the output. It does change what we know about it, but not the output itself. In other words, the code is the same after we inspect it as it was before we inspected it. So code inspection is a control activity, which is throughput-subtract.

So, there are three conditions for a task to be Customer Value-Add (CVA):

1. We must be in a customer valueflow producing a product that the customer wants and is willing to pay for.
2. We must be in the transform stream directly transforming the product and bringing it towards its final customer form.
3. The task must be throughput-add (TA).

By focusing the term value-add on the output of a process, rather than the work of the process, we can now use the concept of *stakeholder value-add* for all valueflows—customer, enabling, and demand.

The Three-Stream model helps to educate people to see burden and waste in processes. The concept of streams makes it easier for everyone to see where the opportunities for throughput increase and waste reduction truly are, regardless of the type of valueflow. So we can apply the concept of throughput-add to any process regardless of whether it is producing a customer product or some other output.

We often separate controls from failure handling from transform work. It is not unusual for an organization to separate some of its control work and its failure work into different organizational units. For example, a service centre may handle failures. So if we attempted to model the service centre's functional processes, we would be modelling a collection of failure streams from multiple valueflows. When we separate the failure streams from the transform streams that actually cause the failure, we have only the option of optimizing the failure handling. But in most cases the true opportunity is in reducing the risk of failure, and for that we need to look at the transform stream. Since these two streams may be controlled by different organizational entities, they are usually managed as if they were two independent processes, rather than one valueflow that has been functionally separated into two.

Add to this the fact that some of the control stream work may also be sourced to some other group and we have the situation of a valueflow being executed within three or more departments or groups, making it appear as if we have several independent processes instead of a single valueflow. This is one factor that can make it difficult for organizations trying to move to a process orientation. They have lost the original sense of a complete valueflow process and are left with pieces of processes. The end result is that they try to deal with functional process pieces rather than complete valueflows. Imagine trying to improve a particular car model if no one was in charge of the model and all you had were different departments making components. What if no one was even aware of the different car models or what they looked like? That's what is happening in many organizations. There is little awareness of a particular valueflow model, only awareness of the separate functional pieces.

The reason we model valueflows instead of functional processes is that it provides the opportunity to reconstitute each variant of the whole start-to-end valueflow. Continuous Process Improvement can't be sustained if the valueflows are not reconstituted because it will become impossible to verify that payoffs are being achieved. When a valueflow is reconstituted and waste is removed, we have the opportunity to explore the potential for organizing along valueflows instead of just along functions. The valueflow gives a context within which to understand the functional processes.

In manufacturing, some companies have converted from a functional organization structure to a valueflow organization structure for some portions of the company and with great success. It certainly won't make sense in every case, but it can have tremendous advantages in specific cases. When we manage an entire valueflow, we increase the visibility, accountability, and consequently the manageability of the valueflow. But even if it isn't possible to execute by valueflow, we should at least design by valueflow and even manage performance by valueflow.

Stream Proportions

If we think of the valueflow as a cable carrying value, would it be thick at the core and thin on the outside or does it have a fine wire as the core with thick failure and control layers? The relative proportion of the three streams will be different for different valueflows and at different stages of perfection.

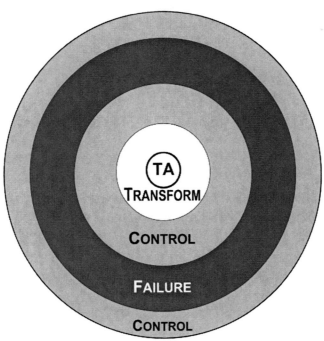

As the processes become more perfect, we approach the situation where the core is thick and the other layers are thin. But in general, the TA core can be quite small. For some organizations the TA transform cores can add up to as little as 5% of total effort. There is no standard for what a particular valueflow should be. It will depend on many things, including the state of the art for that particular process. This is where valueflows are valuable again. Organizations tend to organize functionally. That means that they will often place failure processes and control processes in separate organizational units away from the transform stream that they support. When they do that it is impossible to determine the stream proportions. It can even be impossible to determine if a particular change represents progress or whether we are going backwards.

Understanding how much of the total cost or effort of a valueflow is TA effort is useful in determining how much opportunity for improvement that valueflow contains. A valueflow that has a core that accounts for 10% of total effort should present tremendous opportunity for improvement since it is 90% throughput-subtract. We might be tempted to ignore the core and tackle the failure and control streams instead since they represent 90% of the effort, whereas the transform stream only accounts for 10% of the effort. But what if it is precisely the low capability of the transform stream that is causing the other 90%? We should always look at the core first to determine whether we have the most effective transform process.

The opportunity for improvement through reducible waste elimination is enormous and is far greater than any opportunity related to getting more effort out of people. Getting additional effort represents a one-time opportunity with an upper limit and it will be difficult to sustain higher levels of effort. But the opportunity goes well beyond the direct return on investment. The total engagement of employees in looking for improved ways to achieve better results has a long term impact that can't be duplicated through technology implementation. The continuous search for and implementation of progressive changes is what builds the change muscles of an organization. It is what allows it to be ready for those large changes, which it will at some point need to make. Continuous change makes an organization adaptable in a way that cannot easily or quickly be duplicated by competitors. The organization that continuously improves will be better prepared and more likely to discover and recognize the truly large opportunities when they present themselves, and it will be better prepared to undertake those opportunities. The person who is constantly walking is more likely to be able to sprint when the need arises than the person who sits all day. And he will be healthier as well.

We can draw the model in such a way as to highlight and separate the three streams of work so that we can incrementally understand the valueflow and see which work relates to producing throughput, which to handling failures, and which to controls. Separating by streams is also a form of managing complexity because it separates components that aren't related to the whole valueflow. For example, a particular control may relate to only one of the outputs in the valueflow. Therefore, we separate it. The same holds true for a failure stream. Each failure handler may relate to a specific failure mode of a specific output and not to the valueflow as a whole.

So what is the benefit of using streams? Streams are yet another way to chunk complexity and expand our vision to improve our understanding of the organization. When we separate the model by streams, we can more readily increase our awareness of waste and also simplify the models. One purpose of chunking by streams is to highlight the work that will lead to increasing throughput from the rest of the work—separating the essential from the non-essential. And, of course, finding and increasing the customer-value-add work is an important quest because it is the customer-value-add that leads to value for the other stakeholders. Without that, there is nothing for anyone to share.

Modelling in streams greatly improves our ability to understand the processes and the factors that lead to performance and reduce non-opportunity risks. Let's explore each stream in more detail through a series of progressive examples.

EXAMPLE: TRANSFORM STREAM

So where should we start when we are trying to understand a valueflow? Since the goal is to produce Customer Value-Add (CVA) first, it makes sense to begin with a customer valueflow. And since the transform stream is where the Throughput-Add work is carried out then we should begin with the transform stream of that flow. It is the core of any valueflow process. In practice, you can begin with whatever valueflow needs immediate attention. The transform stream will contain only transform work, i.e., activities that touch the product in some way. But they may be TA or TS, as repeated below.

1. Throughput-Add: Those elements that are transformations of the product (or service) and bring it closer to its final state are throughput-add tasks. And if we are in a customer valueflow they will also be Customer Value-Add.
2. Throughput-Subtract: Those elements that touch the product and are required to facilitate the transformation but don't transform the product are throughput-subtract. Moving a product around is TS. Work required to hand over a transaction to the next person in line is TS. Although such work touches the product or service, it doesn't move the product any closer to its final form.

Let's look at an example. Imagine you arrive at your office building but before you go up to your office, you decide to stop for your morning coffee. You've just been to Italy so you decide to visit a little espresso bar in your building. It's a little place and all they offer is espresso and cappuccino. So you order an espresso. As you watch the staff behind the counter, you decide to quickly record what they are doing. You get your coffee, go upstairs, and decide to draw a process map from your notes. Since service was quick, you had to return several times to complete your notes. Finally you are done and you produce the diagram below.

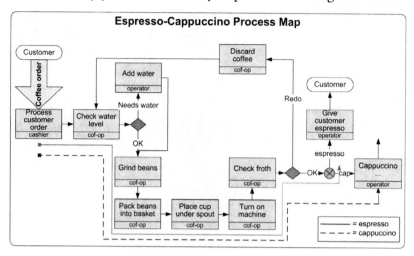

This is what a small task process map might look like. Take a minute or two to review it. Now let's review a few observations about the process map:

1. There are tasks that are required to produce the product.
2. There are also tasks that are checking for failures/errors such as "Check water level."
3. There are two possible products produced by the process: espresso and cappuccino. In this case the espresso path seems to be a subset of the cappuccino path. The two lines (solid for espresso, dashed for cappuccino) below the task boxes show the two paths.

Having recently been introduced to the Relational Process Model, you decide to see if you can come up with a normalized blueprint. So, first you convert your task model into an output model as illustrated below, showing only the outputs and not the tasks.

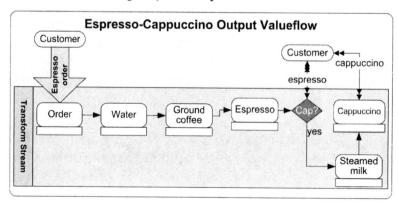

You immediately notice that there are two products and so there are two valueflows combined into one diagram. So you separate out the espresso valueflow, as shown below.

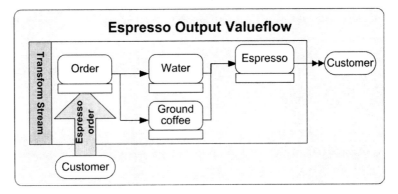

Naturally this is a simple example with the intermediate outputs being the ingredients:

1. Water,
2. Ground coffee, and
3. Espresso.

Notice that in this diagram the first two outputs are shown as being parallel. What this says is that the order of the two doesn't matter as long as they are both ready before we produce the final product, the espresso.

Now we can proceed to the cappuccino valueflow shown below. Notice that this model includes all the outputs from the espresso flow. In essence what the valueflow says is that when we get an order for cappuccino, we make the espresso output and an output called steamed milk. These two outputs are then combined to make a cappuccino.

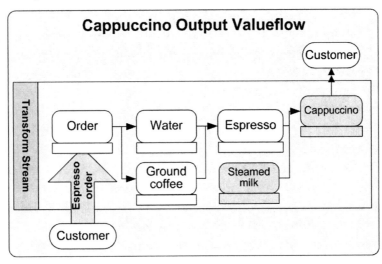

EXAMPLE: CONTROL STREAM

So far the diagrams only show the transform stream at the output level. Now let's show what the diagram might look like if we add in the control stream for the espresso valueflow.

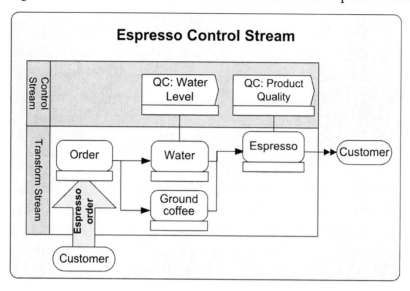

In this example, we have chosen to show the streams in the form of swim lanes. This is just a representation choice, but it does clearly separate the transform stream from the control stream. These swim lanes should not be confused with swim lanes on process maps, which are typically used to separate work done by different departments or groups. The swim lanes here are used to separate the three streams.

Let's review some of the key points of the diagram:

1. At this point we are showing the control stream as an outcome tier. Remember the three tiers from the previous chapter. We have the outcome, output, and task tiers. Why do we have each control as an outcome? A control has a purpose or reason for being there. We are expecting it to achieve some internal process goal or process-related outcome that is measurable. Therefore, we show them as control outcomes.

2. In this case, there are two control outcomes and they are both quality control outcomes. Notice that each control is attached to a transform output. Controls should be specific and are often attached to an output.

3. Since they are outcomes, the implication is that we need to define a Chart of Accounts for each of the outcomes. In the original process map we had a task called "Check water level." We have replaced that with a control outcome called "QC: Water Level," which stands for "Quality Control: Water Level." What this does is

separate the control tasks from the primary transform tasks. And we have promoted the task to an outcome.

So what might we measure with respect to that outcome? Remember there are two key questions for a control. The first is "Is it effective—does it work?" The second is "Is it productive—is the burden worth the benefit?" We could measure the number of times the water level was below the required level. Or we could measure the effort required to do the check. Imagine we went ahead and made an espresso and it was faulty because the water level was too low. Then we could attribute this defect to the Water Level control. This would represent an instance where the water level was low and the control did not catch it (not effective). By separating a control from the rest, we can verify whether a control is effective (does it work) and whether it is productive (is it worth it).

Suppose that checking the water level before making each espresso requires an amount of effort that we can quantify as $25 per day. Further suppose that if we don't do this check it will likely cause 10 rejected coffees during the day at a total cost to us of $5. Based on our business knowledge, we know that this error would be caught before giving the coffee to the customer, so there would be little or no customer impact. Based on that we could conclude that implementing the control is not productive (not worth it). Therefore, we might decide to do without the water level check and simply accept that we will produce 10 rejected coffees, which will need to be redone after refilling the water. Each rejected coffee will serve as the trigger to refill the water. On a purely cost basis we save $20 ($25 - $5). Sometimes a control can be effective (it works) but not productive (not worth the burden). What this means is that sometimes it may be better to allow the failure and recover from it than it is to prevent the failure. Organizations sometimes have both ineffective and unproductive controls. By separating each control and attaching a Chart of Accounts to each one, we can ensure that we don't allow the processes to become over-controlled and under-productive.

Of course, we will need to expand each outcome to the output and task tiers in order to implement the control, should we choose to do so. If we decide not to implement a particular control, we should still include the control in the blueprint at the outcome level. That way the blueprint will record that we are aware of the control, and that we have made a conscious decision to not implement it. That will allow us to attribute failures to it. So if a failure occurs that could have been caught by that control had we implemented it, then we attribute that failure to the control. That way we can monitor the potential benefits of implementing the control so we can revisit the decision if the failure rate increases above some level.

EXAMPLE: FAILURE STREAM

Finally, let's add the failure stream to the Espresso valueflow, as shown below. Our Cappuccino valueflow might have the same failure handlers plus others. Notice that we are continuing to show the streams using a swim lane style. This clearly separates transform, control, and failure.

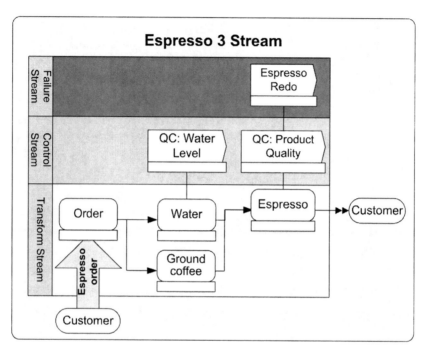

In the failure stream for this example, we show one failure outcome. Again, by separating the failure controls we are showing, visually, the failures that could happen. Notice that the failure control "Espresso Redo" is linked to the quality control "Product Quality." So we can map the potential failures to one or more controls. This makes sense because we implement controls in conjunction with potential failures. When we implement a new control, we can check the Chart of Accounts for the associated failure to see if the control has made a difference, and whether the difference was positive or negative. Since processes are socio-technical-economic mechanisms, a control can sometimes cause things to get worse. For example, when we implement multiple reviews for a document output, we could become lax in our verification if we thought someone else was diligently checking for errors. The practice of getting multiple sign-offs for deliverables is an example of a control that sometimes backfires. People are busy and they sometimes take the view that someone else will catch errors in the deliverable, so they don't have to review it in detail. Of course, when everyone does this, we get a control that costs time and resources but doesn't achieve the purpose. But if we developed a Chart of Accounts for such a control, then we could verify the effectiveness and the productivity of the control.

Example: Complaint Management

Let's look at another example to demonstrate the use of the three streams. Imagine a regulatory agency for professional caregivers. One of their valueflow processes is a Complaint Handling process. The general flow for the transform stream is described as follows:

1. A complainant submits a written <u>complaint</u> through email or regular mail. This is the demand that triggers the whole valueflow process and results in an official Complaint.
2. An investigator reviews the case and determines the Care Issues.
3. The investigator then interviews the relevant parties and witnesses to obtain Discovery Statements relating to the case.
4. These statements are then reviewed and separated in order to obtain the Relevant Facts.
5. A panel of objective evaluators convenes at a regular interval to assess each case. The investigator is available to the panel to answer any questions and to clarify the relevant facts. The evaluators arrive at a Judgment based on the case facts and the regulations that apply.
6. Based on the Judgment and other case information, actions are recommended and packaged into a Disposition, which specifies what actions need to be taken and by whom. All the relevant parties are advised.

Notice that this valueflow is described primarily in terms of the outputs. Therefore, let's first produce the transform stream for the process at the output tier as depicted below with a task placeholder, but no task details.

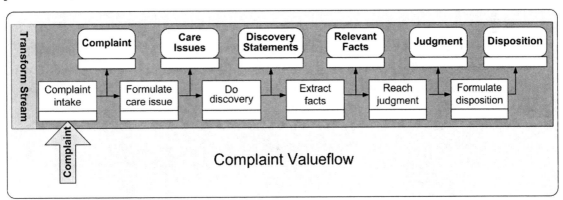

Complaint Valueflow

The transform stream doesn't show any quality or optimization controls, such as quality checks or scheduling functions, nor does it show any failure handling. In fact, it should show how a single transaction would proceed in the absence of any errors or realized risks. It makes sense to understand what a smooth, error-free flow should look like first. We want to paint a picture of the near perfect in everybody's mind. Then anything that must be added is considered throughput-subtract or burden. This helps us become waste aware. The transform stream is the simplest form of the valueflow. At the output tier we can't yet see the TA or TS elements. Notice that an output tier model may include a simple placeholder for the tasks required to produce each output, but no detail. At this level, with only a single task placeholder, we can't yet assign TA or TS status to a task because it's a summary task.

EXAMPLE: COMPLAINT—ADDING THE CONTROL STREAM

The transform stream depicts the process in a state where no errors are made and where transaction sequence doesn't matter. It is the minimal, unprotected, single execution view of the process. The real world, of course, may require us to monitor, check, prioritize, and schedule. Each of these is a control. In order to add the control stream to the valueflow, we need to know what specific controls it requires. If we are modelling an existing process, then these should be known to those who are executing the process.

Imagine that the Complaint valueflow has the following control requirements, as depicted below.

1. Not all cases are the same. Some are more difficult and require greater expertise. If an unqualified investigator is assigned, then the case may not be correctly handled. Therefore, a *quality* control is required to ensure that cases are assigned to qualified investigators. The control is called Case Assign.
2. Not all cases require the same amount of time to complete. Therefore, we need to make sure that we manage the capacity and that there is a proper distribution of workload. Therefore, we need to properly schedule each case, keeping in mind the overall performance objectives for the process. Therefore, we need a Case Schedule *optimization* control.
3. Because of its importance to the rest of the process, the proper identification of care issues presents the greatest risk to the quality of the investigation. Therefore, we want to implement a *quality* control for the care issues called Verified Care Issues.
4. The panel that reviews each complaint comprises a number of external participants with varied expertise who need to be present together. We need to coordinate their

reviews. Therefore, we need another *optimization* schedule control called Hearing Schedule.

5. A Disposition affects a caregiver member who may disagree with the decision. It is important that the disposition be as clear and precise as possible. So, we want to ensure that it is of the highest quality. We will add another *quality* control, Verified Disposition.

Controls can be established in numerous ways. One way is to perform a Failure Mode and Effects Analysis (FMEA) to identify where the likelihood of failure is. If the model is at the valueflow level only and we haven't yet determined the intermediate outputs, then we will define risks and failure modes for the valueflow as a whole. There are many books and articles on FMEA, which can be found in bookstores and on the internet. Alternatively, we can use brainstorming to identify potential failures. Although not as reliable as FMEA, it is a simple approach to use as a starting point.

The diagram below depicts the example model so far with the controls that we discussed above added to the control stream. Again we emphasize that each control is first defined as a Control Outcome and not a Control Output. Each control represents an intention to achieve something with regard to the internal performance of the process. Remember that controls are throughput-subtract and need to be individually evaluated to determine the extent to which they should be implemented. So we first specify the control in terms of desired outcome (thing to be achieved). That forces us to think in terms of how the outcome will be measured and verified. Only then should we proceed to the output and task tiers to design how it will be implemented.

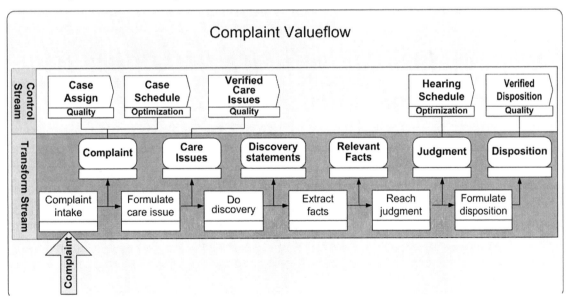

In the diagram, we have shown the controls with a line connecting them to an output. What this signifies is that these controls relate to the production of the linked output. Again, in a task level process map, all we have are tasks in the sequence in which they are supposed to be executed. Such a map has far too much detail for us to fully understand the behaviour of the process. By segmenting each control and relating it to the transform outputs, we are in a better position to define clear accountability for a given output, and then assign accountability for the performance and risk for that output. For each separate risk or failure mode, we can define an associated control and link it to its associated transform stream output.

Once we define the outcome tier for the control stream, including how we will measure its effectiveness and how it might affect value (Chart of Accounts), then each control can be expanded and modelled as if it were a complete process. So we would define the control outcome, outputs, and the control method (tasks). We can view controls as sitting atop the transform stream. Since most transform streams would require similar controls, we can think in terms of standardizing a list of control types and documenting known strategies—best practices—to implement the control.

Initially, potential controls should simply be identified. Later we can determine whether we want to actually implement the control or live with the potential failure. Identifying each control regardless of the degree to which it gets implemented ensures that we have a blueprint that clearly shows what we have decided to implement and what we have decided not to implement. A process map only shows what is in. It doesn't show what is not in. With a typical process map, the risk is that someone will come along and add more controls because they see them as missing. By adding non-implemented controls to the blueprint, we are showing that we have made a conscious decision not to implement them. Naturally, we would want to explain the rationale for doing so. When a control is not implemented, we should still have a Chart of Accounts for that control and we should still attribute failures to the control. Then, based on actual failures, we may later decide to implement a particular control or un-implement one. This also makes auditing much more structured.

EXAMPLE: COMPLAINT—ADDING THE FAILURE STREAM

Failures can occur in a transform stream, in a control stream, or even in a failure stream. Therefore, a failure stream can contain what appear to be transform elements and non-transform elements. In either case, all effort that takes place in a failure stream is considered throughput-subtract or waste. When we are reworking a product or repeating a service, it is because we have already worked it once but a defect was produced. So, in essence, we are repeating effort that has already been accounted for. It is the fact of repeating that makes it waste. A transform task can only be throughput-add (TA) the *first* time it is performed. The second and subsequent times the task is throughput-subtract, since it doesn't add to the potential throughput. Instead it consumes resources and capacity.

In the Complaint Valueflow, despite best efforts, failures do happen. Two such failure handlers are briefly described below.

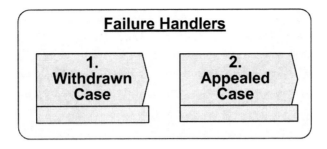

1. Sometimes a complainant will cancel or withdraw his complaint for various reasons. Therefore, we will need a failure handler called Withdrawn Case. Why do we consider the withdrawal of a case a failure? Anytime a valueflow is started but not completed, that is a failure. The reason is that even if withdrawing is the right thing to do, the fact is that we have begun a process that consumed resources and did not add to the throughput of the valueflow. If the process should never have been started, then that should have been caught at the demand stage before starting.

2. Occasionally a Disposition will be challenged by one of the parties in the case. In that situation the case has to be reviewed and may require an additional hearing. Therefore, we will add a failure handler called Appealed Case. This handler will review the case and re-evaluate the judgment and any actions contained in the disposition.

The following diagram depicts the example with a failure stream added.

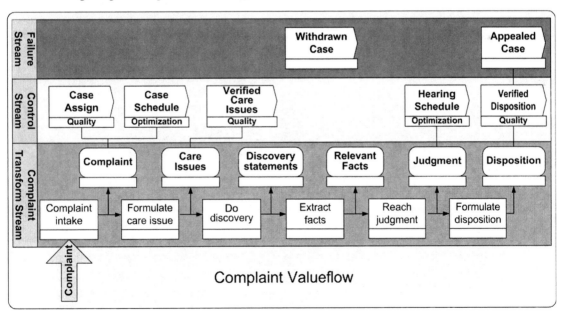

A failure stream contains failure outcomes/handlers. These should be related to the failure modes identified when determining the controls. That's why we have associated the Appealed Case failure handler with the Verified Disposition control, which is in turn linked to the transform output called Disposition. Basically, we don't expect the Verified Disposition control to be able to eliminate all failures. In this case, it is an external person that initiates the appeal and so we need a formal method to handle it.

Essentially, wherever we define a control outcome, we will likely have a failure outcome and possible handler and vice-versa. We may or may not design a standard failure handler for a given control. Nevertheless, we should identify it. When a control does not eliminate the possibility of a failure, a failure handler may still be required. Failures can be shown as being asynchronous or synchronous. An asynchronous handler can be invoked at any time whereas a synchronous handler is associated with a particular place in the flow. The Withdrawn Case failure is shown here as being asynchronous, which means it can happen at any point in the valueflow. It doesn't have to happen after a particular output. The Appealed Case output is shown as synchronous since a case can't be appealed until there is a Disposition.

Note that both the control stream and the failure stream can eventually be modelled all the way down to the output and then to the task level, although we haven't shown this in the example. In this example, we show the valueflow modelled cleanly into separate streams.

EXAMPLE: COMPLAINT—CHART OF ACCOUNTS

Sometimes adding all or parts of the Chart of Accounts directly to the diagram can make the blueprint even more visual. The following diagram does just that to complete the example of a blueprint with all three streams up to the output level with some CoA measures superimposed.

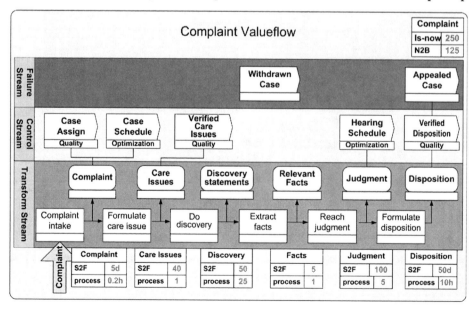

The diagram shows the valueflow with the three distinct streams. In addition, we have added some CoA elements. Notice that we have a Chart of Accounts measure of responsiveness (start-to-finish) for the valueflow shown in the top right corner of the diagram. The current value (Is-Now) of the start-to-finish time for the valueflow as a whole is 250 days, but the target or what it needs to be (N2B) is 125 days.

In addition, at the bottom of the diagram, below each output, we show a CoA associated with each output. The CoA contains the name of the associated output as the title. For example, the CoA for the Judgment output displays two account measures representing actual measured performance.

What this CoA says is that it takes 100 days from start-to-finish (S2F) to produce the Judgment, but that it only requires 5 hours of process time. If we were trying to reduce the start-to-finish time for the valueflow then this output would be a good place to start. The Chart of Accounts begs the question "Why does it take 100 days to complete five hours of work?" This is an example of how we use the Chart of Accounts to focus our attention. So rather than try to map the entire process, we might begin by posing the question to the people executing this portion of the process. They probably already know the answer. In fact, the reason this output took so long was that the committee met one day every two months. And then, if there was a question about a particular case, the committee had to wait until the next meeting two months later to continue that case. Quite often the answer was available within a few days; nevertheless, the case couldn't proceed until the committee met again two months later. This kind of information is difficult to get from a process map. The solution was not to change the tasks but to change the frequency of the review meeting.

SUMMARY

Complexity and sophistication are unavoidable. If we are to solve more complex business problems, then we need a way to deal with that complexity. The Three-Stream model helps to reduce the amount of complexity we have to deal with at any one time by segmenting the business process based on the work being done.

The transform stream contains the core work necessary to producing the defining output for the process. When the transform stream is poorly designed it will lead to more failure and control. That's what leads to poor performance. Only transform stream work can increase throughput.

Failure handling has zero value. We do it because we have to, but it can't increase the throughput of the process. Failure is a direct result of poor design or inherent risks in the process. Therefore, improving the transform design will have a direct impact on the failure stream effort.

Controls are a burden. But they can increase throughput indirectly by reducing failure. Every control has to be individually evaluated as to its effectiveness. Adding controls to a process is often an automatic reaction when something goes wrong. If the effectiveness and productivity of the control is not evaluated, then, over time, a business process can be overburdened with controls, reducing process performance.

But what if we have an existing process map, which may be large and complex? Can we still apply the streams concept? Yes, we can still apply the streams concept if we have a process that has already been mapped using conventional methods. One simple approach would be to take three highlighters and simply proceed to highlight each task as either transform (green) or failure (red) or control (yellow). This would provide a stunning visual effect and make us aware of just how many control and failure tasks are imbedded in the processes. We could also insert outputs and group tasks related to producing that output. Then we could produce a streamed model from our work. However, since individual controls would not be identified, we would need to determine how many different controls there were. By showing each control as a separate outcome, we can individually manage their effectiveness, measure their value contribution, and take action when the control is not contributing to the process performance goals.

By clearly separating each stream, we come close to showing the ideal implementation-independent process. The transform stream approximates the ideal process, from which we should be able to predict the best case performance. Any controls added, no matter how necessary, are a burden and take the process away from the ideal. The more we can reduce control effort and failure effort, the closer we get to the ideal process implementation and performance.

Separating the model into streams simplifies and reduces complexity. As human beings, we are poor at assimilating complexity in one gulp. However, we are good at understanding complex processes and mechanisms if we can divide the complexity into smaller chunks. By reducing complexity, we will reduce failure and improve productivity.

10

THE COMPONENT PERSPECTIVE (4TH NF)

If you can't describe what you are doing as a process, you don't know what you're doing.

W. Edwards Deming

An organization as a system is comprised of a number of valueflows. Each valueflow contains one or more functional processes. And each functional process consists of one or more base process operations. But what goes into the design and building of a process? What are the components that we have to work with to develop a business process? Can we identify a set of key components? As a matter of fact, we can. So let's explore the world inside a process to discover the basic building blocks for any process.

Building a process is like building a house. You work with bricks and mortar and skills and tools. When the house is built, you don't see bricks and mortar; you see a living space. If that living space helps you live a better life, then the house is a success. But you don't just proceed to put bricks one on top of the other. You first have to understand how the living space contributes to a better life. So far the framework has shown us how to articulate intent. But now it's time to build the process. So we need to understand the different kinds of bricks available to us.

In general, a **process** can be defined as a mechanism of organized (designed) and interconnected components (parts) that together do work and produce a defined output. A base process is a complex building block for functional processes. We say that it is a complex building block because it contains several components or pieces that are designed to work together to produce an output. Base processes are combined to form functional processes that are then combined to build valueflows. Let's begin with a summary of the basic bricks used to construct a base process. They are depicted in the following diagram.

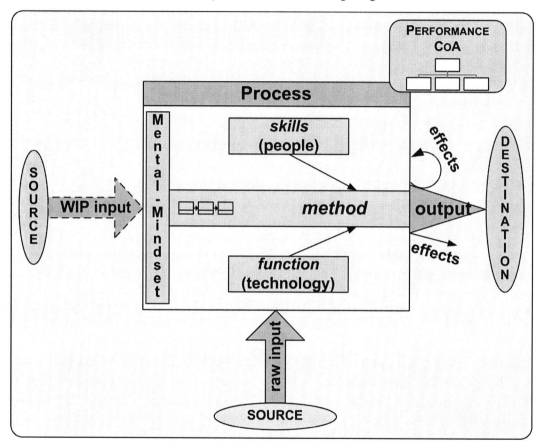

We can think of this as the base process framework, the lowest level building block or organizing principle for how work happens in a process, in an organization. It is a way to see the work that we do and understand how each of the components contributes to the process performance, which then contributes to the overall goals of the organization. It is a kind of microscopic framework that helps us to see inside a process and helps us to answer the central question. At the end of the day, if we want to change the performance of a process, we have to make a change to one or more of the components. But which component do we change?

And what do we change it to? That is the basic question that must be answered every day by organizations.

What part do we change and to what do we change it?

After all, if we want to achieve a different result—outcomes and performance—we must change one or more of the components of some process. Changing objectives and strategies may drive us to change, but changing intent accomplishes nothing if the intent isn't translated into functional process component level changes. Organizations are constantly changing their objectives and strategies but they aren't always successful at translating those into actual component changes.

This base process model provides us with the fundamental building blocks, which we will need to specify when we are designing and implementing a process. Becoming familiar with these basic components is the first step. Let's start by identifying the components from the diagram above and then proceed to explore each of the components in greater detail.

The diagram says the following about a base process:

1. It produces a defined output.
2. The output is received by a destination.
3. The process begins with work-in-process (WIP).
4. The WIP is obtained from a source—a previous process.
5. We might also use raw input in addition to the WIP.
6. The raw input is also obtained from some source.

It is the work-in-process and raw input that are transformed into the output.

7. The transform function uses a particular method, which is a series of tasks or operations.
8. Operations are executed by *people* possessing skills.
9. Or they are executed using *technology* that has function capabilities.

The process design and execution

10. is based on a mental mindset —a set of mental models and emotional mindsets (attitudes).

In addition, the process

11. exhibits measurable performance, and
12. may produce side effects that will impact some other process or itself at some later time.

In order to design and then implement a process, each of the above components must be appropriately specified along with its correlation to the desired performance. The components can be specified as part of a systematic design methodology and process or they can be specified on an ad hoc basis by the people executing the process. The latter approach leaves the implementation to chance or to personal preference.

Many organizations use an informal approach to designing processes. The design teams probably don't think at the level of detail that we have described. For example, they may think in terms of jobs rather than skills. That means that operations are assigned to existing jobs in existing departments. What the framework will permit is a more systematic approach to designing processes. It might seem like a lot of trouble to have to go to this level of detail and specify each of these components for every part of every process in an organization, but that's exactly what is required if we want to design *more perfect* processes. Either we design the process to do what we want, or we become slaves of a process, often working against it while trying to get the work out.

Formal process design for products has led to leaps in innovation for computers, cameras, phones, and many other products. The pace of development would not have been possible using informal practice approaches. The rate of progress is tied to the ability to produce a design blueprint, which is then used as the basis for producing, maintaining, and improving the product.

The same is true for process design. The framework being presented is a crucial step towards more disciplined and formal process designs. It provides a tool for producing a process blueprint that can be used as the basis for executing, maintaining, and improving the process. Disciplined process design has the potential to significantly improve process performance so that greater value can be delivered to all stakeholders. And greater performance can be translated into higher standards of living and especially higher standards of organizational work life.

Of course, attempting to produce process blueprints for all current processes would be an enormous undertaking of questionable value. Producing a blueprint would likely be seen as an exercise in documentation. And often that's what such initiatives end up being. We don't suggest that you take such an approach. Instead, we can begin using the framework to help us to better design the next process whose performance you will be addressing anyway. That should be the process with the largest performance gap and that represents the biggest opportunity for the organization. By applying the framework to your next initiative, you improve the likelihood of producing a more perfect process and you get a permanent blueprint of that process. You can then use that blueprint to execute, to maintain, and to continuously improve that process. And so you have one blueprint. With every additional process you undertake to improve, redesign, understand, or automate, you add to your collection of blueprints. Eventually, all key processes will have their blueprints.

We wouldn't think of building an office tower without a blueprint. And yet we run a business inside that office tower with limited blueprints. Does that make sense? It's what we are used to doing. We design or evolve a process and once that process is running, then the only blueprint left is inside some people's heads. Of course, everyone has their own version of the blueprint. And that causes a lot of needless waste inside organizations. Why is it a source of waste? Because we are each executing from a different playbook and that doesn't increase stakeholder value. Rather, it subtracts from the potential value.

To really understand a process, we must understand the nature of each of these components. We also need to understand how each component contributes to each of the CoA performance accounts. This may be different for different accounts and for different processes. For example, skill level may significantly impact quality and throughput. But it may have a lesser impact on start-to-finish time. So let's explore each of the basic components. We will begin with those that are visible from outside the process. Essentially these are interface components because they can be "seen" by at least two different processes that are connected to each other. Then we will explore the internal components that are seen only by the process itself.

The interface components are:
- Output
- Destination
- WIP or work-in-process
- Demand
- Raw Input
- Source

THE OUTPUT AND DESTINATION

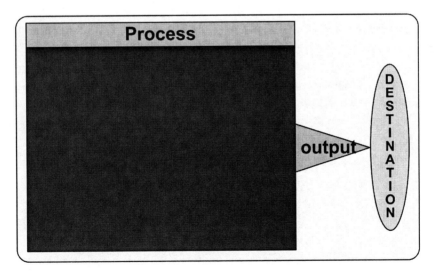

The key *defining factor* that differentiates one process from another is what it produces. The defining output of a process defines the nature of the process. A process that produces a car loan is different from one that produces software, which is different from one that produces a pizza. These are three totally different kinds of outputs. Such outputs look like the defining outputs of different valueflows. But a process can also be as simple as cutting a tube to length. What goes in is a tube of a certain length and what comes out (output) is a tube of the desired length. So a process can be a simple operation on some work-in-process.

The output of a process can take several forms, such as:
- physical output (bread, tube, pen, brick, etc.)
- knowledge output (software, poem, story, etc.)
- decision output, which is a probabilistic choice. For example, if you are sitting in a restaurant perusing the menu, you will likely be making a decision, a probabilistic choice. You may feel like having protein. But should you select the chicken or the steak? There may also be other constraints to your decision such as cost. If you were on a budget, then you might eliminate certain choices based on budget alone. With a probabilistic choice there is never a complete guarantee that the choice you make will lead to the outcome you desire.

This list is not necessarily an exhaustive list. It is only presented as an illustration of what typical categories for outputs might be.

An example of a *physical* output is an automobile steering wheel. We can have a process that produces steering wheels, which later can become a part of an automobile. Another example is a coffee that you might get at your favourite java establishment. Processes that produce physical outputs may seem to be easier to understand because the steps of the process can be seen and followed. Of course, you have to have the expertise to understand the operations being carried out.

A requirements specification is an example of a *knowledge* product. A design blueprint for a building is also a knowledge product. A process producing a knowledge product is not as transparent as one that produces a physical product. We can't see the operations being carried out because they happen inside someone's brain. So a blueprint is really important for these because the only way to see them is to see an accurate model of them.

A *decision* output is a kind of knowledge output. A decision represents a choice among alternatives. A decision process can be complex to understand without a blueprint because there is no real way to immediately evaluate the correctness of the decision. Evaluating a decision really means evaluating the results of actions taken based on the decision. And we often have to wait before we can even perform an evaluation.

Another way to categorize outputs is based on how they are used. We have already discussed these but will repeat them here because of their importance in determining if a process marks the end, beginning, or intermediate part of a valueflow.

1. **Transform Output-Input**: This is the simplest. If a process produces an output that is then further transformed by the next process in line, then we are producing a transform output, regardless of the nature of the output—physical, knowledge, decision. A transform output is essentially work-in-process. There is more work to be done on this output by some later process. Sometimes the later process is within the same organization. So this process would be part of a valueflow. Other times the later process is in a different organization. So this process is part of a supply chain. Our steering wheel is an example of a transform output. It will likely be used as part of something else, like a car.

2. **Component Output**: If a process produces an output that becomes a permanent part of another process, usually in a different valueflow, then it's a component output for some other process. Software is an example of a component output. It becomes part of some other valueflow. A machine is an example of a component output. It becomes part of some other process that uses the machine. A method is a component output of a design process. The method is incorporated into some process, changing the process. Component outputs are generally produced in order to improve the performance of the receiving process. If the performance remains the same, then we have invested without getting a return. Imagine we produce software intended to speed up a particular transaction. We implement the software but get no improvement in the speed of the process. Our Software Development valueflow has produced throughput. But because the performance of the receiving process remains the same, we have not produced any stakeholder value. In fact, we have reduced shareholder value because we have spent shareholder money but no one has benefited. The shareholders can't recoup the investment from the customer, resulting in a zero return on investment. What's worse, we may have to incur ongoing maintenance expenses, making the future worse as well.

The distinction between a transform output and a component output is important in order to separate valueflow processes from function processes. We have already discussed this difference in the chapter on valueflows. Let's briefly review the distinction and its significance.

There are two potential destinations for an output. It will be received by either one of the following:

1. **External Customer**: An output can go to an external customer process as part of a customer valueflow.

2. **Internal Process**: An output can go to some other internal process. Some people refer to all recipients as customers. We distinguish. A customer is really a relationship rather than an entity. The key thing about a customer relationship is that there is an exchange of value. For example, the customer is the source of a demand. The

customer then receives a product in exchange for money. An employee working in one process doesn't really have a customer relationship with an employee working in another process. An internal process that produces an output for some other internal process does not receive something in exchange for it. On the other hand, an external customer must provide something in exchange. We believe it is at worst harmful and at best not useful to view internal entities as customers. One significant risk is that we might begin to focus on the needs of these internal people and departments rather than the intended performance of the process. By referring to an internal process rather than an internal customer, we focus on the stated and designed needs of the process as represented by the Chart of Accounts rather than the ever-changing and personal preferences of an internal employee.

Since the output is seen by the producing process and the receiving process, it is an interface component. What that means is that both processes need to have the same specification for that component.

WIP AND RAW MATERIAL INPUTS

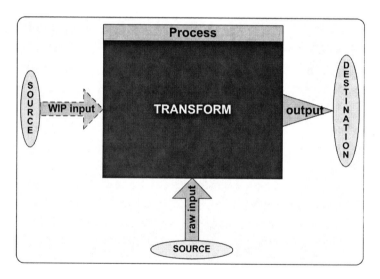

A base process is triggered by its inputs, of which there are two types. A process can receive either or both of these inputs. The first is work-in-process (WIP) from a previous process in the chain. All valueflows will have WIP flowing through them. WIP is basically some not yet completed version of the product. A Requirements Specification is an example of work- in-process. A partiallly assembled vehicle is another example. An assembled but not yet baked pizza is another example. A process that produces WIP is probably a functional process in a valueflow chain. But WIP is the same as ouput. That is, the output of one process is WIP to the next process in the sequence. It just depends on the point of view. So WIP is a process interface component. A process can receive multiple WIP components from different functional processes.

In the output tier model, we define intermediate outputs. These intermediate outputs represent progressions towards the defining output. They are a work-in-process. The transform stream of each functional process transforms the WIP it receives into something that is closer to the defining output for the valueflow. Therefore, the WIP from one functional process is the input and trigger for the next functional process.

A WIP output defines the boundary or transition from one functional process to another. Both producing and receiving processes should have the same specification for the WIP. The output from one process should be directly useable by the next functional process without rework. Often, in processes that have evolved rather than been designed, the WIP-Output from one process is first "prepared or re-worked" by the receiving process before it is ready to be further transformed, as depicted in the diagram below. This can represent a significant burden on the valueflow and can reduce quality and other performance measures.

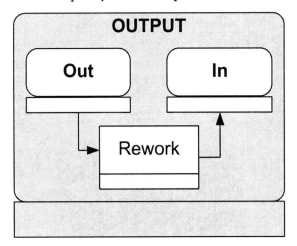

A functional process will have two sources of input. The first potential input will be a WIP input from the previous functional process in the same valueflow. The second will be any additional raw input required to continue the transformation. Both kinds of inputs are transformed by the process to produce the next WIP output. A given process can have both or either types of input. For a process producing a physical product, we will usually have physical inputs or raw material of some sort, but not always. For example, we can have a functional process that shapes a work-in-process component without the addition of any more raw materials. If the output is a soft or knowledge output, then the raw input will be soft input, such as additional information or knowledge. If the output is a decision output, then the input may be additional facts and assumptions.

At this point, we are still viewing the process from the outside only and, hence, the actual transform function is depicted as a **black** box. We don't know what's happending inside the box, and we can only measure some of the performance attributes. We can't know about defects inside the process that are getting corrected prior to the output being produced. This level is useful for performance measurement, but is not useful for understanding how the process actually operates, or for understanding all the risks or failure modes to which the process may be susceptible.

THE DEMAND

The Demand is the trigger for a valueflow. The demand only happens at the beginning of a valueflow and should be viewed as input into the valueflow rather than input into one of the functional processes. Where the demand arrives, there is no other input. In practice, it may look like a demand arrives with other inputs but that's just because of the way the process has been designed. For example, a simple assembly process may have a demand input that arrives with the parts necessary to make the assembly. But that just means that there is a process before it that received the demand and pulled parts based on some blueprint.

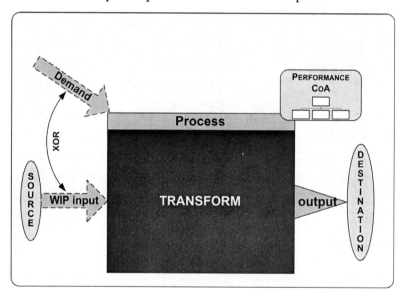

A demand input is an interface between valueflows. The valueflow demand profile can have a strong influence on the performance and the design of a process. It's particularly important to distinguish between actual demand arrival and average demand over a given period of time. As an extreme example, imagine a process called Spread. Spread requires exactly one hour of effort to process each and every one of its transactions. Spread has a capacity of 40 hours of effort per week. The demand coming into Spread is such that a new transaction arrives every hour. That means that just as the current transaction is completed, a new one arrives. Now imagine another process called Bulk. It also requires exactly one hour to process each of its transactions. And it also has a capacity of 40 hours of effort available per week. But Bulk receives all of its 40 transactions at the beginning of every week. The throughput of each process should be the same, i.e., each process produces 40 completed transactions every week. But the start-to-finish (S2F) time will be different. Note that S2F time begins as soon as the transaction arrives. If we needed to have a maximum S2F time of three days, then we would have to design Bulk differently from Spread. The demand will impose external variation that the process must deal with. Demand is normally variable while capacity is usually fixed. Therefore, the demand profile needs to be well understood.

If we know how much capacity is required just to handle demand and how much capacity we have, then that's a good indicator of the productivity and waste of a process. To calculate the productivity of a process, what we need to know is how much effort is required to process a totally error-free transaction—the perfect case. For example, the Bulk process requires 40 hours of effort capacity to process the 40 transactions, assuming perfect execution. If we have four full-time employees assigned to that process, then we have an actual capacity of 160 hours of effort (4 employees x 40 hours). So the process is only 25% effective with respect to effort. In other words, only 25% of total capacity is producing throughput. That should prompt us to ask, "Where are we consuming the remaining 75% or 120 hours per week?"

The above example is presented in order to demonstrate the importance of understanding the demand for a particular valueflow. The demand profile can change the performance behaviour of a valueflow. Therefore, we need to understand what it is and how it can vary before we start making changes to the task level model.

We've covered all the components that can be seen from just outside the functional process. To know more we have to go inside the process, inside the transform function. So let's look at the inside of the process to see how it is working, to see how the input is being transformed into the output.

THE TRANSFORM

The transform function is that part of a process that contains the work that can contribute to increasing the throughput for a valueflow. Note that the transform function for a given process may be implemented in a number of different ways. Therefore, there may be several alternative implementations, each with its own performance profile. In most organizations where there is no standard process, we may find variations in the way the transform portion of a process is executed. This can be a consequence of personal preferences or chance differences from day-to-day. It can also be as a consequence of reactive changes to failures or realized risks that change the process over time. Every time a failure occurs, especially a failure that is visible outside the process, there is a tendency to make changes to the process, often in the form of controls. Such changes are not always sufficiently thought through. The result is that over time the process performance may begin to drift away from the optimal. Because the change is gradual, it may go unnoticed until performance has gotten so bad that it can no longer be ignored. The strength of the transform function will determine the amount of control and failure effort that will be required. Much of the design effort should be focused on producing strong designs with minimal risks. So it would be useful to have a better understanding of the internal components of the transform function.

The diagram below shows the major internal components of a basic process. Let's identify and briefly describe these before we explore each one in greater detail.

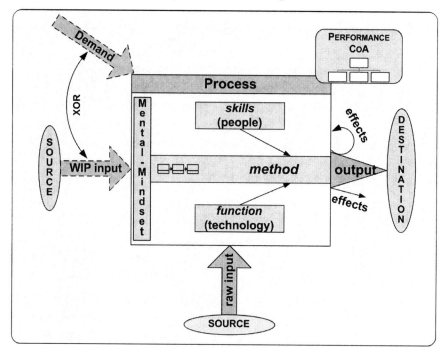

The WIP output is transformed into the functional process output.

1. The *method* comprises the steps or operations along with the logic required for the transformation.
2. Each operation of the method must be executed. It can be executed by *people operators* possessing skills.
3. Or each operation may be executed by *technology operators* that have function capabilities.

The process design and execution is based on a

4. *mental mindset*, which comprises a set of mental models and emotional mindsets/ attitudes.

In addition, a process may produce

5. *side effects*, which will cause an impact on some other process now or in the future. Or it may impact itself at some time. Side effects can be positive but more often they are negative or unwanted.

Let's look at each of these in more detail.

THE METHOD

The method is *not* the same as the process. This is a source of great confusion. The problem arises from the fact that we use the word process in many different ways with different meanings. When we say the process didn't work we are referring to the process. But when we say my process is better than your process we are usually referring to the method. So what exactly is the difference? The process represents the whole or capability to produce a particular output. The method describes the operations required to transform the input into the output. We can have two process instances with two different people executing the exact same method and get different results. If the two people have different levels of skill, then we can get different performance for each instance. On the other hand, we can have two different people with the exact same skill level (clones) using different methods for a given process and still get different performance. The method is the description (abstraction) of the series of steps or operations that are executed in order to produce the output. The process is the whole. When a process is executed we have to have a method, operators, inputs, etc. It is the process that produces the results. If we want to know which of two methods is better, we have to test them inside some process. We can't directly determine which method is better. We have to conduct tests whereby we execute a process holding all other factors the same and varying only the method. We would have to execute the test a sufficient number of times (large enough sample) to statistically conclude that one method was more effective than another. We can measure the performance of a process. But we have to conclude the effectiveness of a method.

The performance of a process is influenced by a number of factors, of which the method is only one. People, their skills, and their attitudes are another. When we take a true process view we are trying to see things from the perspective of the outcomes the process is intended to achieve. So the centre of attention becomes the outcomes. This doesn't diminish the importance of people to a process. After all, the stakeholders should have agreed to the process outcomes. Making the outcomes the focus gives us all a more common and objective focus. It points out the true importance of people as being their ability to reflect on what is being achieved and to change and adapt the process to become ever more effective.

When we switched our view from having the earth as the centre of our system to having the sun as the centre, we didn't make the earth any more or less important. What we did was get a truer and more complete understanding of our solar system. By having people as participants in the process rather than the centre of the process, we do the same thing for an organization.

This is liberating because it allows us to view process performance as being the consequence of several factors. People are only one of those factors. That means that when a process works well or when it doesn't, it isn't necessarily and strictly due to the people.

So the method is the instruction recipe portion of the process. By changing the method we can often change the performance of the process, regardless of who the people are. So when someone is performing a process redesign and their focus is primarily the method, they aren't truly performing a process redesign. They are performing a method redesign. This makes sense if the method happens to be the current constraint. Often it is not.

An example should further help to understand what we mean by method. Let's take the simple problem of finding the product of two numbers—246 by 357. One method is depicted in the diagram below. This is the procedure many of us learned in school. And it faithfully provides the product of the two numbers, when executed correctly.

$$
\begin{array}{r}
2\,4\,6 \\
\times\,3\,5\,7 \\
\hline
1\,7\,2\,2 \\
1\,2\,3\,0 \\
7\,3\,8 \\
\hline
8\,7\,8\,2\,2
\end{array}
$$

In this method we begin by multiplying 246 by the ones digit of the second number, the 7. This gives us the first line product, 1722. We then multiply 246 by the tens digit of the second number, the 5. This gives us the second line product of 1230. Then we multiply 246 by the hundreds digit of the second number, the 3. This gives the third line product of 738. Finally, we sum each column of the three product lines to get the answer—87,822. Since I learned this method in grade school, let's call it the GS (grade school) method.

But is this the only method or way to get the product of two numbers? There are a number of different ways to get the product of two numbers. Multiplication is actually repeated addition. So we could simply add the number 246 to itself 357 times. Of course, that would take us a long time. But there are other methods as well. Let's look at another, depicted below.

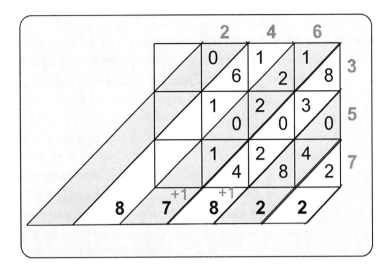

This method uses a grid with one of the numbers across the top and the other down the right side. Let's call it the Grid method. Each square of the grid is divided into two parts by a diagonal line. In order to find the product of the two numbers, we must multiply each digit of the first number by each digit of the second number. The product of each pair is placed into the square that is in the same column and same row as the two digits being multiplied. For example, when we multiple the last digit of 24**6** by the first digit of **3**57 we are multiplying 6 by 3. The product of 6 by 3 is 18, and that's what goes into the square that is in the same column as the 6 and the same row as the 3. Notice that the 8 goes in the lower right part of the square, while the 1 goes into the upper left.

With this method, we are only ever multiplying two digits. There is nothing to carry from the previous operation. When all digits have been multiplied, we add up all the digits within a diagonal—depicted in the diagram as alternating bands of white and grey strips.

If all we needed to do was multiply these two numbers, then it would matter little which method we used. But what if this was the time before computers and we had to produce the product of two numbers by hand (no technology)? And what if we had 10,000 orders, each for the product of two different numbers? So now we need to design a process, a capability. One of the things we would need to decide is which *method* to incorporate as part of the process.

A process that requires two numbers to be multiplied can use either *method* to get the product. But the performance of the process would depend in part on which method is chosen. It would also depend on other factors such as the skills of the people available to do the multiplying, the conditions under which the process is being executed, and other factors.

The methods differ in a few important ways. With the Grid method, we only ever multiply two digits. And we don't have any carries, so we don't need to remember the previous result. The GS method requires that we remember the carry from the previous result and that we then add it to the current product. So, on the surface, the Grid method seems to require a lower level of skill. On the other hand, when we get to the end we have more digits to sum up with the Grid method. So which method is better? The answer is that whichever gives us the best process performance is best for the process. Of course, to determine that we have to define what performance is required for the process. Then we will have to test the two methods. The problem is that we can't directly determine which of the two methods is superior without testing each inside an actual process. That means we will introduce other factors such as skill level, legibility of the orders containing the numbers to be multiplied, noise, and other environmental distractions, etc. To evaluate effectiveness we would need to execute both methods under controlled and similar conditions. We would need to generate a big enough sample of data to be able to reach a statistical conclusion. We couldn't, for example, have two different people each executing one method alone. Why not? Because the process performance would include impacts from the method as well as from the person executing. So we wouldn't know if the winner was due to the method, the person, or some other factor that we hadn't considered.

We can imagine that if we have low-skilled people with regards to multiplication, then the second method may produce fewer multiplication errors. On the other hand, the second method requires more numbers to be summed at the end, and so may produce more addition errors. The first method can be used if all that is available is a sheet of paper and a pencil. The Grid method requires preparation. We have to provide the operators with material that contains the grid. In order to know which method is more appropriate in a particular process, we would need to conduct an experiment that accounted for all of the factors and not just the multiplication part. Even then it is likely that each method may be superior to the other under specific conditions. So when conditions change, we may want to change methods in order to achieve the best possible performance. This is why best practices can sometimes be an illusion. The conditions under which a particular practice was seen as superior may not be the same as the conditions under which we are trying to implement it. So we need to know all the factors required to make one method preferable to another.

The method is in essence one way to abstract the *operations* of a process. Every method in a process must be matched to all the other components in order to achieve maximum delivered value. When a method is changed we need to make sure that other components and conditions are matched to the new method. Most process maps are primarily method maps. If we compare a process to a complete automobile then the method is like the engine.

Methodologies, as the name implies, are focused on the method to the exclusion of other factors. Methodologies often fail not necessarily because they are bad but because they are not superior under all conditions. They are not more perfect. So when an organization tries to adopt a single universal methodology, its success will tend to deteriorate over time. Initially we have wide latitude in selecting problems for which the methodology is well suited. But soon we run out of the well-suited problems and we get to ill-suited problems. The methodology starts to fail. The champions of other methodologies point to the failures and try to get us to switch. And thus is born the methodology-of-the-year syndrome. The thing is that the choice of which methodology to adopt makes less difference than we would think. That's because soon enough every methodology will run out of its favourite problems. The low-hanging fruit for that methodology will have been picked, so to speak.

The framework, on the other hand, can be used to produce a process blueprint regardless of the chosen methodology. So it can be used to compare results obtained from alternative approaches.

SKILL AND FUNCTION—THE OPERATORS

The steps or operations of the method must be executed. And they will either be executed by a person with the *skills* required for the operation or they will be executed by a piece of technology that is able to carry out that *function*. Sometimes it takes the two together. For example, we might use a saw to perform a cutting step. That saw might be completely automated or it might be a hand saw. Either way it is performing a transformation by taking a length of something, say a pipe, and producing two pieces of pipe, one of which should be of the desired length.

What we need to specify with regards to people is the *knowledge, skills, and emotional mindset* that they require in order to perform a particular operation. The tendency during design is to assign the operation to a job early during the design, rather than just specify the skills required. Job design is really part of an organization design activity. When we design a job we certainly need to take skills into consideration. But we also need to take emotional mindset, accountability, responsibility, authority, and other factors into consideration. Jobs may also be designed with employee stakeholder interests in mind, such as career progression, stability, security, personal challenge, and other needs that are not directly related to a specific process. That means that job design comes after process design. We need to understand the requirements across multiple processes before we can begin to design individual jobs.

Specifying skills is not the same as designing jobs. This distinction is often not made. When skill requirements change, we often try to shoehorn them into existing jobs. This works well enough when the changes are minor. But over time many small changes lead to jobs that no longer make any sense and represent a clear and present danger to both the organization and the employees. When job designs are suboptimal, the organization has to work harder and may have to undertake unnecessary risks to remain competitive.

When we design the process setting aside (not forgetting) job considerations first, we give ourselves the option of designing jobs whose boundaries align well with process boundaries, for example. We also need to design jobs so that their boundaries align well with accountability and authority. Such decisions can only be made when we understand the design requirements for multiple business processes, not just one. Regardless of how we design jobs, the skill specification for an operation remains the same.

When it comes to technology, what we need to know is what functional capability the technology or machine needs to be able to perform in order to carry out the operation. Software is an example of a situation where we can build a technology operator that does exactly what we want it to and nothing more (such as custom software or a custom machine). On the other hand, we can buy off-the-shelf software, which may do more or less than we need. Then we have to be able to understand the performance impact of each alternative. Of course, we should always design the process first rather than select the application first. Some people will disagree. They will argue that there is no point is designing the process when the software dictates the process. What they probably mean is that there is no point in detailing the *method* because a method will already be imbedded in the software application. But remember that the method is not the process. We agree that there is little point to producing a detailed method for the process when the application software probably dictates part or all of the method that can be used. But the software doesn't specify performance, accountability, responsibility, or authority. Each of these is part of the process design.

Naturally we must know the performance requirements of the process to be able to determine how best to implement a particular operation of a method, for example, whether we should have a human operator or a machine.

THE MENTAL MINDSET

The mental mindset is comprised of two complementary components: the mental model and the emotional mindset. These work together.

Processes tend to be developed much like the cowpath. A cow will move along a path based on moving around obstacles. If there is a large rock in its path, it will go around it. It makes no difference that the cow will make the journey around that rock a thousand times. It will simply never think of removing the rock so that it can continue going straight. We can hardly blame the cow because it really makes no difference to the cow.

The problem is that processes often develop based on the same principle. When we run into a process obstacle, we often do something to get around the obstacle rather than remove the rock. Why do we do this? In the short term, going around the obstacle is virtually always faster and requires less effort and energy. The problem is that removing the obstacle permanently requires present cost with future return. We call that an investment. That requires a long term view. Quite often, even when an employee has that long term view and wants to remove the rock, he doesn't have the authority to remove the rock. First he has to think through how he would remove it (solution), then he has to figure out who would need to be involved, then he would need to convince his boss, who would then need to convince her boss. In the end, the person's job might even be in jeopardy. And so it seems to make more sense to go around the rock.

Of course, over the years, your process probably contains a lot of steps that have to do with going around rocks. What these steps do is obscure the reasoning or theory behind the process design. So even though you might understand a process from the operations' perspective, it might not be clear why it was designed that way. All too often it wasn't initially designed that way; it just turned out that way. What we want to do is make the reasoning or theory behind the process explicit. That way we can gain further insights into the process. What if the underlying reasoning is wrong? How will we ever know? For example, many approaches to requirements elicitation are based on the premise that the subject matter experts *know* what the process requirements are. But what if they don't know what the process requirements are? They may understand their craft but they may not know which factors affect start-to-finish time. So they can't provide proper requirements with respect to that particular measure. If we explicitly stated the premise as "The subject matter experts are the source of reliable requirements," then we could evaluate what turned out to be wrong requirements at implementation and make a determination of whether the requirements were wrong from the start or if they were misunderstood.

The *mental model* refers to the theory behind the process. It includes the assumptions and pictures that we hold about the process and its components. If we believe that the employees are all lazy and will try to do as little as possible, then the process design will reflect that. On the other hand, if we believe that everyone is always giving 100%, then the design will likely reflect that. We aren't suggesting that one model is correct, only that how we think about the process has an impact on how it is designed and how it is executed. The assumptions need to be understood and made explicit in order to truly understand the process. The mental model should be made explicit. That way it can be shared, understood, challenged, and verified. The mental model used to design a process should be consistent with the mental model held by the participants of the process. If you design a process based on "Everyone is honest" but those executing believe "Everyone is dishonest" then they will be confused about the design and they will probably execute quite differently from the intended design. This may require training and communication to resolve. Or it may require you to verify the assumptions. Otherwise, there will be an execution gap. A process designed on the basis that everyone gives 100% in an environment where people do as little as they can will not perform to expectations.

One problem is that for many processes there is no mental model behind the process. It is a cowpath process. The process may have initially focused on "producing the product." So all the focus has been around the functionality to produce the output regardless of other performance, except perhaps cost. The process as a performance unit was never truly designed. Quite often when we redesign, we should think of it more as a first design, rather than a redesign. That means that we should set aside all current constraints when redesigning, as if we were starting from scratch. Of course we can't ignore current constraints, but we can temporarily set them aside for the purposes of redesign. Then we can determine which conditions would need to change and which constraints would need to be resolved in order to achieve the required performance

The mental model really refers to the theory or paradigm behind how the process is designed. By identifying it as a separate component, we are nudged into making it explicit.

This brings the theory out in the open, where it can be understood and even challenged. Quite often the problem with a process is that it is based on faulty theory. Other times it isn't based on anything other than the fact that it worked at some point—the cowpath.

The *emotional mindset* reflects the attitudes required for the process to achieve peak performance. Take a selling process for a product or service that has a naturally low closing rate, say one sale per 100 prospects. Such a process would need to tolerate the high failure rates. Imagine a salesperson who becomes so demoralized after 50 failed prospects that she reduces her call rate. That process is not going to succeed because the person's emotional mindset is out of tune with the process. Or imagine a policy that stated that if a salesperson has 75 failed attempts in a row, then he gets fired. Would such a policy make any sense for such a process? Again the policy would indicate a mindset that was out of tune with that required. A doctor in a cancer ward may need a different attitude from one in a maternity ward. The decoration in the cancer ward might also need to be different from that in the maternity ward. This is all part of the process design.

There is the mental mindset that is optimal for the process in order to achieve its performance objectives, and there is the actual mental mindset as represented by the method, policies, or people that are part of the process. Any gap will cause a reduction in the performance or even outright failure.

The mental mindset reflects how we think about the process (mental model) and how we feel about the process (emotional mindset). Let's look at an example. Suppose you are designing a Risk course intended primarily for financial institutions. This offering is meant to address what you believe is a gap in knowledge for Risk Executives. And let's further imagine that the gap is real. So you invite a number of Risk Executives from competing organizations to a round table discussion to get their views. What mental attitude is required in order for your inquiry process to produce an accurate description of the current conditions? We probably need a high level of openness, right? That means that the executives must be forthcoming about the actual conditions within their organization. They need to be candid. That's what the process requires. However, let's look at how the process is designed. It will bring these highly competitive individuals—likely type A people—together and expect them to express weaknesses in front of their peers from competing organizations. What is the likelihood that this will happen? Of course it's not going to happen. The personal need to look good in front of others will trump the need of the process for openness. The process will likely fail to produce the correct results.

The problem here is that the participants cannot act in accordance with the emotional mindset that is required. It is for this reason that when we ask for feedback comments, we often make them anonymous. We permit the openness we need. So the process would need to be redesigned somehow to take the actual mindsets into consideration.

Many processes fail to produce correct results because the emotional mindset is never considered. Meeting processes can be poor because a meeting may contain different processes trying to produce different results running simultaneously.

Take brainstorming sessions. These can be highly productive or a total waste of time, depending on how they are designed and carried out. Part of the brainstorming session is to produce ideas and part is to filter out those ideas that we don't believe will survive. If the two steps are carried out together, then what happens is that when one person makes a suggestion that someone else torpedoes, we have a conflict in the mental attitudes. Making suggestions require us to open up. If our idea is then attacked, we feel *we* have been attacked, which produces a certain feeling or attitude. What often happens is that people may clam up and stop making suggestions because they feel they are being attacked. Or they may fall back and make only safe suggestions that they believe everyone will go along with. Many potential solutions never come to light because they were seen as too risky to suggest.

But if we separate the part of the process that produces the idea from the part that evaluates the idea, then we can get a different result. If we further declare which part of the process we are in, and make the required attitudes explicit, and we give people a minute or two to prepare themselves to adopt the required attitude, then we might get a much better result. When one part of a process requires one emotional attitude and another part requires an incompatible attitude, then separating the two is a good design approach. People can't automatically and quickly switch from one attitude to an opposite attitude on the fly. They need to get out of one and get into the other. It's a bit like changing outfits. Superman can do it quickly but the rest of us need some time. So any process that requires competing attitudes or feelings should be split, so that people know which attitude is required, and so that they have the time to *get into that attitude.*

To achieve peak performance, a process must be based on a valid and effective mental mindset and it must be implemented in accordance with that mental mindset. The mental mindset is not the same as the culture but can be impacted by it. Whereas the culture applies to the organization as a whole, the mental mindset applies to a particular process. Naturally we would expect the two to be compatible. When the mental mindset required for a process conflicts in some way with the current culture, the culture will usually pull the mindset back into alignment.

Why do so many companies fail when trying to implement methodologies or strategies such as Lean or Six Sigma or Continuous Process Improvement? Part of the reason is that they attempt to implement methods that will only work within a process that has a specific mindset derived from a particular culture. When you attempt to implement that method inside a culture that is not compatible, the culture wins. Why does the culture win? Because people are the caretakers of culture and people are the only ones who can affect changes to it. So people may reject a process that requires a foreign mental mindset in much the same way that the body rejects a foreign organ. Change is often rejected not because of some built-in change resistance but because of mindset conflict. The resistance to change may be overstated because realistically we accept all kinds of changes every day.

SIDE EFFECTS

Side effects may include nausea, vomiting, drowsiness, constipation…We've all seen or heard commercials for various drugs on TV. What they all have in common is a long list of side effects. Of course, side effects are usually unwanted and undesirable impacts of the primary solution. Why are they always undesirable? Well, if they were desirable, then they would be part of the primary selling points.

When we try to solve a problem we often focus so much on the problem that we may tend to ignore potential impacts on those around us. The evidence of this is all around us. From landfills to rude drivers to running red lights to global warming, we seem to have a tendency to solve one problem while at the same time creating another one, usually for someone else. Often, the someone else is us in the future.

Process solutions also have side effects, mainly unwanted. These tend to be negative impacts on other processes. Of course the processes that are impacted tend to be those for which we are not accountable. When a process produces such an unwanted side effect, we refer to it as *creating an externality*. When a manufacturer creates packaging that sells his product but that is difficult to dispose of, he is creating an externality—a problem that someone else has to pay for and solve. Externalities due to side effects can significantly reduce overall organizational performance. Systematic process design with a good Chart of Accounts can help us to identify these externalities and their impacts. But that isn't enough. An organization should take the view that improving one process at the expense of another isn't really an improvement. It should become standard policy not to accept any externalities from a process without explicit agreement. If externalities are unavoidable, then the impacted processes must be reviewed and modified or have their Chart of Accounts updated to reflect the impacts.

We can also have positive externalities, unlike most drugs. For example, when we start walking to the grocery store to reduce gas consumption, we also improve our health. And so it is with processes. They can be designed to produce positive externalities and that's what the goal should be during process design.

Side effects are an important part of a process, though they aren't really components. They are really consequences that are not directly related to the production of the defining output. Therefore, given a choice between two implementations, each capable of producing the performance, the one with the most favourable side effects is usually the better choice.

PERFORMANCE

Every time a process executes, it will exhibit measurable *performance*. Of course, performance is not a component, but the CoA is. Performance is an attribute of the process or some part of the process. Performance is measured through the Chart of Accounts for the particular functional process and should be linked to the CoA for the valueflow. We have already discussed measures in great detail. So we won't give this topic much more attention.

There is one important distinction that needs to be made. When we reach the component level, we will have to specify the components. Specification is not the same as performance. We can still have a CoA for the specification but the values in the CoA don't change every time we execute the process. For example, we can specify certain skill requirements. We can even specify the level for a particular skill. We might even go further and test the skill level for a particular person to ensure that she meets the specification. But when we execute the process, there is no guarantee that the person will actually function at that skill level all the time. Nevertheless, we should have a periodic evaluation of the status of the specification. Let's say that we have identified a skill level for a particular job but are unable to hire at that level. So we go ahead and hire at a slightly lower level. Our specification CoA would show a gap between the target skill level and the actual skill level. This would get re-evaluated periodically to see if there has been movement. But it wouldn't get measured every time we execute.

Process execution performance is a measure of excellence that can change every time a transaction is executed. So performance is dynamic, ever changing. A specification is static across transactions over a period of time. That doesn't mean it won't change over time. In fact, we would expect skill level to rise. We just don't expect it to change from one transaction to the next. A specification acts as a reference. Measuring the performance of a component inside a process can be difficult or even impossible. That's because performance is the net effect of all the components from input through transformation to output working together. And this can change for every transaction.

Often the only way to determine how a component contributes to performance is through experiments. If we want to know which of two methods provides the best results for a given Chart of Accounts, then we might need to execute a particular transaction a number of times with one method, and then with the other method. Since all components contribute and can change the performance, we would have to hold all the other components stable to get reliable results. If we had one group execute one method and a different group execute the other, then we could not know if the difference in performanc was due to the method or to the skills of the different groups. The components relate to performance in that each component will impact one or more performance account measures. Understanding the account measure impacted by each component and the degree of impact is crucial to the pursuit of *more perfect* processes.

SUMMARY

We really can't properly specify the functional aspects of a process until we understand what the process as a whole needs to accomplish and how the process will be measured and evaluated. When we understand the performance requirements in addition to the functional need then we can design the process by specifying the building blocks. The building blocks are all we have to work with. But there are so many options at the component level that specifying them without reference to the higher level performance we desire will of course never lead to an optimal process. All the work done up to this point was to prepare us for component specification and design.

When we go from performance measures to a specification, we are translating a characteristic into something we believe will deliver that characteristic. So once the process components have been specified, then we need to measure to determine the level of success. This is an experimental trial-and-error process. What this process gives us, or rather should give us, is a set of design principles along with design conditions. An organization improves as it refines its principles. The principles are a resource for the enterprise and must be treated as such. If they are stored only in the heads of the employees, then we lose them when we lose the employee.

When we design, we need to keep in mind that different components have different impacts on the various performance accounts. The relationship between a component specification and each performance account is crucial to design. For example, if we choose a higher skill level to populate a job and if the higher skill level costs more, what impacts will that have on the various measures? Will the impact be the same on cost as on start-to-finish? Quite often a higher skill level means that a task might be completed with slightly less effort, which would certainly impact costs. But less effort on a task doesn't necessarily translate into a faster process, particularly if the wait time between operations is large. So the crucial thing about components is to understand how each one impacts each performance measure. And this may be different for different processes. Actually creating such a profile for a component is a great way to use some of the tools of Six Sigma.

The process framework presented here is not just a way to understand a process; it is also a framework for storing the process knowledge and process design principles so they can be used as a base for organizational progress. When the process is in third normal form and when it explicitly specifies each of the basic building block components, then the process is in fourth normal form. These building blocks form the last tier of detail that we will discuss for the framework.

PART IV

APPLICATION

11

THE MASTER VALUEFLOW MAP

Because men often get lost, and because they don't like to ask for directions, maps were invented.

Raffaela Baratta

We can view an organization as being comprised of a production system and a management system.

Organization = Production System + Management System

The Production System is the collection of valueflow processes that are required to produce the customer products and services. Naturally, these will be different depending on the industry of the organization. Similar industries will tend to have similar, if not identical, production systems. That's because they are dependent on the technical nature of the product or service. Therefore, two organizations are more apt to have similar production systems if they produce like products.

The Management System is the collection of valueflow processes that are required to manage the production system. Unlike the production system, the management system is less dependent on the nature of the product and more dependent on the character of the organization itself. The management system will be impacted more by the philosophy and beliefs of the organization. Therefore, two organizations are more apt to have similar management systems if they have like thinking.

To make the jump from intent to execution, we have to link processes to strategy. By now we should know that identifying the valueflows is crucial to achieving this. If we can't identify them, then we can't develop a normalized model, since the valueflow is the first normal form. We have learned techniques for determining the scope of a valueflow starting from any functional process but is there a general map that can help us to figure out where to start to look for key valueflows within virtually any organization?

The short answer is "Yes, there is!" We have compiled a general map for this purpose. The Master Valueflow Map is intended as a guide to help us locate key valueflows. In addition, it helps us determine where an already identified valueflow fits into the greater scheme of things. But remember it's only a guide. Organizations can differ greatly in how they are designed and your organization might be somewhat different from the model we have developed.

Our Master Valueflow Map contains three distinct valueflow segments. Each segment serves quite a different purpose. Every organization has valueflows for each segment. We haven't come across any organization that is missing any of these basic segments.

1. Breakthrough Strategy Deployment Segment (Manage Shift)
2. Customer Value Segment (Manage Customer Value)
3. Core Strategy Sustain Segment (Manage Drift)

The first and third segments, Breakthrough Strategy Deployment and Core Strategy Sustain, are part of the Management System. The Customer Value segment is part of the Production System.

To get an understanding of how the three segments relate to each other, we'll resort to an analogy. Let's imagine we own a large fishing boat. Our intent is to go out and catch some fish. That's where the customer value is. But where should we go to catch these fish? Think of the various potential locations of the fish as being the potential markets. So we determine where we think the best fishing will be, taking into account that competitors will also be going after the same fish. Then we set course for those fish. Once we have set the course, we need to maintain it to get to the fish. But there are many reasons why we might go off course. Perhaps the ship is being blown off course by the wind. Or perhaps we aren't always paying careful attention to the direction. Perhaps the navigation equipment is not very sensitive such that we can really only tell if we are within 10 degrees of the right direction. For these and many other reasons we might drift off course. The destination is still the same. Our intent is still the same. We are simply drifting away from the proper direction. Naturally, the farther off course we drift, the greater the likelihood of not catching any fish. So one thing that we have to be able to manage is drift.

But what if we are right on course? We haven't drifted at all. Nevertheless, the fish themselves might move. They might shift their position. In that case we need to know that they have shifted position and we need to know their new position. Then we need to set a new destination and based on where we are, set a new course. Note that setting the destination is not the same as setting the course, which depends on where we are as well as where we want to get to. If we fail to detect that the fish have moved (shifted), the risk is that when we get to the destination, we won't find any fish there. Or perhaps we get to the right destination but there never were any fish there. So another thing we have to manage is shift.

Once we get to the destination, it's time to catch some fish—customer value. We might catch a lot of fish or we might only catch a few. We might catch them efficiently at low cost, or we might spend more resources than necessary. How well we do will affect what we make from the fish catching. Perhaps we catch the fish well, but have difficulty selling them. And so we also have to be able to manage customer value.

Now we're ready to introduce the Master Valueflow Map and use the analogy to explain it.

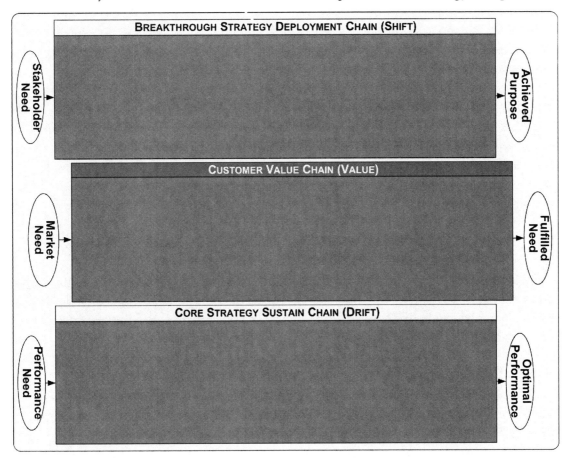

Our map contains three segments. The middle segment, "Customer Value Chain," is all about catching the fish and selling them to customers. This is *Customer Value* management. Every organization is built around managing some sort of customer value. We could say that this is the core of an organization from a customer point of view. If an organization fails here, it cannot survive for long and it certainly can't thrive. To the customer, this is all that they care about. But remember that an organization has other stakeholders as well. So just because this portion is the most important from the customer view, it isn't necessarily the only important segment.

The top segment, "Breakthrough Strategy Deployment," is all about determining destinations and setting the course. It is here that we take into consideration the needs of all the stakeholders. It is here, also, that we monitor the fish to see if they are moving. It is here that we monitor the stakeholders to see if expectations have changed or shifted. It is also here that we monitor the competitors to see how their relative position may have shifted. This is Shift management.

The bottom segment, "Core Strategy Sustain," is all about maintaining the direction and adjusting the course that has been set. It is about detecting when we are beginning to go off course, or are no longer on course. Then we take action to make changes to get us back on course. It is also about detecting any deterioration of component parts as compared to their specification. If the components are beginning to vary from the specification then this will eventually lead to us going off course. This is Drift management.

An organization needs to excel in each of these three segments in order to thrive in the long term. Many organizations begin with a product idea and so they focus their attention on how to best get that product to the customer. Because they are small, they tend to implement the shift and drift segments informally. Often they see the work that belongs to the Breakthrough and Core Strategy segments as just an extension of the Customer Value Chain. *But they are not.* As the organization grows, the valueflows in the Customer Value Chain become more formalized and more disciplined. The people within those valueflows are carefully selected based on their subject matter expertise and experience within the Customer Value Chain, which we can consider as being the heart of any organization. But just as a human can't live with only a heart, so an organization cannot thrive on the Customer Value Chain alone.

An organization must develop its capabilities with respect to Breakthrough Strategy Deployment and with respect to Core Strategy Sustain in order to survive and thrive. These are process groups which, in the long term, are even more critical than the Customer Value Chain. These constitute an organization's Management System. And these are not well identified or defined in most organizations. Approaches like Lean, Six Sigma, Business Process Engineering, and even Project Management are primarily in support of the Breakthrough Strategy and Core Strategy segments. One of the reasons that these approaches and methodologies have a tough time succeeding is that in many organizations, there is no home for them. Those companies that have had greater success with project management, for example, tend to be those that have formalized the use of project management as part of their Management System.

To the customer, what she buys is the product of the organization. But to the shareholders and to the employees, it is the business itself that is the product. To these stakeholder groups, it is the Management System that is the product. And this product requires the same level of attention and detail as does the customer product. There are many organizations that have failed even though they had a great product. But because they had a weak Management System, they were not able to adjust and adapt. Because they didn't see the shifts and the drifts, they eventually found themselves shipwrecked while other organizations with less perfect customer products thrived.

Describing in detail the processes that are required to support Breakthrough Strategy Deployment and Core Strategy Sustain would take a book on its own. So we won't do that here. We will, however, describe the Master Valueflow Map to put the three segments into perspective. Note that the Relational Process Model can be used to model valueflows from any of the three segments of a business.

The middle segment centres on the customers and their needs. Let's explore this segment first, since customer value is the source of all other value and since this is the segment with which most of us are familiar.

CUSTOMER VALUE MANAGEMENT

Every organization has to deliver value to its customers, based on some need. And so it must have a number of product-related valueflows for delivering that value. This segment explores the broad category of customer-related valueflows.

At one end (left of diagram), we have a market need that is waiting to be fulfilled. At the other end, we have the fulfillment of an individual customer demand related to that need. In between are a series of related valueflow categories. These are all part of the Customer Value Chain. Let's briefly describe each category before we proceed to exploring each in greater detail.

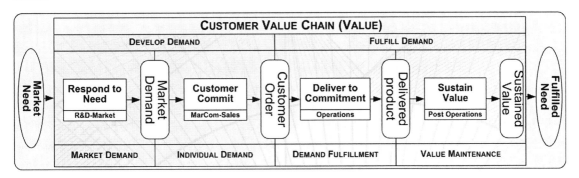

The diagram summarizes the four major sections that make up the Customer Value Chain.

1. **Market Demand**: We start with a Market Need and we develop product and service responses to that need. Then we use those product responses as the basis

for generating a specific market demand for the products and services. That's the purpose of a Market Demand Valueflow, to create market demand.

2. **Individual Demand**: But market demand is not the same as a purchase. Based on the Market Demand, we work to get individual customers to commit to our response to the need. We work to get an individual Customer Order for a specific product (good or service). The purpose of an Individual Demand Valueflow is to go from a general market demand to a committed customer order.

3. **Demand Fulfillment**: Based on a Customer Order, we then produce or deliver the product or service. That's the purpose of a Fulfillment Valueflow—to deliver to the order.

4. **Value Maintenance**: Some products or services lose their value over time and need to be maintained, such as a car, computer, skill set, etc. In order to sustain the product value, we implement a Value Maintenance valueflow. Often these can be viewed as additional products and services.

We begin with a need, develop a market, get individual customer orders, deliver the product, and then maintain its value. The centre of attention in this segment is the customer and his needs. Let's explore each valueflow section in greater detail, beginning with Demand Fulfillment, which is the most important from the customer perspective.

DEMAND FULFILLMENT

Every organization must deliver some product (good or service) to an external customer based on individual customer demand—the customer order. Giving the customer what he has asked for is the purpose of the Demand Fulfillment valueflow. Every organization will have one such valueflow for each and every product (good or service) that they produce. Remember that we identify valueflows based on output, destination, demand, and Chart of Accounts. Demand Fulfillment is the primary source of all value because it is here that the organization exchanges value with the external customer world. This is the only category of valueflow that contains customer value-added work.

When you order a pizza you are creating an Individual Demand. When that pizza gets delivered, your demand has been fulfilled and you exchange value by paying for it. Pizza order to delivery is an example of a Fulfillment valueflow. When you place an online order for books and those books arrive at your door and your credit card is charged, that's another example of a Fulfillment valueflow. Both of these are examples of fill to order. The fulfillment begins after the order is received. Sometimes we also fill to forecast. When you walk into a pizza shop and order a slice that has already been baked, that's an example of fill to forecast. Although the valueflow technically begins when you order, some of the fulfillment functions, such as making the pizza, have already been executed. In this case the Fulfillment valueflow begins to execute before the actual customer order arrives.

Customer Fulfillment valueflows are the ones that are of most interest to the customer and they are the only ones that deliver measurable customer value. So the search for valueflows should begin here because ultimately this is the only place where we can directly measure customer value throughput. We might say that this is the source of the energy required to sustain the organization. When this energy dries up, so does the organization.

But just because it is the source of exchanged value doesn't make it more important than any other valueflow. The thing we should always ask ourselves is not "What value does this add?" but rather "Is this necessary to get to the value?" Importance is an emotional question that can blind our vision. Necessity is a more objective question that leads to better choices. But how is a Demand Fulfillment valueflow triggered?

INDIVIDUAL DEMAND

In order to deliver something to a customer, we must have some sort of product order, which is a demand request. An order is produced by an Individual Demand valueflow. Its purpose is to generate commitment to a particular product at a particular price. It defines the value to be exchanged. An order says "We, the organization, will provide you, the customer, with a product and you will provide us with something of value to us, usually in the form of money." The Individual Order is like an exchange contract.

There should be a distinct Individual Demand valueflow for every product that we sell, even if they are sold in exactly the same way. At the least they might have different Chart of Accounts values. The Individual Demand valueflow will typically contain the Sales function. But it contains more than just the Sales process, which might be the last process in the valueflow chain. Notice that the valueflow ends with an individual customer order, which is a trigger for the Fulfillment valueflow. Notice also that it starts with Market Demand. What this is saying is that we are trying to generate an individual order based on a collective market demand.

The Individual Demand valueflow for a profit-oriented, customer organization may differ substantially from that for a not-for-profit, consumer-payer organization. In the profit scenario, the customer can evaluate both value and price and that serves to control the demand. Whenever the price changes due to cost increases, for example, customers may re-evaluate the exchange proposition. That evaluation has a direct impact on the demand for the product. An organization driven by customer demand would try to increase demand since it makes a profit on each individual order for its product. The customer acts as a brake or demand dampener in this case.

On the other hand, a not-for-profit, consumer-payer organization will behave differently. When the cost of a medical procedure changes, for example, the consumer won't see this effect. So she won't play a role in moderating demand. The payer, on the other hand, may or may not feel the impact. If the medical procedure is funded by the government through taxes, then the payer won't see the effect either. Eventually he may see it as taxes rise, but there will be a long delay. Neither the consumer nor the payer can act as a moderating influence on demand. So how will demand be managed? The simple answer is that in many of these types of situations, the demand is not managed and tends to increase. That's one reason that government-run programs often come with escalating growth in costs. It isn't necessarily mismanagement (that may be a part of it); it could be runaway demand. When something is free to a consumer the tendency will be to consume more.

In a consumer-payer situation, the consumer will likely evaluate the product/service against a zero price. Therefore, virtually all products will appear to be "worth it." The consumer, rather than controlling the level of demand, is more likely to tend to increase it. That means that, left alone, the Individual Demand valueflow in a not-for-profit organization will tend to act as a demand accelerator with no natural brake. Such an organization would need to design-in demand controls that are otherwise unnecessary in a for-profit customer business. Otherwise, demand will forever increase.

And it doesn't stop with the consumer. The suppliers can often act as *demand accelerators* as well. Again looking at a medicare example, medical specialists can act as demand accelerators by requesting more and more tests. They don't pay for the tests so they are likely to view the potential benefit of the test regardless of cost. We aren't saying that doctors or anyone else are ordering tests that aren't required. We are only saying that such systems need demand regulators because without them the tendency is towards increased demand, regardless of individuals involved. This is another example of creating an externality. When trying to determine the value of something that has zero personal cost, too many things appear to be valuable.

This is why approaches that work in a for-profit organization may backfire in a not-for-profit. Imagine a *public service* organization that embarks on an improvement campaign to lower its transaction costs and deliver better service. Suppose it succeeds in lowering functional transaction costs and improving service levels. Initially this may look like a success. But if the increased service levels attract increased demand, then total costs may go up. This is great for a profit organization, because it means more profit. But for a not-for-profit, greater demand usually means higher total costs. When we treat the valueflow, we make this potential impact visible because demand is part of the valueflow Chart of Accounts.

MARKET DEMAND

In order to generate an individual demand, there must be some sort of larger market demand for each of the products and services. And how is market demand created? The left side of the Customer Value Chain diagram says that in response to some need out there in the market, we produce responses in the form of products and services. These responses take into consideration both the value to the customer and the value to the shareholder in terms of potential profits.

Once a product response has been formulated, we need to make that market aware of the product and service responses. The goal is to generate a Market Demand for our products. After all, if no one knows about our product, it will be more difficult to get anyone to commit to buying it. As with Individual Demand, this valueflow should likely have a different implementation for for-profit organizations versus not-for-profit. In a profit organization, the desire is to have a growing market. So we want to see the market share rise over time so that we can achieve greater profits. A growing market share is also important to the survival of the firm. If an organization becomes too small compared to competitors it may be swallowed up or die off. In a not-for-profit the issues may be different. The emphasis should be to define the market precisely and to ensure that those who are not intended to be part of that market are kept out. Because the price is zero or close to it, we may attract demand for which the product was not intended. Or we might attract fraudulent demand. Everyone wants free stuff and they may cheat to get it. For example, if we have an Employment Insurance benefit, then what we want is for everyone intended to receive that benefit to receive it and for everyone else to not receive it. In a profit organization we don't care as much about who buys the product as long as they pay for it. If people buy our product even though they were not the intended market, we still benefit. It's profit either way. Again, in a not-for-profit, we typically need to manage and limit the market demand rather than encourage it.

The behaviour of for-profit and not-for-profit organizations should probably be quite different with regards to market demand. That means these valueflows may need to be designed quite differently for each.

VALUE MAINTENANCE

In the real world things tend to deteriorate. Slowing down deterioration is the purpose of the Value Maintenance valueflow set. An example is ensuring that regular maintenance is performed on your vehicle. Maintenance doesn't add more value to your car. It simply helps to maintain the value that is there. So Value Maintenance is really a kind of control valueflow for the customer. It increases value to the extent that it can prevent failure. Every Fulfillment valueflow can potentially have a set of corresponding Value Maintenance valueflows. Because we can only maintain something we already have, it is at the tail end of the Customer Value chain.

When you get your toaster repaired or your car serviced, you experience examples of Value Maintenance valueflows. From a customer's perspective, those transactions are really handling a failure and, therefore, undesirable. But from the organization's point of view, they are additional services that generate profit and, therefore, they are desirable. We can see that from a value perspective this represents a conflict between two stakeholders. The customer wants to experience no failure handlers since they don't add value, only cost. But the business wants those transactions because they are a source of revenue. This is the motivation that leads to planned obsolescence.

And that brings us to the end of the Customer Value Chain. Customer Valueflows are the only ones that can generate directly measurable value because the customer provides something of value in exchange, usually in the form of money. But an organization can neither survive nor thrive on Customer Valueflows alone. It must also be able to sustain defined performance as well as set new directions for the future. Let's explore another segment from the Master Map.

BREAKTHROUGH STRATEGY DEPLOYMENT

Breakthrough Strategy Deployment is about looking into the future and setting direction. It can be compared to the cerebrum (largest part of the human brain). The cerebrum is the thinking part of the brain and controls the voluntary muscles—the ones that move when we want them to. Similarly, Breakthrough Strategy Deployment is the thinking part of an organization that controls the voluntary actions—the actions that can change and lead to greater opportunities.

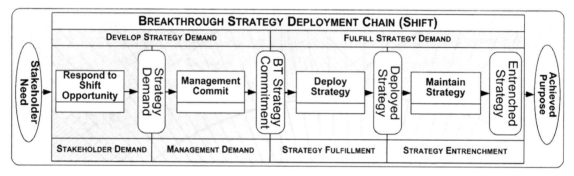

Let's explore in a little more detail the map for Breakthrough Strategy Deployment and briefly discuss each section or valueflow type.

1. **Stakeholder Demand**: In the Customer Value Chain we focus on the needs of the customer. Here we start with the needs of the other stakeholders. Those needs have been translated into purpose, objectives, and strategy. Based on stakeholder needs, we formulate strategy responses and then determine whether there is a demand from management on behalf of the stakeholders. That's the purpose of the Stakeholder Demand section.

2. **Management Demand**: Based on the results of Stakeholder Demand, we work to get specific management commitment to a particular Breakthrough (BT) strategy for a shift to which the organization may need to respond. This valueflow is equivalent to the Individual Demand valueflow in the Customer Value Chain. If there is "no sale" here then there is no commitment for that particular change

from management. The purpose of this valueflow is to secure commitment and accountability for a specific strategy change.

3. **Strategy Fulfillment**: Once management has committed to a strategy change, we have an order that needs to be fulfilled. Now we must engage the rest of the organization. The objective of deploying is to ensure that those who must act do so, and that those who only need to observe and not act, also do so. The purpose of this valueflow is to deliver the blueprint for executing the strategy change.

4. **Strategy Entrenchment**: Just because the organization has been steered in a new direction doesn't mean it will be able to hold that direction. Organizations can be considered to have status quo memory. They will tend to want to return to the status quo state unless all the forces pulling them back are replaced with alternative forces. It takes time, effort, and energy to ensure that the new strategy in entrenched. Once entrenched, it becomes the new status quo. At that point it can be transitioned to Core Strategy Sustain status. A common mistake is to stop paying attention before it is entrenched. The purpose of this set of valueflows is to transition a Breakthrough Strategy to a sustained Strategy at the appropriate time and under the appropriate conditions. Once transitioned to Core Strategy Sustain, we are mainly concerned with managing drift.

Notice that the sections of this chain of valueflows are similar to those of the Customer Value Chain. Each valueflow chain must produce a payoff for the organization, otherwise it won't be sustained. The payoff from a Customer valueflow is directly measurable. The payoff from Breakthrough Strategy Deployment is indirectly measurable but no less important. This is an essential business valueflow.

Breakthrough Strategy Deployment is a part of the Management System. It is not an extension of the Customer Value Chain. Unfortunately many organizations treat it as an extension. As such, it doesn't receive the level of attention that it deserves. The mindset required in this segment is different from that required inside the Customer segment. Decisions made here affect the organization's future. Therefore, we need to insure that Breakthrough decisions are made here and not as a consequence of casual decisions made inside the operational Customer Value Chain. By separating this group of valueflows we can ensure proper accountability. All too often Breakthrough Strategy decisions are inadvertently made inside functional processes rather than as part of a systematic strategy deployment.

Let's explore each section in a little more detail.

STAKEHOLDER DEMAND

This is analogous to the Customer Chain. The other stakeholders—employees, shareholders, suppliers, etc.—have needs as well and we need to respond to their needs. The competitive position can change as well, potentially impacting the stakeholder interests. So an organization needs to continuously scan the external stakeholder environment and the competitor positions to detect or predict any shift to which the organization might need to respond.

We are looking for shifts from any of the stakeholder groups, not just customers. Changes in employee attitudes and conditions may require a response from the organization. As workers become more educated, for example, an organization can modify its valueflow processes to take advantage of the changed condition. Of course, we know that this doesn't happen often. Instead, organizations may simply shift their production to countries where the general level of education more closely resembles familiar conditions.

Management needs to understand any potential future gaps that must be addressed. Then new strategies need to be formulated. Just like developing alternative product responses for customers, here we develop alternative strategy responses for the stakeholders. Then we need to communicate those strategies to create an internal market for change. Although we are responding to stakeholder needs, executive management is typically the proxy for those needs. The risk is that some management teams may cease to represent the stakeholders in favour of themselves or that they may favour one stakeholder over all others.

Customers buy product responses. Management has to buy strategy responses. But someone has to create those strategy responses. That's what this section is about. Its focus is to create a market for strategic change. This is an important part of a complete Management System.

MANAGEMENT DEMAND

We have developed a number of strategy responses, which are like an internal product. But who are the buyers? Management is the buyer in this segment. A customer exchanges her money for something of value. In this valueflow some member or members of management must commit time, effort, money, and other resources in exchange for some strategy change. Management is acting like a customer in the sense that they are saying that the value of implementing a particular change will result in stakeholder value increasing by more than the investment required. This is where the Chart of Accounts is useful. It will help us to understand which stakeholder values will increase as a consequence and which stakeholder values will decrease as a result of the required investment. An investment may look positive based on numbers alone. But what if one group of stakeholders is reaping the benefits while a different group is stuck with the investment? That would present a different picture.

It is here that we should measure the strength of the internal demand for adapting and thriving. It is here that we need to define accountability for outcomes. If the strength of the demand is weak or if there is no accountability for the outcomes, then it's probably wise to go no further. With weak demand the likelihood is that as soon as we run into difficulty trying to deploy the change, the initiative will be defeated. Many change initiatives fail to even complete because the demand for them was weak from the start. In practice, a business case may represent the order. Where many business cases fall short is when there is no accountability specified in the business case. Imagine a customer placing an order for a product without accountability for payment. Would you accept such as order as being a firm order?

STRATEGY FULFILLMENT

An order represents a promise. It doesn't guarantee delivery. This is especially true for Breakthrough Strategy Fulfillment. When we are delivering a standard product as a result of a customer order, the risk of not being able to satisfy the delivery request is small. However, the risks associated with delivering the outcomes required by a strategy are more significant. There is always uncertainty with regards to delivering to a strategy.

Strategy Fulfillment is about engaging all those impacted in creating the full blueprint for delivering the strategy change. It is here that accountability gets propagated to other units in the organization. It is here that we make the changes required by the strategy. Unlike the Customer Value Chain, every deployment here is unique. There are no standard responses here. So this is more like an organization that produces custom products than one that produces repeatable products.

Strategy Fulfillment produces the new modified blueprint that incorporates the changes required. It is a valueflow that should get repeated whenever a strategy *shift* response is required. Ideally it should be a continuous process rather than a once-a-year event.

STRATEGY ENTRENCHMENT

A change in strategy means a change to the status quo. Inertia will tend to make an organization resist change. In addition, there may be built-in forces that tend to pull the organization back to the status quo. Such forces have to be defeated and counter forces put into place. Strategy Entrenchment is a maintenance process intended to stabilize the organization around the new strategy. Once the new strategy has become normal, or entrenched, then we can consider the change as part of the Core Strategy.

CORE STRATEGY SUSTAIN AND CONTINUOUS CHANGE MANAGEMENT

But what about after a strategy has been deployed? How do we stay on course? Once a Breakthrough Strategy has reached the point of being entrenched, it must be protected from drifting. It must be successfully transitioned into Core Strategy. Core Strategy Sustain is like the body's autonomic nervous system *(ANS)*. It acts as a control system and should function largely below the level of consciousness of the organization, getting our attention only when things deviate from the standard. Its purpose is to continuously keep us on the course that has been set by constantly monitoring where we are compared to where we should be. It should instruct us on making small changes and warn us when active attention is required.

There are three key differentiating concepts central to Core Strategy Sustain and Continuous Change Management.

1. **Core Strategy**: We are dealing with the core strategy here. And by "core" we don't mean important versus unimportant; we mean the current entrenched strategy that we should be following. This includes all the things we must do well every day in order to reproduce (sustain) excellent results.

2. **Continuous**: Drift management can't be done effectively on a scheduled basis, once a year or twice a year. Some organizations have planned reviews of their skills or methods, etc. Although this can be part of drift management, it isn't on its own. Since drift can happen at every moment, every day, so should drift management. That's where the whole concept of the Chart of Accounts comes into play. With a CoA and assigned accountabilities, we can continuously manage through the CoA. That means we manage by detecting gaps in the Chart of Accounts. So when a gap from target develops, we swing into action to close the gap and bring the organization back into alignment.

3. **Change Management**: True change management is not about how to get other people to do what we have decided to do. Core Change Management is about making changes based on performance drift and desired improvement (momentum). It includes knowing what to change (based on a gap), what to change to (based on a standard), and how to validate the changes. Yes, we do need to then deploy those changes and for that we do need to engage the right people. But knowing what to change and what to change to is by far the bigger challenge. The amount of change in most organizations exceeds by far the amount of progress.

Core Strategy must be controlled. That means that someone needs to be accountable for seeing that it gets done. It also means that we need the capability to get it done. And capability requires both capacity (time & resources) and ability or know-how. If the organization takes the view that maintaining performance is simply part of everyone's job, then it isn't likely to be done because it will become the *least* important part of everyone's job after getting out the product or delivering the service.

Sometimes people will think in terms of strategy and routine. But a strategy is a specific way that you chose to deliver to your purpose. It is still your strategy even if you have been executing it routinely for years. Walmart's strategy hasn't changed much over the years—it has been refined. The strategy should never be allowed to fade into the background. On the contrary, it should be the core of how you achieve your purpose. That's why we call it Core Strategy. It has reached the point of being stable but is always at risk of drifting away from purpose. Core Strategy maintenance includes Continuous Change Management because it does need to be continuously changed in small but numerous ways to remain optimal. In addition, we should always be making forward progress because there is always waste somewhere in the system. It is this continuous exercising of the change muscle that allows us to undertake the breakthrough strategies. Otherwise, we settle into change resistance, which is nothing more than a reluctance to engage a part of us that rarely gets used, the ability to adapt. So, continuous change is not only a necessary trait for the organization but also for us as individuals within the organization—reducing the risks to both. As an organization manages its Core Strategies, it builds its capabilities and becomes stronger.

Core Strategy Sustain is truly the autonomous nervous system of an organization. It should operate largely automatically and under the level of consciousness of the organization. However, when it comes across a gap that won't close, then it should bring this to conscious attention.

Let's explore in a little more detail the map for Core Strategy Sustain and briefly discuss each section or valueflow type, starting on the left.

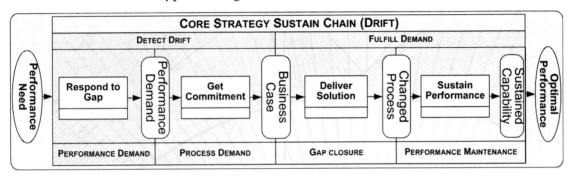

1. **Performance Demand**: Our Chart of Accounts is at the heart of this. It is the performance framework that we use to detect gaps (needs). If we have deployed the strategy for each objective to each valueflow and for the functional processes, then we have the ability to detect performance gaps at all levels. The purpose of this valueflow group is to respond to performance gaps and to generate potential responses that have payoffs. These should then become internal demands capable of generating profit every bit as much as market demand. Of course, we may not always generate new profit. Sometimes it is more about recovering profit we used to have. Many organizations have no systematic way to execute this and hold no one accountable. The result is that gaps go undetected until they are large, by which point a lot of value has already been lost.

2. **Process Demand**: Based on a performance demand from a process, we may produce a business case for gap closure. This is the internal equivalent of the Individual Demand order. Of course someone has to generate this order. What the business case does is create an order to close a particular gap based on a particular solution. This requires accountability. If no one in the organization stands behind such a demand, then the gap won't get closed. Many organizations build up capability

to deliver solutions to performance gaps before there is any internal demand for it. Then the delivery organization tries to sell its services. That's like getting the factory floor worker to sell the car that he assembles. Of course the factory worker's interest is to keep up demand for his skills. Unfortunately, the factory worker is not in a position to properly close a sales order. The same is true for other internal groups such as Information Technology or Process Improvement. They shouldn't be generating demand for their own services. We know this model doesn't work.

3. **Gap Closure**: This is the valueflow that develops the changes and implements them and produces the new changed process. It is at the end of this that the payoff begins. If there is no payoff, then it's like selling a product and getting no revenue. Like revenue, there is gross and net. The gross payoff would be what we get without regard to what was spent. If this is zero, or worse, negative, then that's the worst case scenario. Note that this can be more risky than selling a product. The worst case with a product is that you can't sell it and, therefore, have zero revenue. But when you change a process, you can potentially increase the cost (make things worse) going forward. That means that you not only have to pay to get to implementation, but you also pay going forward.

4. **Performance Maintenance**: Physical things, whether they are machines or raw material, can wear down or deteriorate over time. That's why we maintain them. Otherwise, they will become less productive and will also break down. Processes and their components are no different. They need to be monitored and maintained according to specification in order to remain productive and not slide backwards. The purpose of this group of valueflows is to ensure that any maintenance to the components of the process is carried out. Training falls into this category. Of course, in order to maintain parts according to a specification, you must first have a blueprint for those parts. Many organizations don't have such specifications and, therefore, can't easily maintain the components. In this case, what is likely to happen is that the process components will deteriorate over time, degrading the process performance slowly, then suddenly. At some point the performance will be so poor that action must be taken. This is analogous to someone who allows their health to deteriorate to the point that something dramatic happens—such as a heart attack—and emergency action must take place. Of course, at that point, your options are limited and irreversible damage may have been incurred.

PERFORMANCE DEMAND

At any one time, there may be a number of gaps that can be attended to. This is the equivalent of the market need. Similarly to selecting a market opportunity to respond to, we need to select which gaps are worth responding to. Then we need to create a gap response. These gap responses then have to be communicated to management, not sold to management. We sell to customers. But we want management to buy gap closures. This is creating an internal market for change based on drift from our processes. That's the purpose of this valueflow.

Few organizations have a disciplined approach to this. Most organizations rely on their Information Technology or Process Analysts to create this market. But that's like getting the production department to develop new products. That's not likely to lead to the most innovative or impressive results.

This valueflow needs to be explicitly identified and capacity needs to be dedicated to it. If this were implemented as an extension of everyone's job, then it would be unlikely to succeed. The CoA is particularly useful here because it can be used to quantify the value of closing a particular gap. That's primarily what this section is about: identifying which gaps should be closed based on the potential value from closing those gaps. Again, the market that we are communicating to is an internal one made up of executive management and process management.

In this valueflow what we need to do is develop a response to the performance gap. This is like R&D for a product cycle. Process Improvement and Process Engineering are methodologies that are used to develop responses to close performance gaps.

Process Demand

As with the Customer Value Chain, we need to generate specific commitment to closing a specified gap. We need a firm order to close a particular gap. We call this valueflow Process Demand because the demand should originate from a valueflow process. But, in the end, we need someone or some team to be accountable for this demand. If we don't have a firm commitment, then failure will be the likely result. At this stage, we are talking about an order to close a performance gap, and not an order to implement a particular solution. It is important that the commitment is for the gap (solve the problem) rather than for a solution.

A commitment to a solution is risky. What if we discover that the solution originally proposed ends up being the wrong one? Because we have committed, we are emotionally tied to the solution, more than we are tied to solving the problem. We need to close a performance gap, not implement a specific solution. So that's what the order should be for here. What we need is for someone to be accountable so that closing the gap will produce the gross benefit. That way we can refine and even switch the actual solution as we learn more.

When closing the gap requires time, effort, money, and other resources in significant quantities, then a project structure is probably the best way to proceed. So this valueflow can be part of a project lifecycle.

Gap Closure

This is the equivalent of Demand Fulfillment. It delivers and implements the actual solution. Again, we can compare this to a custom-designed product. The solution to closing a performance gap won't likely come off the shelf. It will need to be developed based on specific requirements. Examples of valueflows that are in this section include Software Development, Training Development, and many others.

Sometimes a project might be required to close a gap, especially if the gap is significant. That's because the level of resources required are such that capacity may have to be redeployed away from other processes. When capacity is taken away from other processes, the throughput of those processes will likely be impacted. Organizations rarely account for such effects and they behave as if taking people away from operational processes and putting them on a project will not affect the operational process. But when effort is transferred from an operational process to a project, there is less time available to the operational process. So there should be a potential negative impact on the operational process in the short term. If it is proposed that there will be no impact, then either there is excess capacity, or management is implying that the participating employees will do the project work on their own time and for free. Of course these assumptions are often not made explicitly. When what is said differs from what is meant, or when assumptions are left in a fog, we could call it a form of *mist* management.

Such behaviour attempts to make the individual employee accountable for capacity, which is a process attribute. It is the process manager who should be accountable for process capacity and not the individual employee. Essentially, in this example, management is trying to transfer accountability. That would clearly demonstrate a lack of accountability. Of course, this will usually elicit a response from the employee. The usual strategy is to try to somehow kill the initiative because that will free the employee and solve her capacity problem.

Many initiatives fail here not because of any technical obstacles but due to socio obstacles that could easily be avoided. Time can neither be created nor destroyed. However, it can be wasted. When effort is diverted away from operational processes to a project, the impacts must be taken into consideration explicitly. Otherwise, the employee will interpret her participation as "best effort," which means she will participate as long as everything else is going well. That's a sure way to failure. Closing a performance gap requires a positive investment and it should be treated that way.

Performance Maintenance

Maintaining performance requires us to have a blueprint specification for each valueflow and its processes. That can serve to produce a maintenance schedule for the components of each process.

Maintenance requires two main activities to take place. Firstly, we need to monitor the performance through the Chart of Accounts. Secondly, we need to perform maintenance activities. This is easy to understand when we are talking about machines, but what about skills and other conditions? How are skill levels maintained? How are they evaluated? If we are expecting skill levels to increase with experience, how do we validate that this is happening? What about working conditions? If we used to dedicate 100 square feet of space per employee in an office and now we are at 50 square feet, do we take action or let it slide? If the standard was 100, then why is a level of 50 now acceptable? There are many things that change or drift in a process and are ignored, quite often because there is no one accountable for those things. Remember that the things for which no one is accountable will deteriorate. Why is this so? Because if a problem can be solved by creating an externality in a location that is unobserved, then it will happen. Why do people dump garbage in unobserved fields? Because they can. The same thing happens in organizations. If you purposely leave aspects of your process unmanaged, then you can be certain those aspects will get worse, not better.

Performance Maintenance is about improving performance by detecting gaps and by maintaining the individual components that make up the processes. What is not properly maintained will fail more often and at inopportune times.

SUMMARY

To the customer, it is what she receives that is the product. But to the remaining stakeholders, it is the business itself that is the product. And so that is the scope for both the shareholders and the employees. That is the world they need to better understand. Every organization needs a Production System to produce the customer product and to survive. It also needs a Management System to go beyond survival and thrive.

The Master Valueflow Map ties the three key segments that make up the Production and the Management systems of any organization:

1. A set of processes and valueflows that deliver the customer value product, which is the source for all other value—Customer Value Chain. This is part of the Production System.
2. A set of processes and valueflows for determining the best way to deliver the customer value and for navigating in the ever changing, ever risky, competitive environment—Breakthrough Strategy Deployment. This is part of the Management System.
3. A set of processes and valueflows for detecting when we go off course and for taking quick and appropriate action to get us back on course—Core Strategy Sustain. This is part of the Management System.

An organization must develop and excel in all three segments concurrently. If it focuses on delivering customer value while neglecting the other two, it may become great for a while, but it will falter. Like someone who suddenly becomes rich without having developed the skills required to manage wealth, the wealth will soon be gone. An organization is like a whole body and must develop that body in balance. The Master Valueflow Map is a starting point for mapping out the different parts of the greater organizational body and for specifying all its parts.

The three segments are distinct. The Customer Value Chain is the most visible to the customer and, therefore, there tends to be a focus on it. Many organizations behave as if this is the only important part of an organization. They argue that if customer value isn't delivered, then the organization will fail. And so they may conclude that this is the most important part of the organization, neglecting other parts. That's like concluding that your heart is more important than the rest of your organs because if it fails then you will die. That logic is incorrect. The fact that the whole will fail when a particular part fails means that the part is necessary to the proper functioning. It does not in any way imply that it is sufficient.

Organizations are like bodies. They require many different organs or parts, each of which is necessary but none of them are sufficient on their own. If you ignore your other organs you will also die and perhaps more painfully.

An organization must excel at delivering customer value through the Customer Value Chain in order to survive. We have identified two other segments. Breakthrough Strategy Deployment and Core Strategy Sustain comprise a set of valueflows and functions that, together, can be considered the organization's Management System. An organization must also excel at these, if it is to thrive in the long term.

Each segment has a different purpose and different accountabilities. Each segment addresses different decisions. When decisions come through the wrong segment, then that introduces unnecessary risk into the organization. That's why it's important to distinguish among the three. That's why it's important to ensure that we understand what segment we are in when making a decision, and we should ensure that we are in the right segment for that decision. When someone in a function unit tries to convince management to adopt a policy or approach that has strategy implications, then we need to move that decision to the Breakthrough Strategy segment and make that decision there. Functional decisions are made from a different perspective.

But what does it mean to make the decision in a different place? Does it mean that we go to a different physical place? That can certainly be part of it. But what it really means is that we understand what process should be executed for the decision. Then we make sure that we have the right people and the right emotional mindset for *that* process and that we follow the blueprint for that process. This is especially true for decision processes. When we try to make a strategy decision inside an operational context, we tend to make an operational decision. We may tend to skip steps, leave out some key people, and make the decision from the wrong mental model and emotional mindset. In other words, we are manufacturing the decision outside the production line that was set up specifically for it. The result is that we are more likely to increase the number of defects and that will affect the performance.

**We should not manufacture a decision outside the
production line that was designed specifically for it.**

The Master Valueflow Map is intended as a guide for locating the key valueflows. It is also meant to increase our awareness that outputs need to be produced by the processes that were designed for them. And if those processes have never been designed, then maybe it's time to begin designing them, one at a time. The purpose is to develop an ever more complete and useful blueprint for the organization.

12

MODEL MATURITY AND NORMALIZATION

We spend much more time solving the solution than we spend solving the problem.

There is so much work to be done that we often rush to get to a solution to a problem. Often we stop at a solution that is satisfactory for us without sufficient regard to other stakeholders. We don't have the time or energy to invest in truly understanding the problem so that it can be solved *once* and *for all*.

Solve a problem *once* (the first time) and *for all* (stakeholders).

So we implement a far less than perfect solution and others must cope with that solution for years to come. A poor solution creates other problems that must be solved. And so, in the end, we spend more time solving the solution than we ever spent trying to solve the original problem. And because we are so busy continuously solving the solution, we rarely seem to have time to solve the next problem properly. If we are to break this unproductive and vicious cycle, then we need to be more systematic in our approach and we must dedicate the right amount of time (capacity) to solving underlying problems.

A model is a vehicle for learning about some aspect of the world. This book is about modelling an organization's process world. Models are extremely important in science as a tool for understanding the bigger world we live in. Similarly, in organizations we can use models to help us understand the behaviour of the organization. The Relational Process Model is a framework that also serves as a process blueprint. Like the scientific community, which is on a quest to discover how the world was designed, we should also be on a quest to discover how the organization within which we work is designed.

Of course, there is a difference. Science is mainly about discovering the design of the universe. We aren't out to redesign the universe because that is not within our power. We are only seeking to understand it better. Scientific discoveries don't change the universe itself. Instead science helps us to better understand the environment so that we can change our behaviour to better live in that world. But within the organization, we have a different opportunity. Firstly, as with science, we can use the modelling to understand the organization as it's organized today. But we also have the power to use models as blueprints for creating better designed organizations—organizations that create more value for the stakeholders and provide a better working environment for those within.

Animals are born with instincts. Humans are not. In essence, animals are born with pre-designed blueprints from which they deviate little. But we are not born with blueprints. We have the opportunity and obligation to develop our own. Of course, in order to do that, we must be able to design and to learn. People, of all the organisms on this planet, are the only ones who can *consciously and deliberately design* how they live. In that sense, we could say that design is the most human discipline.

Design is the most human discipline.

Reading is not writing. We first learn to read. Then we learn to write. Modelling is to design as reading is to writing. It is necessary but it is not sufficient. We must also explicitly design. So learning to model is the first step towards design. It is through the discipline of modelling that we begin to see how poorly the current processes may be designed. It is this eye-opening experience that helps to create a demand for better and systematic designs.

It is both a great tragedy and a great opportunity that process design, as a discipline, has been neglected in organizations. It is a tragedy because poor designs have caused and continue to cause both waste and personal hardship for all stakeholders. Shareholders suffer because they may not make a reasonable return on their investment. Taxpayers suffer because they experience more money being taken from them while at the same time quality of services may be reduced. The customer suffers because he receives less value for his money while at the same time having to put up with poor service. And, of course, employees, a group that includes pretty much all of us, suffer because we have to deal with the day-to-day stress caused by poor design.

Systematic design presents an opportunity because if we improve the quality of design, then we can reduce waste and turn many organizations into rewarding places to work instead of places of frustration and stress.

This chapter introduces a simple method for incrementally producing a normalized model of an existing valueflow. And so it can be used to augment virtually any methodology, whether it be for process improvement or requirements elicitation or process troubleshooting or even training. The first step in design is to be able to understand the current design of an established process. That will help us begin to understand the current process behaviour. It gives us a strategy for "reading" existing processes. Only after we have learned to read the processes should we attempt to redesign them.

But be aware that many, even most, processes were never systematically designed in the first place. Rather, they have evolved based on practice—the cowpath. These processes may function but are certainly not optimal. And understanding the thinking behind them may prove difficult.

Once we have identified a valueflow and connected it to the proper strategy and objective, exactly what are the steps for producing a normalized model that will connect to the functional processes? Is there a method that we can follow? Yes, there is. We will present a general method that we can use to produce a Relational Process Model. A general method is one that can be applied to any business, to any valueflow process. The method we will explore models a single valueflow but is scalable for any number of valueflow processes.

The approach is called the Six Simple Steps method and it leads to a normalized blueprint. It contains six simple steps, each subsequent step building on the previous. It is based on modelling a single valueflow. What this method does is tie together the key components of the normalized process model.

PROGRESSIVE STAGES OF AWARENESS AND MANAGEMENT

But where does one start to model? Should we model all of an organization's valueflows? There is normally little, if any, appetite in most organizations to embark on a modelling "documentation" project. And in most cases there shouldn't be any such appetite. Modelling on its own will not increase stakeholder value. And modelling a bulk of valueflows might incur costs with no return on investment. So how can we make use of the framework and what strategies can we use to begin to use this framework?

If we want to get fit and lose weight there are probably two things that one should purchase. On their own they won't help us lose even a single pound; nevertheless, we should have them. These items are a scale to measure your weight and a tape measure to determine your physical dimensions. In other words, we need some way to get feedback so that we can evaluate the success of our actions. It's the same with processes. The Value Chart of Accounts is the process *value* scale and so that should be one of the first things we need to have. The Capability Chart of

Accounts is the process *capability* scale and so that should probably be the second scale that we acquire for a given valueflow. Finally, if we are to make any changes to the processes, it would be a good idea to have a blueprint of the current process. We can rank the manageability of a process based on which stage of modelling has been completed, as described below. Each stage provides us with greater ability to manage a process.

So let's introduce all six progressive stages for a Valueflow Model:

- **Unidentified**: At this point we are not aware of the valueflow as an entity whose performance should be managed. All valueflows are initially at this status. Unfortunately, since they haven't been identified, we can't list them.

- **Stage 1—Indentified**: This is really the first true stage. At this point, we have identified a valueflow. We have defined its scope or boundary but we don't yet know any more about it other than that it exists. We also haven't yet tied it to any business objectives and strategy. Since it isn't yet tied to business objectives, we can't determine its effectiveness. And since we don't know what's inside we can't determine its efficiency. What we do know is that we should consider taking the valueflow to the next stage.

- **Stage 2—Value Performance Aware**: At this stage we have connected the valueflow to the business objectives and strategy. We have also developed a Value Chart of Accounts for the valueflow. Now we can begin to set performance targets and establish accountability. We have a framework for measurement. We have a way to determine the stakeholder value that a particular valueflow is producing. We don't yet know the capability of the process, nor do we know what it looks like inside—the design.

- **Stage 3—Tiered Model**: We need to translate our value measures to capabilities. Before we can do that, we need to go inside the valueflow. We need to create the Three-Tier model. This provides a greater understanding of the internal processes and provides the foundation needed for attaching capability measures.

- **Stage 4—Capability Performance Aware**: There are two parts to this stage. First we will expand the model to include the valueflow level Capability Chart of Accounts. So now we have a framework for understanding elements such as the valueflow throughput, quality, and demand. Then we expand the Capability CoA to the output tier of the valueflow. So now we can explore the capabilities for each of the major intermediate outputs of the individual functional processes. But we still don't know the actual internal design. For that we go to the next stage.

- **Stage 5—Streamed Task Model**: This is the last and perhaps the most labour-intensive step—develop the three streams. This requires us to take the existing tasks and organize them according to the streams. Of course, existing processes are unlikely to have clear controls defined. Therefore, there will be some work required to deduce the control outcomes from the control tasks.

- **Stage 6—Process Blueprint Aware**: At this stage we have completed the valueflow model. We have expanded the model to streams and completed the component specifications. We have a full task-tier, streamed, specified *blueprint* of the current design. We have everything we need to fully manage the valueflow and its functional processes.

Each of these stages applies to an individual valueflow. And each of these stages defines the progress of the valueflow model. Therefore, different valueflows can be at different stages. The more valueflows we get to the highest stage, the more able we are to better manage process performance for the enterprise.

SIX SIMPLE STEPS TO A NORMALIZED BLUEPRINT

The Six Simple Steps method is a stepwise approach to producing a full valueflow blueprint, one step at a time, *one stage at a time*. The diagram depicts the six steps and the corresponding stages (S1 to S6).

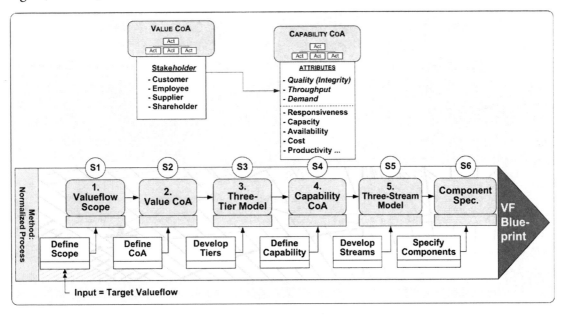

The Six Simple Steps (S³ method) method applies to modelling a valueflow and the functional processes that make it up. Notice that modelling is itself a process and so we are using a normalized model to represent it.

We want to understand a process from intent to execution and so we begin at the Outcome and Output (intent) tiers before we model the task streams level. An output tier model is much

241

less bulky and is only a fraction of the size of a full task level model. It should easily fit on a tabloid-size sheet (11" x 17"). Our S^3 method is depicted and described as a tiered model. This is a great way to chunk a process for further modelling.

Before exploring each Output in greater detail, let us summarize each of the steps and relate them to the stages of model maturity previously discussed.

1. **Valueflow Scope (S1):** We need to select a valueflow and define its boundaries. This includes the defining output produced by the process and the demand request that triggers the process. We shouldn't create models just for the fun of it, although some organizations do create models just to have them. The best time to undertake modelling is in conjunction with a performance gap (drift or shift) closure project. Understanding the boundaries is important in order to identify the functional areas that are crossed. It is important to select a valueflow process, not a functional process. This step is moving the process towards first normal form. This represents Stage 1—Identified.

2. **Stakeholder Value Chart of Accounts (S2):** Ideally the reason we are modelling is that there is a performance gap in either the Value Chart of Accounts or the Capability CoA. If we don't have a Value CoA then we need to develop one before proceeding. This is an essential step that can't be skipped. It defines the target performance for the process and measures the actual performance from the value perspective. It specifies how we will evaluate any changes to the current process. The valueflow is now in first normal form. This represents Stage 2—Value Performance Aware.

3. **Three-Tier Model (S3):** This step defines all the intermediate outputs that will be produced in order to get to the final or defining output. It includes the identification and definition of all outputs beginning from the last or defining output all the way back to the demand and inputs. This is a first step in connecting to the functional processes. Often each intermediate output is produced by a different functional process. If these outputs can't be mapped to functional processes, then it may be an indication that accountability will be difficult to establish. This represents Stage 3—Tiered Model.

4. **Capability Chart of Accounts (S4):** Each functional process in the valueflow needs to have a Capability Chart of Accounts. So we need to develop one that is representative of the process being modelled. As always, it should contain both target and actual values for each account. This brings us to Stage 4—Capability Performance Aware.

5. **Three-Stream Model (S5):** Each output requires a series of tasks or operations to be carried out in order to produce it. So we can expand all outputs to the full task level and separate them into the three streams. Any appropriate representation

method can be used to produce the task level model, including the classical task-based process map. This is Stage 5—Streamed Task Model.

6. **Specified Components (S6)**: When all the outputs are produced, we can specify the components. This provides us with a full blueprint of the process in normal form. This brings us to the final Stage 6—Process Blueprint Aware. At this point we have a complete process blueprint for the valueflow. Now someone can be accountable for maintaining the blueprint. We can now manage to the blueprint and apply lessons directly to the blueprint to achieve continuous *progress* improvement.

As we progress from the first output step to the last, we are increasing our knowledge of the process. And, we are increasing the model maturity level, but with a difference. When the classical process map is detailed, it is often compared to peeling an onion. When we remove a layer of onion, what do we get? Of course, we get more onion, i.e., we get more of the same. And so it is with a process map. As we detail the tasks, we get more tasks.

The Relational Process Model approach is radically different. Each tier adds not just more knowledge but also knowledge of a different kind. We can still detail an output and detail tasks but when we move from the outcome tier to the output tier, for example, and then to the task tier, we are exploring detail of a different kind. When we add the Chart of Accounts information we are adding performance knowledge rather than task method knowledge. This is a significant extension to existing frameworks. With that in mind, let's explore each of the six steps in greater detail.

OUTPUT 1—VALUEFLOW SCOPE

Modelling is a communication tool. Of course, in order to use a valueflow as a framework for communication, we have to identify it. Therefore, this step can only take place after we have identified a valueflow.

The first step in communication is to define the limits or scope of the discussion. We need to determine the universe of discourse, the context for understanding. The primary purpose of this step is to define the boundaries of the valueflow that we are modelling. Giving the valueflow a name and clearly defining its boundaries ensures that different people have a common understanding of exactly what the valueflow refers to. If we only give it a name without defining the boundaries, then that will leave the scope to personal interpretation. That would encourage poor or imprecise communication.

So what do we mean by boundaries? A boundary definition for a valueflow includes:

1. The defining output, and
2. The demand trigger.

The first step in defining the boundaries is to clearly articulate what the defining output is for this process. It is the defining output that characterizes the process. The defining output is the output that will be consumed by or become part of the next valueflow. This will also tell us if the valueflow is a customer valueflow or an enabling valueflow. A clear understanding and agreement on the definition and specification of the defining output should be the start of alignment. If people can't agree on what the output is, or if people have different perceptions of its specification, then it may prove difficult to obtain agreement on the details of the process. Getting agreement on the defining output is especially important between whoever is accountable for the process that produces it and whoever is accountable for the process that receives it.

The defining output clearly identifies the end of the process. But is it the end of the valueflow? If you need a review on finding the end of the valueflow, refer back to Chapter 5: The Valueflow.

Next we need to locate the demand trigger, the thing that sets the valueflow in motion. Again, refer to Chapter 5: The Valueflow to review how to do this. The defining output and the demand trigger together define the outer boundaries of the valueflow that the process is a part of. Even if we think we only want to model a functional process, we should know which valueflow it is a part of. Without identifying the valueflow we will not be able to attach meaningful value and capability measures.

It is important to note that the demand request is the trigger that starts the valueflow that leads to the process instance. The demand trigger is not the same as work-in-process input or raw material input. Whereas the demand acts as the trigger to start the valueflow, the supply inputs are necessary in order to perform transformations and produce the defining output. The supply input can be physical raw material if we are producing a physical output. On the other hand, if we are producing a decision or knowledge output, then the supply input will be information.

All valueflows share some common characteristics. At the end point of the flow we have a definable value and a maximum cost. At the beginning of the flow we have zero value and minimum costs (zero variable costs). In addition, there should be a minimal amount of exchange between the producing valueflow and the receiving valueflow.

Let's look at an example of a steel company valueflow called Steel Delivery.

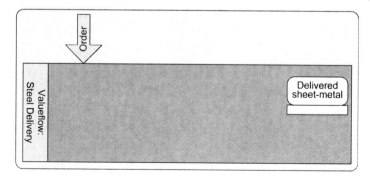

The defining output is shown as "Delivered Sheet-Metal." This is what the valueflow produces. The demand trigger is an "Order." So we have a valueflow that receives an order for sheet-metal and fulfills that order, probably for an external customer.

This shows a valueflow model that is at Stage 1—Identified. The amount of effort required to get a valueflow to this stage is, of course, minimal. It simply makes us aware of the valueflow. We can't do a lot at this stage because we don't yet have a framework for evaluating performance. On the other hand, there can be significant informal value to having a valueflow modelled at this level. At least we are making people aware of a potential value-producing process. In any case, we have to get a valueflow to this level before we can even begin to think about assigning accountability.

OUTPUT 2—STAKEHOLDER CHART OF ACCOUNTS

We have taken the valueflow model to Stage 1—Identified. What comes next? First of all, let's be clear. We are at Stage 1 for the specific valueflow. Different valueflows can be at different stages. We don't have to get all valueflows to Stage 1 before proceeding to Stage 2. Such a decision would depend on what we were trying to accomplish.

Once we have identified a valueflow we can establish a way to measure the value produced by that process as seen by the major stakeholder groups. The tool we use for that is the Stakeholder Value Chart of Accounts. So we can develop the Value CoA. In order to do that we will likely need to engage more participants. It is the Value CoA that provides us with the framework necessary for measuring and managing the valueflow to the desired outcomes. It is the Value CoA that should link back to the objectives and strategy.

Let's look at an example of an enabling valueflow. Imagine that we have identified a valueflow called Application Software Development. The defining output is a software application that will be used by some target business process. The demand trigger is some performance gap in the target business process. And let's say that the bulk of the effort takes place within the organization's IT (Information Technology) department. How could we measure the value produced by such a valueflow? We could measure the amount of code but that isn't value. If the software, once produced and implemented, doesn't make a difference to the target business process using the application, then what would the value be? Wouldn't it be zero? On the other hand, what if the implementation of the software led to additional customer business and the value of that business was $100,000? What would the value be then? We could conclude that the particular software increased the value throughput of the target business process revenue account by $100,000.

The value contribution for an enabling valueflow can't be measured in the enabling valueflow itself. It has to be measured where the effect takes place; it has to be measured in the process that is impacted. That is always the case for an enabling valueflow.

When we ask, "What is the value of this process?" we need to be careful with the response. A process doesn't *have* value. Value is delivered after we complete a process transaction. It is the output of the process that *may* result in value. So the Software Development Process might produce a zero value for one execution and a $100,000 value in another execution. Value has to be measured each time a process executes. The Value CoA provides the framework for value measurement. If we keep track of the value produced each time the process executes and if we keep track of the investments required for each execution, then we can determine the net value delivered for a specified period.

Let's look at another case. What if the organization had to make a change in order to comply with some new law? For example, some privacy laws limit the use of social security numbers. If an organization needed to change software to comply with such a law, then that change could have a value of zero dollars. That would not imply that the change should not have been made; only that it added nothing to the organization's value. We might imagine that value was created for the customer in that case, but at a cost to the shareholders.

A specific execution of a process can sometimes produce positive value throughput, sometimes zero throughput, and sometimes negative throughput. Value is something that is attached to the result produced by the process. It is not automatically inherent in the valueflow itself. Understanding this distinction is crucial to being able to evaluate the effect of changes and knowing what to change. The impact that a change will have on the Value Chart of Accounts should be predicted prior to making the change. That way we can verify how we did. In other words, as in pool, we should first call the shot and then take the shot.

This concept of value relating to a specific execution of a process is not always appreciated or well understood. Management may ask, "What is the value of process X?" This is a tough question to answer because it isn't clear what is meant. We can't place a value on a process. What we can do is equip a process with the financial reporting equivalent of the annual report. For example, organizations will typically have a profit and loss statement for the year and a balance sheet, which provides the cumulative net value that has been produced by the organization. We can do the same for a valueflow. Every time the process is executed, we essentially have a profit and loss statement transaction. And so, we can have times when the process produces a net positive value and other times when it produces a negative value. The process balance sheet, on the other hand, can capture the cumulative value delivered. For example, every time we execute a software project or a process improvement project, we can evaluate the value delivered and the associated costs. That is, we can produce a profit and loss statement for each project. But we can also keep track of all projects so that we have a balance sheet for all software development projects and for all process improvement projects. That way if someone asks, "What is the value of software development or of process improvement?" then we can answer the question in terms of value produced over a particular period of time by a particular process. This would probably be a much more meaningful way to measure project success than just the measure of budget and schedule. The Value Chart of Accounts is the framework that allows us to produce this kind of meaningful information.

Many organizations have great difficulty defining appropriate metrics. Measuring throughput can be especially difficult. A couple of common mistakes that organizations make are:

1. They are trying to define value for a functional process rather than for a valueflow. Functional processes incur costs. They don't individually produce measurable value. Nevertheless, they may be necessary in order to produce the ultimate value.

2. They conclude that they can't measure the throughput value for their process when in fact the throughput value is zero. They make the assumption that every process produces value. This is not the case. There are many processes or instances of processes that produce zero value but are nevertheless required under the current conditions. For example, an organization may go through a process at the beginning of each year to modify the tax tables for their payroll. This process doesn't generate any value. It is a maintenance process that is necessary, but the organization is not worth more after the change than it was before. Maintenance activities are control activities. That means that they are a burden on the organization. Nevertheless, they may be desirable in the sense that the organization would incur even higher costs without them.

We should not confuse producing customer value—something that a customer wants and is willing to pay for—with necessity—something we must do under the current implementation. In addition, value delivered is a valueflow measure, not a component measure. It is not a measure that should be applied to the employee executing the process. Employee performance can certainly be measured but should not be equated to process performance directly. An employee will certainly influence the performance of a process. But the extent of the influence depends on each individual process and that should be well understood when evaluating employee performance. Imagine that we have a process where an employee's job is to throw a six-sided die with 1 to 6 on the faces. If the die comes up with an even number (2, 4, 6), we score that as a loss but if it comes up with an odd number (1, 3, 5), we score that as a win. How much influence does the employee have on the outcome? Probably little. If we want to change the outcome profile for that process, we probably need to focus on the die, perhaps loading it towards odd numbers, rather than focusing on the employee. Certainly different employees may have different levels of success and failure over a period of time. But they may not be the cause of the results.

It is sometimes the case that we aren't able to determine an appropriate value-measuring metric without a deeper understanding of the process. But just because we find it difficult doesn't mean that we can abandon the search for an appropriate value-measuring metric. The Stakeholder Chart of Accounts is the output that begins the important step of understanding and defining how we will measure the effectiveness of the process. It is the key step for creating manageability and accountability. If we attempt to design or improve a process without understanding how the value throughput will be evaluated, then we won't know which measures are important and we won't be able to connect the valueflow outcomes to a higher outcome. We won't be able to tell if the changes we are implementing are making the process better or worse. In the absence of measurable evaluation we will resort to opinion.

Of course the key thing here is to have a framework that will allow us to determine whether we have a performance gap (positive or negative). A gap is defined as a measured difference between two sets of measurements. Typically, one of the sets acts as the reference target while the other is some sort of actual measure that can vary from one execution to the next. Let's explore a few potential measurement categories:

1. **Core Strategy Target**: This is some stated value that the organization is trying to achieve based on the current core strategy. Target metrics can be time sensitive. So we can have different targets for different time periods. An example could be beer sales revenue by season. A target is what we need to reach in order to achieve a business objective or strategy.

2. **Current Actual**: Every time a process executes, it generates an actual value. This is the current measurement, which represents actual performance. Actual measurements can change with each execution and over time. They can be specified by transaction or as a cumulative value for some given period. Naturally, the structure for current actual measures should match the structure for target measures. So if the target is quarterly, then we need a corresponding quarterly actual and it should represent the same quarter.

3. **Breakthrough Strategy Target**: When a strategy changes, some account measure targets may need to change as well. Some measures may need to be updated based on a change in some portion of the strategy. The breakthrough strategy target, once entrenched, will become a core strategy target.

4. **Near Perfect**: This is the current estimate of what might be possible under near perfect conditions of:
   a. Zero errors
   b. No burden

   The near perfect performance is great to have because it can be used to determine the best case performance for a process. The near perfect performance can be determined for each measure, separately. Its purpose is to let us know what the best case performance is for a particular measure within the current paradigm. If we need the performance to be higher, then we will probably need to re-engineer the process.

5. **Standard**: This is a specific target metric that represents what the performance of a particular process should be on a day-to-day basis. A standard may be condition specific. For example, we may have different standard measurements based on

different levels of demand. An example could be in the time from request to fulfillment for a particular transaction. This metric might be variable based on the number of transactions arriving. When demand goes up, then response time gets longer. The time required to renew and receive an updated passport is an example of such a metric. Standards are usually applied to single instances of execution.

A performance gap is the difference between two sets of measures from a particular CoA. Some typical performance gap types are summarized in the table below.

Gap	Description	Caused by
Breakthrough vs. Current	When an organization changes its strategy and sets a new target, there will be an immediate Strategy gap. This should trigger the Strategy Deployment process and we should re-examine all the impacted valueflows. This gap will be generated and detected by the Breakthrough Strategy Chain.	Shift: Something has changed externally and we have responded with a new strategy, causing a planned gap.
Core Target vs. Actual	When there is a difference between the core strategy target and the actual performance, then this should trigger action at the valueflow level to close the gap. This gap will be detected by the Core Strategy Sustain chain.	Drift: The process performance has drifted away from where it needs to be to such an extent that action is now required. The drift can be gradual or sudden.
Breakthrough vs. Core vs. Actual	This is a double gap. It says that there is a new breakthrough target that differs from the core target, which creates one gap. In addition, we already had a gap between the core target and the actual performance. That means this process was already underperforming before we created a new target. So now we have a double gap to close. This requires a more serious response.	Shift + Drift: Something has changed externally while we had an existing drift gap. This means we have two issues to deal with together. This may be a good signal to redesign some processes.

Detecting performance gaps early is important if we are to manage the processes by exception. When there is no performance gap, then the process may not require much attention beyond executing transactions. But when a gap is detected and it is judged to be important in its impact, then resources need to be marshalled to address it. The response may be different for a negative gap than for a positive gap. Without a way to measure the gap there is the risk that performance will degrade slowly in such a way that it is not noticeable from one day to the next. People may get used to a pattern of degrading performance when it is gradual because we tend to compare today's performance to other recent performance, such as last week's, or last month's. In such a case the gap may be ignored until the degradation becomes intolerable. Of course a lot of throughput value will have been lost in the meanwhile. That's why valueflow performance accountability is needed. If no one is even aware of the valueflow performance, then how can a gap be detected?

It is probably a good idea to get all key valueflow processes modeled to Stage 2—Value Performance Aware. This level of modelling, if done across the enterprise, will move the organization to a higher level of awareness and provide it with a framework for process learning. If we find that there is no performance gap for a particular valueflow, then we can switch our attention to another valueflow rather than modelling it further.

Let's return to the Steel Company example. This valueflow is modelled to Stage 2. The diagram illustrates some key accounts for the Value CoA.

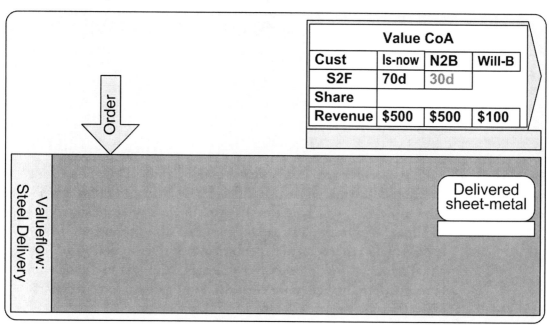

The Value Chart of Accounts is shown in the upper right-hand corner. Under customer (Cust), we have a responsiveness account called S2F (start-to-finish). It represents the calendar number of business days elapsed from the time a firm order is received by the company to the time a completed order is received by the customer. It has a current (Is-Now) average value of 70 days. However, due to new customer requirements it needs to be (N2B) 30 days. The customer has advised the Steel Company that he needs to have his orders fulfilled within 30 days rather than the current 70 days. If the Steel Company does not comply, then it will lose its preferred supplier status along with 80% of its current business with this customer. The value of that business currently amounts to $500 million in sales revenue. This is depicted in the "Revenue" line. What it says is:

- Current value (Is-Now) is $500 million.
- Needs to be (N2B) is $500 million—this means we want it to be the same.
- Will be (Will-B) is $100 million—this reflects the fact that if nothing changes then the company will lose 80% of $500 million in revenue. That would leave it with only $100 million in revenue once the customer's policy takes effect. In this case, the current target is the same as the needs-to-be (N2B) target. The gap is not a present day gap. It is a potential future gap which will develop if no action is taken.

Gaps can be current gaps or potential future gaps. A gap represents the difference between where we want to be and where we actually are. A future gap can be the result of some known change in conditions or circumstances. In this example, the company took the future gap seriously because the future event was considered to be certain.

Quite often there are projected future conditions that are not quite as certain. These may be listed as risks. By attaching the CoA to these risks, we can better quantify the potential impact should the risk materialize.

An Identified valueflow with a full Value Chart of Accounts represents a Stage 2 maturity model—Value Performance Aware.

OUTPUT 3—THREE-TIER MODEL

The Three-Tier Model is where the framework truly diverges from the normal process-mapping approach. Outcomes and outputs force us to think in different terms. We can view a process as progressively producing its defining output. There are stages in any process where we reach distinct milestones that are increasingly closer to the final output.

The outcome gives us an evaluation framework. The output is something that the process needs to produce in order to achieve the outcome. Someone needs to be *accountable* for the defining output of a valueflow and for each progressive output of the functional processes. Each output can have a different accountability in addition to the accountability for the defining output. Accountability for an output implies leadership in following through in the face of difficulties.

When modelling a current process it might be the case that there is no clear accountability for the output design or for the execution. If that's the case, then that's what the blueprint should reflect.

Part of modelling a process includes establishing outcome and output accountability for design in addition to accountability for execution. Typically, there is no accountability for the design. The implication is that designing a process is simply part of executing it. Of course, in manufacturing, where things are made from blueprints, design accountability is separated from "make" or execution accountability. The blueprint represents the output design. The actual output represents the product of execution. In most knowledge- or service-based organizations this distinction is rare. So, in practice, outputs will differ from one person to the next in these organizations. Of course, this leads to significant waste and makes management of the processes more difficult.

An output is not a task. An output is what we are left with after we execute a number of tasks. Outputs provide us with yet another tool for chunking a process into more manageable pieces. Outputs also allow us to view a process not in terms of the operations performed but in terms of a progression towards the final and defining output. The modelling process that we are describing produces outputs as shown in the diagram without specifying a particular method for producing the output.

A Requirements Specification is a generic example of an output. It can be an output of a process improvement project or an IT Software Development process. A Design Specification is another example of an output. Perhaps the Requirements Specification was first produced and then the Design Specification was produced from it and other inputs.

Outputs are natural convergent handover points. They represent a work-in-process. As such, it is crucial that those accountable for the process producing the output and those accountable for the process consuming the output have the same understanding of the output. That's why every output should have a single specification. This is a weak point in many processes, especially in those that do not produce any physical product. Quite often the producing process has one specification for the output while the receiving process has a different specification for the same output. That means that the receiving process will rework the output before new work can begin.

By output we don't mean a report or some sort of document. The outputs we are referring to are the ones that are directly related to the defining output. So if the defining output is software, then a specification might be an intermediate output. The code would be another output. A status report would not be, since it is not directly required to produce the defining output of software. However, the information on the status report could be part of a control output.

The advantage of an output tier model is that it is a good tool for synchronizing people and for communication. Whereas outputs are determined by the nature of what we are trying to produce, tasks are determined by how we decide to produce them. A given process may have few alternative output tier models. But it will have many more potential alternative task level implementation models. Outputs also allow us to implement clear accountabilities. Although you can assign task responsibility to people, correctly executing the tasks doesn't guarantee that the output will be of appropriate quality. So assigning output accountability improves the whole accountability structure in an organization. When no one is accountable, that signals the presence of a significant risk.

The output tier model allows us to reduce the complexity and build incremental alignment. Once a team has agreed to the output tier model and has standardized the specification of each output, the task level models can then be developed by different sub-teams for each output. What this means is that each team can work independently on the task model for their output as long as they have the same specification for each output. As long as those producing the output and those consuming the output have an identical understanding of the specification of the output, then they don't need to concern themselves with the details of how it will be produced unless they are the ones producing it.

What does this mean in practical terms? With teams working in parallel, producing the model can go significantly faster. We're not saying that it will require less effort but rather that the start-to-finish time will be much faster. We do think that in total it will require less effort as well, because each of the teams can be smaller and more knowledge focused. A desirable side effect of this is the potential for higher levels of engagement, wider participation, and distribution of effort.

One last thing about outputs—some outputs can be evaluated with regard to quality without reference to the method used to produce them. On the other hand, some outputs cannot. For example, a pie can be evaluated without knowing how it was produced. A decision, on the other hand, cannot. That's because a decision is actually a conclusion reached as the result of executing some decision process. In order to evaluate the likelihood that a decision is a good one, we would need to know the facts and assumptions that went into it and the rationale or logic behind it. In other words, someone would need to walk us through the decision-making process actually followed. What this means is that the level of required transparency of a process will differ depending on how independently we can evaluate the output.

In addition, there is a difference between a good output and the correct output, especially when we are talking about decision outputs. Decisions are probabilistic or risk based. A decision process cannot provide the correct conclusion 100% of the time because of other factors that are not within our control or influence. That means we can produce a good and valid decision that leads to the wrong results—incorrect decision. We need to be careful because the term "incorrect" can be misleading. Since a decision is probabilistic, no one can be right 100% of the time. There is an old saying that the strong don't always win but it's the way to bet. So we need to keep this in mind when we come across a decision that was made correctly but leads to an incorrect result. It may still have been the "way to bet."

Outputs tend to map directly to the underlying functional processes required to produce them. So an output tier map is a good way to take a complex process and chunk it into the functional processes that produce the transformational outputs. Here again is the Steel Company example expanded to the three tiers.

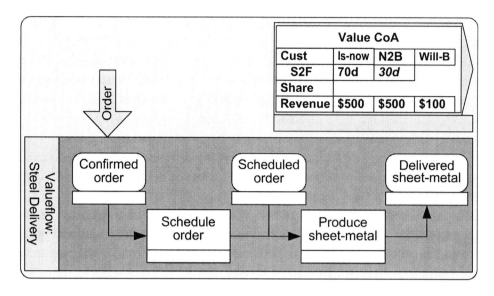

Expanding the model to the three tiers, especially the output tier, is a necessary step to get us to Stage 4— Capability Performance Aware. But it doesn't quite get us there. For that we also have to complete the next step. Nevertheless, it may be useful to take the model to this point. It takes little effort and it makes clear which functional units are involved in executing the valueflow.

OUTPUT 4—CAPABILITY COA

By now you may be forgetting what the **S³** model looks like and how the maturity stages map to it, so we repeat it here:

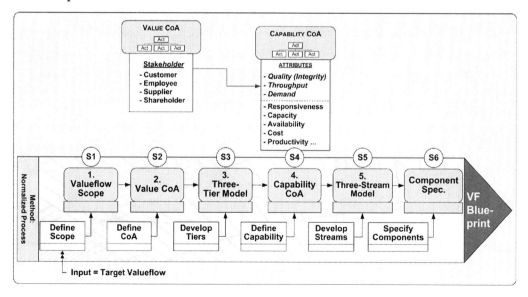

Whereas the Stakeholder Value CoA evaluates the process value as seen from the external stakeholders' point of view, the Capability CoA measures the process from the inside as seen by the executors. It is a way to determine the internal health of the process as a whole and of the functional processes that make up the valueflow. It is a way to measure how well the value is delivered—the efficiency and internal operational risk.

Establishing a Capability CoA involves two key activities:
1. Propagating or distributing the measures from the Value CoA down to the output tier.
2. Establishing internal Capability account measures.

What do we mean by propagating or distributing? The outputs inside a process will each have a greater or lesser impact on a particular valueflow level account measure. The purpose of propagating a particular one is to determine the extent to which each output contributes directly to the value of that measure. Propagating a valueflow level metric down to each output is not always possible, but when it is possible, it is useful.

Let's continue the Steel Company example. And let's focus on the responsiveness account measure. Remember that this account, which measures the start-to-finish time for an order, was the one that the company has to reduce; otherwise it faces a potential drop in revenues.

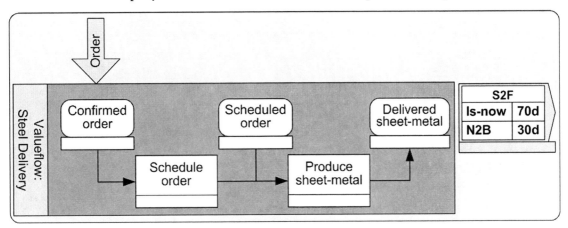

The diagram shows the Steel process modelled at the output tier and containing three outputs. It also shows the single account measure of responsiveness called S2F (start-to-finish). This represents the time it takes the process from start to finish, from a confirmed order to a delivered order.

It has a current or actual value (Is-Now) of 70 days, as illustrated on the right side of the diagram. That means that today it takes about 70 days to go from a firm order to a delivered order to the customer. It also has a target N2B (needs to be) of 30 days. It needs to be 30 days because that's what the customer is dictating. It doesn't show the date by which we need to achieve this target. We have taken it out to simplify the diagram but in a real situation that would be a crucial part of the CoA.

What all this means is that we have a potential future gap of 40 days for the S2F account metric unless we take corrective action. In other words, we need to reduce the start-to-finish time by at least 40 days overall to reach the target. But where should we focus our attention?

In order to answer that question, we need to see if we can distribute the S2F metric over the outputs of the valueflow. Imagine that we did that, and that the results are as shown in the diagram below.

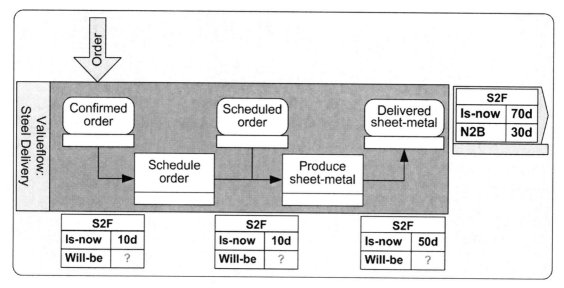

Also assume that we are using the start of one output as the end of the previous output. That way there are no S2F time gaps to account for. We can see that the 70 days were not evenly distributed across the three outputs.

1. The Confirmed Order output has a current value of 10 days.
2. The Scheduled Order output has a current value of 10 days.
3. The Delivered Sheet-Metal Order has a current value of 50 days.

The Delivered Sheet-Metal has the greatest impact on this particular valueflow level account. Interestingly, this output alone puts us over the target of 30 days. So the responsiveness capability for the functional process that produces the Delivered Sheet-Metal is 50 days. Therefore, even if we were able to reduce the actual value for the first two outputs, we could not reach the target of 30 days by addressing those two outputs alone. The conclusion is that we would be advised to address the functional process for the output called Delivered Sheet-Metal first, since that measure *must* be reduced no matter what. As it turns out, this is an example from a real client and they *did not* address that process first. The result was that they spent tens of millions of dollars trying to reduce the other two before realizing that they were focusing their attention on the wrong processes. Why did they do that? They had a preferred solution focus. Their preferred solution was technology—specifically software. So what they did and what many companies do all too often is look for those parts of the process that would most readily accept a technology solution. And that led them to the first two outputs. Unfortunately, they realized rather late in the process that no amount of effort in those first two outputs could achieve the result of 30 days without addressing the third output, which accounted for 50 days of elapsed time all on its own.

Propagating or distributing a metric across the outputs helps us to focus on the critical portion of the process that requires our initial attention for a given account metric. So the likely starting point for closing this gap would be to first look at the Delivered Sheet-Metal output rather than the whole process. If we are able to reduce that metric from 50 days to 10 days, then we don't need to look at any other part of the process. On the other hand, if we can't reduce it to below 30, then it will be virtually impossible to achieve the goal.

If we had been interested in another account measure such as cost, then it's possible that the relative distribution would have been different and perhaps the focus would have been different. The point is that distributing the measure of interest across the outputs helps us to determine where we should begin the search. Sometimes the initial focus will be different for different account measures. Distributing the measure can also help rule out areas that don't have an impact on the target account. Distributing the measure doesn't tell us what to do but it does tell us where to look.

The advantage of the output tier model coupled with capability metrics is that we have a context within which to make changes that are highly likely to achieve actual improvements. Without the proper capability metrics being defined, we will attempt to change the process to look like our idea of what a "best practice" might dictate. That approach won't necessarily get us to where we need to be. That approach may also lead us to modify aspects of the process that, although imperfect, don't have an impact on the actual goal of improving responsiveness. That leads to investments of time, effort, and money that won't provide a proper return or lead to the desired outcomes. It also leads to personal career risk because people often get the blame for digging in the wrong place even when someone else chose the spot to dig.

The danger with a task level process map is that it could easily lead us to make changes in those parts of the process that are easier to address but that won't achieve the target. When we know where the initial focus needs to be, we can then delve deeper to better understand what actually goes on inside the relevant functional process.

When the model has been expanded to the Accountability CoA, then the model has reached Stage 4—Capability Aware. When the model has reached this stage, we have both a value CoA and a Capability CoA and we have defined accountability. We have a complete framework for managing the performance of the valueflow. The more key valueflows we model to this stage, the better we will be able to manage total process performance across the organization.

Output 5—Three-Stream Model

The Three-Stream model is a task level model. The difference is that the work has been segmented into the three streams. It can look much like what we are used to, but with some differences. First of all, we have already produced an output tier model. That model has taken the larger valueflow and created an organized framework that can now be populated with task level detail. If the output model has seven outputs, for example, we can produce seven corresponding task tier process maps. So rather than producing a large monolithic model, we produce more but smaller, segmented models. In addition, we can focus our attention and energy on those processes that contribute more heavily to whatever account measure we are trying to improve. Or we can expand the model one output at a time as needed. If we are simultaneously developing the process models and exploring opportunities for improvement, then we can postpone the production of a detailed task level model unless we are exploring a performance gap that we can't explain without the task details. In many cases we can explain the performance gap without understanding the task details at all. For a given performance gap, we rarely need to understand the entire task level model, but only that portion that may explain the gap.

Returning to the previous Steel Company example, we could conclude that we really do need more information to understand how to produce a Delivered Sheet-Metal order. This is depicted below by the oval.

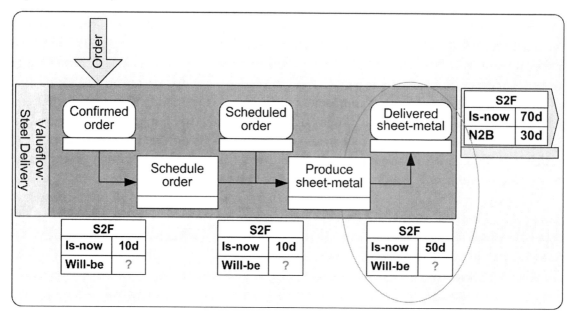

It is not necessary, at this point, to explore the entire task level model. In fact, if we engage the right people we might not have to produce any detailed documentation at all because the people who are executing those tasks may know why that portion takes that long. But if we needed more detail, we would produce the Three-Stream model related to the output called Delivered Sheet-Metal. We won't do that here because such a model would be large.

A detailed task level model can be expensive to produce and is rarely used beyond the initiative that created it. By only producing it when absolutely necessary, we can achieve a better understanding of the valueflow while avoiding significant time and cost.

The Three-Stream task level model can be represented in many ways, depending on what we are trying to accomplish. A task model using the task symbol is one way. On the other hand, an actual detailed procedure may sometimes be more appropriate. In other cases, an example is a better tool to use in order to convey understanding. Or perhaps a checklist is sufficient. It all depends on the circumstance and type of process.

In the *Relational Process Model*, the task level model has a different, more democratic purpose. It should be a tool for those people who are executing. Therefore, it should be produced by the task experts and should reflect whatever standard work they have developed. In this way it becomes a base for executing, training, and improving. It becomes a tool used by the task experts to achieve mastery in their functional area rather than a consultant tool. As such, the level of detail for a task level model may vary significantly. If an organization does not currently use task level models to guide people during their job execution, then it will likely be counterproductive to produce a highly detailed procedure. On the other hand, people may accept and use a simple checklist. This is a start for engagement. As people use the checklist, there will be a tendency to add useful details as they begin to benefit from its use. Functional excellence, however, must always be achieved within the context of the valueflow performance requirements.

When the model is expanded to a streamed task model and used as a tool by the subject matter experts who are executing, then the model is truly useful.

OUTPUT 6—SPECIFIED COMPONENTS

The final step is to complete the specification of the components—skills, functions, mental mindset, etc. Of course some of this will have been done along the way. But now we need to complete them. This comprises the full blueprint for the whole valueflow. Even if we are modelling just a functional model, we should always model it in the context of the valueflow. This is the knowledge management framework for this valueflow. We now have a framework to which we can attach all kinds of knowledge, including performance-related and risk-related lessons. This also becomes the framework for managing the valueflow and for connecting strategy to execution.

Here is the final diagram for the example. However, this is not the whole blueprint. We would need to fully define the Value CoA and the Capability CoA. We would also need to fully specify each of the outputs and get the model to the detailed Three-Stream task level. But this is a sort of Master Blueprint Map for the valueflow.

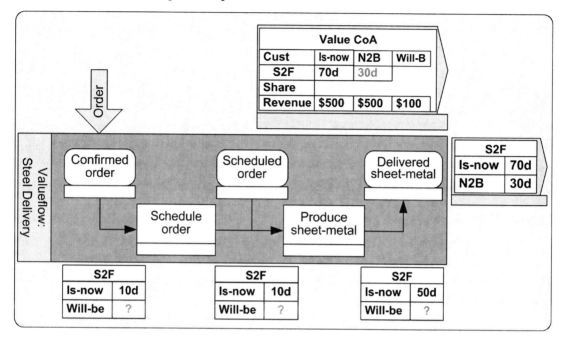

THE NORMALIZED VALUEFLOW BLUEPRINT

When a valueflow has been modelled all the way down to the task tier and all the components have been specified, then we have a full normalized Valueflow Blueprint. When that blueprint is used as a tool for both design and execution and when it is kept current, then we can say that the model has reached Stage 6—Blueprint Aware. A valueflow that has been modelled to this stage has a blueprint that can be used to fully manage that valueflow.

As an organization achieves this stage of modelling for more and more valueflows, it should see a significant increase in process awareness and that should translate into higher performance. But modelling on its own won't do that. We also need to develop the discipline of continuous enterprise process performance management. In the next chapter we will explore how such discipline can be cultivated and maintained.

SUMMARY

A valueflow can be modelled in many ways. You can use your own methodology along with the framework. This chapter has introduced you to the Six Simple Steps method to going from an identified valueflow to a full normalized process blueprint. The method can be used to model a complete valueflow or to model a single functional process inside a valueflow.

Modelling by itself only produces documentation and does not deliver any direct value. Therefore, we should always model in conjunction with some other objective, such as closing a performance gap. Of course this could be a catch-22. If we don't have a performance measurement framework, then we can't detect a gap. If we don't see the gap, then there is no gap to close.

A valueflow can be modeled to Stage 2 (Value Performance Aware) with minimal investment. Consider it like buying a scale when going on a diet. So we should consider modelling a few key valueflows to this stage just so we can determine whether we have performance gaps.

We introduced the six stages of a model. Each stage requires a little more effort than the previous. But each stage has potentially greater use. The last stage, which gets us to the task level, will likely require an order of magnitude or about ten times more effort than the others. For that reason a model should only be taken to this stage when the potential benefits warrant it.

For most organizations, process knowledge is in people's heads. Of course this is an unreliable storage place. Not only can the knowledge change from day to day but also from person to person. In addition, when a person leaves, the knowledge might leave with them.

Reliable products are mostly produced from explicit blueprints. To the shareholder, the business is the product. Yet there is no blueprint for the business. But every day a business has to be reconstituted from the collective memories of the employees and from what few written procedures exist.

Modelling is a necessary step on the road to managing performance based on designed blueprints. Since producing these blueprints can be expensive, we have introduced a method for developing them in stages. In this way they can be developed indirectly as a side effect of some other objective. The model is used as a tool in achieving the performance objective and becomes a desirable and free side effect.

Modelling increases process transparency and awareness. Process Modelling, as a tool, takes only days to learn. But Relational Process Modelling, as a discipline for learning, takes years to master.

Relational Process Modelling: It takes days to learn, but years to master.

13

The Office For Strategy Achievement

Sustainability is the capability to continue to produce a specified outcome by executing a blueprint—indefinitely.

We have presented a comprehensive framework for modelling an enterprise's processes and linking them directly to strategy and to accountability. We've also introduced the Master Valueflow Map, which comprises three segments:

1. Breakthrough Strategy Deployment for managing external and stakeholder shifts
2. Core Strategy Sustain for maintaining the course by managing internal drift that might take us away from the target performance
3. Customer Value Chain for managing the execution of the customer delivery processes

We also explored a method for developing a full blueprint for a given valueflow and we introduced the idea of modelling in progressive stages. But modelling by itself is not the end game. Its true purpose and usefulness stems from its role as part of a systematic approach to deploying, executing, and managing the strategy. The deployment of the strategy should be considered a key management activity in any organization, be it private or public, for profit, or for purpose. But quite often companies falter not because of a poor strategy but because of lack of follow-through during and after deployment.

Most enterprises are organized functionally around their Customer Value Chain. They may even be organized around the concept of profit centres versus cost centres. They are rarely organized around the concept of value centres for valueflows. The whole idea of a valueflow is to collect both the value and the cost required to deliver that value under one entity, the valueflow. That gives us a much better idea of what needs to change in order to deliver greater value.

The Master Valueflow Map clearly shows that in addition to delivering the all-important customer value through the Customer Value Chain, there is also a whole Management System that needs to surround the customer delivery processes. Strategy deployment is part of that Management System. The deployment of strategy is the continuous process of aligning everyone and everything to carry out the organization's purpose and achieve its objectives. That makes it a force for integrating the often disparate parts of the organization.

Strategy deployment requires that we integrate three key elements: the strategy itself, the execution processes, and the change projects. These three elements cross both functional boundaries (horizontal) and authority boundaries (vertical). So where is there a home for carrying out the strategy deployment effort? Is there a way and a place to integrate strategy, processes, and projects to increase performance?

In many organizations these are treated as separate pieces rather than parts of a whole. But strategies, processes, and projects need to work together in order to achieve the business objectives. That means that we need to constantly realign them when external and internal conditions and circumstances change.

In order to manage something as a whole, we need accountability for the whole. The purpose of the Office *For* Strategy Achievement (OFSA) is to help provide that accountability, to provide a home for the effort required to integrate the three components of strategies, processes, and projects.

The diagram below depicts the three components and their relationship to the Value and Capability Charts of Accounts. Managing these three components as a unit is essential to moving the performance forward.

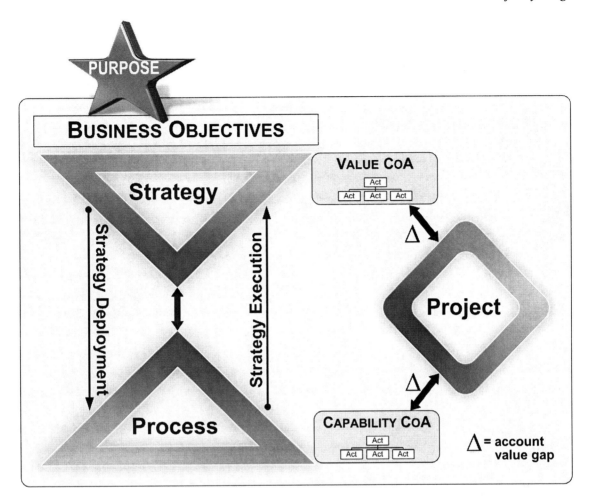

CALLING THE SHOTS

"Calling" is the rule in pool where players announce the pocket where they plan to sink a ball. They let their opponent or referee know what their intention is beforehand. For example, "3-ball in the side pocket" is a call (announcement) of the ball and the intended target pocket. If the player sinks any other ball or if they sink the ball they called in the wrong pocket, then they don't get credit for the shot. Calling the shot is a higher, more difficult level of play than one where we don't call the shots. After all, when we don't call the shot, we can miss the intended shot and still sink a ball that was ours. No one will know the difference. Unfortunately, when we have to call the shot we can't take credit for such fortunate misses.

Imagine you are not a strong pool player. Now suppose you wanted to demonstrate to someone that you are a better player than you actually are. How might you go about it? One way could be to play and record many, many games. Then you could review the recordings and carefully select only the most impressive and exceptional shots. You could use the selected shots to develop a presentation that included only the chosen shots and none of the missed shots. Maybe you could insert a few really close calls just to make it look a little more realistic. That presentation, after careful editing and perhaps adding some background music and a few special effects, would be what was shown to others. Of course that could present you as being much better than you actually were.

Now let's look at a different scenario. Let's say that you had to call all your shots and that you had to show, or account for, the results from *every* shot you made, not just the ones you liked. Let's say that you recorded entire games. Would that portray a different picture? Of course it would. If we can hide the bad shots and emphasize the good shots, then the temptation is to focus on the perception of our ability more than our actual ability. On the other hand, if we had to call the shots and then account for every shot, we might be more highly motivated to improve our game. But how does this relate to organizational performance?

We have all probably attended corporate gatherings where someone stands up and delivers a presentation titled "Accomplishments." Maybe it was at a strategic planning session. Or perhaps it was at a project review meeting. Or perhaps it was a business unit presentation. Virtually all such presentations have several things in common: they look at everything that has happened over a period of time, pick out the really good stuff, intended or not, and they present those as if they were the intended results. Such presentations are virtually always biased towards the "positive." But they should be biased towards reality, which means they shouldn't be biased at all.

In order to achieve the strategy, we need to call the shots and show or *account* for the result of every shot regardless of whether it went in or missed. We don't do this so that we can blame people, but rather so that we have the visibility needed to *learn and improve*. But this is a difficult thing to do. Even those with the highest integrity will tend to try to forget the bad and focus on the good. They tend to think of the unwanted results as being one-time events rather than the consequence of the processes. They may think that this shows a positive attitude. But hiding our head in the sand when it comes to failures is not a positive attitude. If we are to call every shot and examine the result in order to improve, then we are going to need a different level of discipline. Such a level is rarely achievable at the personal level.

The OFSA can help an organization achieve this higher level of discipline by ensuring that shots get called and that the results are all accounted for. It can help us manage the three components of strategy, process, and project. With that in mind, let's look at each component in more detail to understand how they interrelate and how they help an organization to improve and learn by "Calling the Shots."

STRATEGY—INTENT

The first component in the diagram is the strategy. The strategy is a statement of intent that describes *how we intend* to achieve the related business objective. The strategy flows from the purpose of the organization as seen from the perspective of each stakeholder group. The purpose gets translated into specific and measurable business objectives that are cast in the form of a Value Chart of Accounts.

Organizations may begin with similar business objectives. But each may choose a different way to achieve the business objective. Or they may choose a different way to achieve a particular objective. For each objective, an organization develops a set of strategies or ways to achieve that objective. Strategies are important in that they can change the risk-reward profile for a particular business.

Let's use an analogy. Imagine a foot race with five participants. They all start at the same place and the first one to reach the finish wins. But this race is a little different. There are several different routes that lead to the finish and contestants are free to select whichever one they want. But they must make their choice one week in advance of the race. No changes are allowed afterwards. Each route might have certain advantages depending on conditions. For example, one route might be shorter but because it is packed with dirt, it would cause difficulty under wet conditions. So the strategy can have an impact on the performance, apart from the individual's ability to run fast. If two people choose the same route (strategy), then they are competing more on excellence in running the race. The strategy or route doesn't give them any advantage over each other. On the other hand, there might be an advantage or disadvantage as compared to those who have picked a different route. Business strategies are similar. They have advantages and disadvantages under various conditions. There are also different risks depending on the strategy chosen. Unlike the foot race, companies don't have the same starting point. And so a strategy that might make sense for one might make no sense for the other based on their starting point. That's why there may not be such a thing as the "best" strategy, but rather the most appropriate strategy given current conditions for your organization.

During the development of the strategy, we want to engage people across the organization (for horizontal accountability) as well as up and down the organization (vertical accountability). Strategy deployment needs to engage those who will be responsible for execution as well as those who will be accountable for results. We are engaging those who will call the shots. And we engage those who will be taking the shot. So it's probably good to find out early when a shot can't likely be made. Engagement is required for both control and for commitment to the shot.

But calling the shot is just one bookend. The other bookend is being able to verify whether or not we made the shot. Execution, of course, lies between the two. Since we must be able to verify what we said we were going to achieve, we need some framework for evaluation and measurement. The Value Chart of Accounts provides that framework at the objective and strategy level. Basically, it records the intent sufficiently, clearly, and completely so that we can verify what has been accomplished as compared to what was intended. And so we have a Value CoA attached to each objective and to each strategy. But it isn't enough for the CoA to specify what we want to accomplish. It also needs to specify how to perform the evaluation because there are often multiple ways to measure, with each approach leading to slightly different results.

Commitment is built up during the development of the strategy. Commitment doesn't mean acceptance. We don't and can't get everyone to agree to a particular strategy. In fact, for some strategies, we might need to limit the knowledge of the strategy. Commitment is the process of building a *stake* and deciding who will be the *holder* of that stake (stakeholder).

As we execute the functional processes and valueflows, the results get recorded so they can be compared against the Chart of Accounts. Now we have a solid basis for determining which intended shots were made and which intended shots were missed. We can also track the shots we made that were never called. It is important to know what we have called and achieved as well as achievements made that were not called. The latter can provide new information. Perhaps we did something that created a positive result that we didn't anticipate. Let's find out how the desirable result was achieved.

Separating the calling of the shots from the making of the shots is important. And calling the shots before they are made is also important. How often are shots called after they are made in your organization? If you are doing this, then it's a sure sign of a failure to commit. And a failure to commit is a failure of accountability.

When commitment and accountability are properly developed, then the Value Chart of Accounts helps us to detect gaps in strategy achievement. Then we can engage the right people to determine why the gap exists and to propose alternative responses. Gaps can have many sources, such as:

- changes in the external customer environment
- changes in the external competitive environment
- changes in stakeholder expectations, which reflect on business objectives
- execution wasn't done well enough to achieve the objective
- execution was done well, but we were mistaken about what was needed
- etc.

Any of these changes and others can cause a gap (difference between the shot called and the shot made or missed). When a gap develops, action is required. That's where accountability is important. If there is no one accountable for a particular account, then the gap may not get detected since no one is looking out for it. But even if it is detected by someone, if that person isn't accountable, she may not be able to take action. Or she may choose to take no action. So the gap may be ignored.

The Office *For* Strategy Achievement through a well-designed Value Chart of Accounts can ensure that all value gaps receive the appropriate attention and a response. Valid responses can include:

- direct adjustments to the *strategy*
- determining which processes are associated with the strategy and making adjustments to one or more associated *processes*
- launching a *project* to determine an appropriate solution
- etc.

Detecting strategy achievement gaps requires a high level of maturity and discipline that is not always achievable at the individual level. The OFSA is an organizational mechanism meant to ensure that the discipline is always practiced regardless of any individual weaknesses. The OFSA should be seen as a support structure that brings objectivity and discipline to the organization. But strategy is just intent. So where is intent carried out and achieved?

PROCESSES—EXECUTION

At the end of the day, we must execute to change the values in the accounts. Execution is what achieves intent. Excellence in execution is necessary. But it is not sufficient. Nevertheless, it is execution that produces results. Intent is calling the shot, but intent can't sink the ball. Execution does that. And where does execution take place? It takes place inside the processes. That's why we deployed the strategy from objective, to strategy, to valueflow, and then to the functional process. We execute functional processes. Then we record the results at the functional, valueflow, strategy, and objective levels. Of course, even if the results are not recorded they will still happen, but we won't have visibility into cause and effect. If we don't record, then we will have difficulty in assessing the results against what we said we were going to do and how we said we were going to get it done. Why is this important?

Firstly, if we don't track the results, then we won't accurately know what we have achieved. That leaves us open to false claims of success. We could end up rewarding people for results that never were. Without knowing what has been achieved, we can't know if there is a gap in performance or how large the gap may be. Secondly, without that knowledge we will have a difficult time determining the response that we should make. Again, if a gap is not detected, then it might be ignored until it is so big that it can be detected, even if not formally measured. If you don't get tested for an illness it will eventually make itself obvious. But by then it may be too late to respond. So we measure and test to achieve early detection. It's the same with a business process.

At the process level we primarily use the Capability Chart of Accounts to detect gaps in execution performance and gaps in specification performance. But we also use the Value Chart of Accounts for the valueflow. That helps us link back to strategy.

The Office *For* Strategy Achievement (OFSA) can use the Value Chart of Accounts and the Capability Chart of Accounts for each valueflow to ensure that accountability is assigned for each and every account. That ensures that performance gaps can get detected and receive the appropriate response. Valid responses to a capability performance gap can include:

- direct adjustments to the valueflow
- direct adjustments to one or more functional processes
- changes to one or more components
- launching a project to determine an appropriate solution
- etc.

The effort and discipline required to manage the process performance is quite apart from and in addition to the effort required to execute those same processes. The OFSA helps to ensure that this discipline is maintained. As each response changes the blueprint in a progressive way, we move towards the development of a *more perfect process*.

When a change is small, it can be made directly without significant additional resources beyond the process capacity. But sometimes a change will require more time, effort, and resources than that available through normal process capacity. In those cases, how would we affect more major changes to our processes?

Projects—Transition

When changes require greater capacity than is available, or when multiple accountabilities are involved, then we might need to resort to a project. Let's review the definition of a project according to the PMBOK book published by the Project Management Institute (PMI) (Project Management Institute, *A guide to the project management body of knowledge (PMBOK) (3rd ed.*, 2004).

> *The PMBOK poses the question, "What is a project?" and then answers: "A project is a temporary endeavor undertaken to create a unique product, service or result."*
> *The PMBOK makes a distinction between projects and operational process work. It states that "operations are ongoing and repetitive" in contrast to projects. Further, it states:*
> *"Projects are different because the project concludes when its specific objectives have been attained …"*

Another way to look at projects that is consistent with the above definition is to view them as transitional and transformational mechanisms. When a gap is detected in either strategy performance (through the Value CoA) or in process performance (through the Capability CoA), and when the gap can't be closed through simple local actions, then we may need to initiate a project to address the closing of the gap. Sometimes the gap is too large or too complex or requires engagement from multiple units. In these cases, the project paradigm may be the answer. So that's when a project may need to be initiated.

Processes are instruments for stability. Projects are instruments for change. A process requires capacity to produce its outputs. Projects also require capacity apart from any normal process capacity. And where does this capacity come from? Many organizations have a pool of project resources such as project managers, business analysts, and other skilled resources. This is one source. Sometimes resources are brought in externally for limited periods of time. Sometimes capacity is diverted from existing processes for the life of the project. This is especially the case when specific subject matter experts are needed. Usually, capacity comes from all of these sources. Capacity is crucial to projects. Sometimes projects fail because capacity is insufficient or not available at the right time.

Processes are instruments of stability and sustainability. If we think in terms of a ship, then processes are the bulk of the ship. Projects are like the rudder on a ship, helping us change direction. Without the rudder, it's tough to change direction. So of course we need both and they need to work in harmony with each other. The point of a project is to get us from one stable process to another, more perfect, higher performing, and stable process.

A project can be used to help an organization return to a previous desired state after it has drifted away from it. Or it may help the organization define and achieve a new state in response to a market or other shift. Either way, the endgame should be to close a performance gap, not to implement a preferred solution.

Most of the time an organization is trying to sustain its performance. And then at opportune times, it is looking to move that performance forward. Organizations continue to struggle to sustain the gains they have made. One problem may be that they don't yet realize that gains can't be held. They have to be *reproduced* every day. Performance gains are not like money in the bank that can be stashed away and protected

That's the purpose of a well-designed process—to be able to reproduce a certain level of performance indefinitely. But processes are subject to many of the same laws as the physical world. They are subject to erosion and entropy. Internal and external conditions can cause a process to slowly drift away from its peak performance. Processes will also tend to move towards the state that requires the lowest level of emotional energy, unless constant effort is expended to maintain it.

The Office *For* Strategy Achievement (OFSA) provides an organizational control that links process performance gaps to projects. Since the true purpose of a project is to close a performance gap, one of the key success factors for projects is their selection. It's kind of like drilling for oil. If you drill in the wrong place, it doesn't matter how well you drill—you won't get oil. It just isn't there. Many projects fail not so much because we didn't know how to drill but, rather, because the project was drilling in the wrong place. In a functionally focused organization, people tend to drill where they are comfortable: in their own backyards. What that means is that projects are initiated to solve what appears to be a problem or headache to the local function, often without regard to external impacts.

Projects should be initiated based on gaps in *specified* performance, rather than based on personal preference. By initiating projects based on performance, we know in advance what the outcome result needs to look like—we are calling the outcome. But we may not initially know what the actual solution will look like. On the other hand, when we initiate projects functionally, we typically know what the solution will look like—we are calling the solution. But we may be unaware of what the total impact across the organization will be.

A project initiated based on the solution will tend to protect the solution at the expense of the performance outcome. That's because it's the solution that has been sold to management. Therefore, we are compelled to stay with the solution even when evidence points elsewhere. Solutions have to be sold against the solutions of others. So it's a competitive situation. People are emotionally attached to and have a personal stake in a solution. So, to them, it is the implementation of the solution that represents success. That makes the existence of more perfect solutions invisible to them. When someone sells a project on the basis of a solution, we should still set up an evaluation framework in the form of a Chart of Accounts. The seller of the solution should be accountable for that Chart of Accounts. They should be accountable for the desired outcome, not the solution.

A project initiated based on achieving a certain level of performance outcome will exhibit a different behaviour. Firstly, the desired performance is stated at the start of the project. The performance comes as a result of strategy deployment and not as a personal preference. The solution is more flexible. It can change as we learn more about the processes that we are trying to change. Since we are committed to achieving the outcome, we are freer to modify and adjust the solution as we learn more. Since the focus is on the performance, we are more likely to achieve that performance. Think of it this way: "Is it more important to reach the destination or to take a particular route?" If it's the destination, then we are freer to adjust the route. But if we commit to the route, then we have to accept where it will take us. Sometimes, in organizations, individuals are more concerned with the route because it is more personally advantageous to them, at the expense of others. We need to be able to see such situations and to avoid them.

OFSA IMPLEMENTATION

Many organizations have Project Management Offices (PMO) whose purpose is to ensure that project investments produce good results. Unfortunately, for many organizations, the PMO hasn't always lived up to the initial expectations. There is nothing wrong per se with a PMO. But most PMOs select projects from a pool of projects supplied to them from functional units. They may pay a lot of attention to project selection, but there is a big assumption embedded in any selection process. The assumption is that the pool from which we are selecting already contains the best candidates. The constraint with many selection approaches may not be with the method used to select, but rather with the method used to populate the pool from which the candidate projects are selected. Part of the role of the Office *For* Strategy Achievement is to manage the generation of projects to maintain a healthy pool.

If your pool contains projects generated by functional process units, then it is probably missing many of the highest opportunity projects. By generating projects based on performance gap closure, we are much more likely to have a pool full of rich opportunities. Only then does it make sense to focus on which project opportunity to select first. And only after that does it make sense to focus on how we do project delivery. A more perfect pool would contain only great opportunities. Then selection becomes more about selecting the sequence than selecting the projects.

Another key function for an OFSA would be to provide independent measurement and verification of value delivered through projects and processes. An organization is a socio-technical-economic mechanism. We have to understand the human behaviours (socio) as much as the other two. We can't accurately measure process performance and people performance together, especially if the people doing the measurement are also part of the process being measured. Such conflicts of interest will clearly hurt the organization. In addition, projects will tend to be closed when the product of the project has been implemented, rather than when the outcomes have been achieved and validated. Most of the value delivered through the project—the outcomes—will occur later, perhaps over a period of years. If there is no one to capture this information, then we will never really know what was truly delivered and what was not.

This may not be true in your organization, but in many there is little or no accounting for actual business results from project investments. Outcomes may be based on forecasted results rather than actual results. Project failures are unfortunately so common that when a project has delivered its product, few have the motivation to measure the business impact, which requires post-project measurements over some period of time. We are usually so glad that it's over that we really want it to be completely over. With many projects—some even suggest most projects—measuring business value from the project would simply drag out the already bad news. Certainly those who were on the project usually don't have the time, the mandate, or the motivation to do that. The irony is that for learning sometimes the bad news is the good news.

Sometimes the bad news *is* the good news.

At the organizational level, it is the bad news that can lead to progress. It is the bad news or the not-as-good news that, when acted upon, leads to more perfect performance. In order for continuous process performance improvement to succeed, we need some bad news Perhaps we should change the name to "gap news"—news of a performance gap. *For continuous improvement, the gap news is the good news.*

But bad, or gap, news can reflect negatively on specific people. So that's why we need to understand not just the technical and the economic aspects but also the socio impacts. Sometimes what is best for our future is too difficult to admit to ourselves. That's where the OFSA as a concept can lead to better, more objective evaluations. It can ensure that the bad news does come to light, and that it isn't used for political gain. It can be a place where bad news can also be good news. Of course it shouldn't be *all* bad news.

But how might an Office *For* Strategy Achievement be implemented? Is it an actual staff unit with a permanent staff of people working in it full time or is it more of a project that comes and goes? The answer is that it will depend on your particular organization. There is unlikely to be a universal answer and since few organizations have such a unit, there will be some experimentation required to properly answer the question.

But let's make a few predictions about the characteristics we would expect such a unit to possess:

1. The unit would contain some core, persistent, permanent functions.
2. The unit would draw on resources from the business units depending on circumstances. For example, during strategy deployment we would need to engage management from across the organization. For a project to close a particular gap, we would engage more specific resources.
3. The unit would report quite high up in the organization, possibly to the CEO.
4. The unit would map accountability required to accountability assigned. The problem with accountability is that it is usually more about blame than about who's looking after which accounts. The Chart of Accounts is intended to make accountability more visible by defining what we need to keep our eyes on and assigning that to someone specific.

So the Office *For* Strategy Achievement is always engaging people from all parts of the business to achieve the objectives of the organization through its strategy. It is continuously building stake.

OFSA AND CONTINUOUS ALIGNMENT

So how can the OFSA help in managing strategy, process, and projects? It can provide a home for necessary control functions that form part of a good Management System. Continuous performance progress requires a level of discipline that *must* be institutionalized. We can't depend on individual discipline because it is not reliable. Individual discipline can fluctuate widely depending on specific managers. If we want consistent levels of discipline, we need organizational level discipline in addition to the individual discipline.

The OFSA can supply the organizational discipline in much the same way as a personal coach. The coach is there to tell you what you need to hear, not what is pleasant to hear. The OFSA needs to have three functions that work together to tell you the news as it is. These functions need to work together as part of a PDCA cycle (plan, do, check, act).

The diagram below shows the three key control functions of Strategy Deployment.

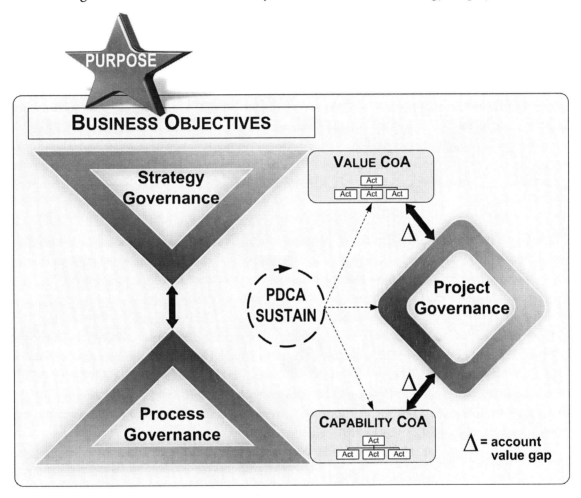

Since there are three components—Strategy, Process, and Projects—each of them needs to be properly governed.

1. Strategy Governance
2. Process Governance
3. Project Governance

Strategy Governance is the process of evaluating and managing the extent to which the strategy is working to achieve the objectives. *Process Governance* is the process of evaluating and managing the performance of the business processes to detect gaps. *Project Governance* is the process of selecting which gaps need to be closed first and then evaluating the degree to which each project was successful in closing its gap.

Once we have established the strategy and defined the process performance, how do we sustain the outcomes? Strategy Governance, Process Governance, and Project Governance, along with the Chart of Accounts, work together to implement a PDCA Sustain cycle. We could say that the OFSA is the keeper of the PDCA Sustain Cycle.

The PDCA *("Plan-Do-Check-Act")* cycle is a classic approach to sustaining. It is an iterative four-step management process used in some organizations. It is also known as the Deming Cycle or the Shewhart Cycle after its originator. The PDCA cycle is a classic approach that has remained unchanged for more than 50 years. Nevertheless, few organizations have formally implemented such a cycle and maintained it. Part of the problem is that although the PDCA cycle is a great concept, it has a tough time finding a home in many organizations. The OFSA represents one approach to providing a home for the execution of the PDCA concept with some powerful added tools. Let's recast the PDCA cycle in terms of the OFSA by exploring each of the PDCA steps.

Planning is the process of clarifying the purpose of the organization (or some unit), translating the purpose into achievable and measurable objectives, and then developing a set of strategies for each objective. Strategy deployment is the planning portion. Planning is about calling the shots and setting up the Charts of Accounts so that we can verify which shots were made and which missed and which should have been called but weren't. Planning, in the form of Strategy deployment, is the art and science of engaging the organization and building all the right connections and checkpoints up and down the organization such that the functional process (execution) level connects to the strategies via the valueflows. We need to properly specify each component and we must have the necessary framework to continuously validate any shift or drift away from the plan. This is in the form of measurement. We must be able to verify the objectives, strategies, and processes through the use of measures.

The most critical element of deployment is engagement. It is direct and active engagement that is at the heart of excellence. Deployment is the systematic and incremental engagement of the company's people in moving from objectives to strategies to valueflow capability to functional specifications. This is a clarification of what should be happening in the "planning" cycle. It is here that we think through, align, and set up mechanisms that will allow us to verify and validate what we are doing. This stage creates all the navigation Charts of Accounts that we will use to check whether we are on course.

Do is about execution. We have called the shots and now it's time to take the shots. Again, the CoA and blueprints provide those that are taking the shots with guidance as to what they are supposed to do. Of course, it's important to do what we said we would do. Otherwise, we can't evaluate whether the plan worked. We need to *execute the blueprint*. After all, if we don't execute the blueprint, then how do we know what it was that succeeded or failed? During the execution, everyone needs to understand which CoA accounts apply to their particular function. They need to know how the work is supposed to be done, and they need to know the expected performance. That way everyone can account for the results that their particular work is supposed to achieve. Accountability needs to be propagated both widely and deeply in the organization.

Control is about verifying that the course set is the correct course. All three governance functions have a strong element of control. This is about verifying where we are and also about making sure that we don't drift from the intentions. But control is not about blindly and diligently following orders. It is about thinking and reflecting on what is going on. It is during the control cycle that we make most use of the Chart of Accounts that we have set up. These serve to warn us as to when we need to pause to take a look at what is going on. What we are trying to accomplish during this stage (which is always active) is to detect exactly when a particular strategy, process, or component requires our attention. Then we immediately move to Act and Adjust.

It is during this stage that we use the accounts to verify that the right outcomes are being created backwards from Functional processes to Valueflows all the way to Strategy and Objectives. When a variance outside the acceptable tolerance is detected for a particular measure, we need to pause and analyze why the variance exists. It doesn't matter whether the variance is favourable or unfavourable. If it lies outside the tolerance we need to understand what conditions created it.

Control requires that accountabilities are set up for each account measure. If no one is accountable for a particular measure then no one will pay attention to it. Visible and defined accountability is crucial for proper control. Control is so important because it is based on focusing on what is going right most of the time and only stopping when there is an exception, when we begin to drift. Then we organize all necessary resources to analyze the situation and determine what actions need to take place.

Analyze/Adjust/Act is about stopping to look at and understand what has happened to create a variance or gap. Analyze looks at the data and again engages those concerned. The purpose is to understand what has happened and what the root causes might be. This step cannot succeed if the accounts and the process behaviours are not well understood. It also can't succeed if the organization does not immediately respond to problem situations and resolve the root cause. A deep understanding of the process under consideration is really essential here. This is not the time to stop to understand the process. Someone must already have a strong enough grasp of the process to quickly analyze most situations. This is where all the deployment work, when properly done, will pay off. Once we know what has happened, we can move to correct it. This requires discipline, and the OFSA can be the organization unit that promotes that discipline.

Adjust is the closing action for this cycle. Once the situation has been understood, we need to determine what actions need to be taken in order to resolve the issue at its root cause. Adjust is an implementation step that implements a change somewhere in the enterprise and reflects the change in some blueprint. An organization that isn't constantly making changes is either perfect or not following a PDCA Sustain and Improve cycle. And since no organization is perfect, then it must be that we are not engaging in systematic and continuous process improvement.

In the *adjust* phase, we will be making changes that can be broadly classified as falling into one of three buckets. So the changes will take one of these three forms:

1. **Execution Components**: There are many types of execution breakdowns. These can be related to skills, method, technology, input, etc. Execution changes are about doing things right or as specified and usually require us to address some sort of component issue.

2. **Process Design**: We may be doing things right according to the plan, but there may be a constraint in the design of a functional or valueflow process or a strategy. In such a case, we have to back up to one or more valueflows and re-examine the design. Design changes can be more serious than execution. Whenever a design change is made, we will need to propagate it back down towards functional execution and functional components. This will ensure everything remains aligned and that we aren't causing unintended consequences.

3. **Objective-Strategy**: It may be that the strategy, objectives, or the purpose itself needs to be adjusted. This is typically an even more serious situation. In that case, we have to go back to the beginning of the Plan step, adjust, and then redeploy the particular objective or strategy that has been adjusted.

SUMMARY

Achieving business objectives through the strategy is the end game. Everything else needs to be aligned to that. But that is such a difficult thing to do, as most organizations will attest to. Organizations may expect that the discipline for achieving strategy is somehow embodied in everyone. But this is rarely the case. The level of discipline required and the effort involved cuts across functional silos. And that's where the discipline often breaks down. We need a way to integrate knowledge and effort across those functional boundaries.

The Office *For* Strategy Achievement can help to reduce some of the risks and difficulties associated with this goal. By integrating strategy, process, and project governance across functional silos, we increase organizational discipline and reduce risk. This makes the PDCA cycle more predictable and increases engagement for everyone in the organization. It brings together the governance for strategy, for processes, and for projects. Governance is a distributed function but it needs an integrating component. The OFSA can be that integrating component.

It is an organizational structure that ensures that we can get peak performance and motivation by sharing the work associated with control and improvement. It is not a complex process to understand but it is difficult to achieve because it requires engagement, accountability, discipline, and a commitment to continuous improvement. It also requires capacity and ability (*cap*ability).

When an organization does not set aside time, effort, and resources (capacity), then the PDCA cycle will not be executed. The result will be that the organization will only react to those situations that are so urgent that they demand attention. Of course, when we react only to the urgent, then the available options are limited. Usually they are limited in effectiveness and they are expensive. It is a fact that the greater the time horizon, the more options we have and the less expensive they are. If our car is running low on gas, we have an option to pull into the next gas station and fill up. That might cost us $25 to $50. But if we ignore the situation, and wait until we are out of gas, then not only will we still have to pay for the fill up, but we might also have to pay to get towed to the gas station. We will have to pay in time and aggravation, in addition to the gas.

Functional units have the capacity to produce their outputs. That is their number one job. When they fall behind on that job, all resources will be applied to catching up on production (even in service organizations). What get neglected are the control functions of monitoring and improvement. By putting some of the capacity and accountability for that work into a unit that isn't hampered by production responsibility, we ensure that necessary management system functions are not neglected.

The path to innovation and continuous improvement can be systematic. We have introduced an organization design concept, the Office *For* Strategy Achievement, as one way to implement the PDCA cycle. It will allow organizations to govern strategy (intent), processes (execution), and projects (transformation) together to better achieve the organization's stated purpose and finally close the strategy-execution gap. Of course, you must have the motivation and will to make it happen.

14

THE MYTH OF UNIVERSAL SOLUTIONS

Don't come to me with a solution. Come to me with a problem worth solving.

There is an old management saying:

"Don't come to me with a problem. Come to me with a solution."

How many times in your life have you heard this phrase from a manager or boss? I consider this phrase and the thinking behind it to be one of the greatest barriers to progress and innovation today.

Imagine a mechanic working in the bowels of a cruise ship. He notices water coming into the engine room where no water is supposed to enter. This is a problem. But he doesn't have a solution. Should he keep quiet until he finds a solution?

"Don't come to me with a problem if you don't have a solution."

But if I have a solution, do I still have a problem? I suppose that I might if I wasn't able to implement the solution on my own—if I needed others to assist. But then if I need others to assist, shouldn't they participate in finding a mutual solution? Upon careful reflection, we should be able to see that deep down the phrase makes no sense. So how did the saying originate?

I don't know the answer but I can propose a few alternative scenarios. Sometimes an employee might run into some problem that they should be able to resolve on their own. But for whatever reason they might try to off-load the problem onto the boss, to get the monkey off their back. So we can imagine the boss, being fed up with this, might one day have shot back, "Don't come to me with a problem until you have a solution." Such a boss was probably trying to get his or her employees to stop the practice of off-loading their problems. Or perhaps people were constantly finding "problems" with other people's work. Again, the boss, being fed up with this, might have come up with the saying to stop people from criticizing the work of others unless they had a better alternative.

We can sympathize with such bosses. But maybe it would have been better for all of us if that person, whoever they were, had given the quote a little more thought. With the benefit of hindsight, I'd like to propose the following replacement quote to fill the original intent, which was meant to encourage people to think through and own problems that they should rightfully have solved for themselves. Here is the replacement quote:

Don't try to turn your problem into my problem. But should you need help, I'll be glad to assist.

The boss may have been trying to ease their management burden. Meanwhile, we have spread a negative behaviour that must now be replaced. If you have a local problem that you are able to resolve, then of course you should do so.

But if we are to make progress and if we are to innovate, then we need a new mantra. I propose the following:

Don't come to me with a solution. Come to me with a problem worth solving.

Today we still need to solve the local, functional problems. But we especially need to solve those problems that will lead to progress. And more and more of those can't be solved by any single functional entity. They require a team to solve them. And they can be difficult and may require resources to solve. Therefore, we don't want to attempt to solve them unless they will lead to significant meaningful progress for the organization. That means that we need to separate the recognition of the problem or situation from its solution.

The Strategy Deployment framework and the Relational Process Model are intended to help us to identify "the problems worth solving." Identifying these problems, getting commitment to solving them, and validating that we have done so is the central purpose of the framework.

Finding problems worth solving, rather than solutions that can be implemented is a paradigm shift in thinking.

But what happens if we don't do that? You can probably look inside your own organization to answer that. If we don't choose which problems to solve, then, as with everything else in life and nature, the shortest path will be taken. There will be two kinds of problems that are most likely to be pursued with enthusiasm. The first is a problem for which we already have a perceived solution—the easily solved problem, the low hanging fruit. The second is the problem that has a solution that would be particularly rewarding personally—the preferred solution problem. These are the problems that will get solved. But are these the problems that need to be solved?

In order to achieve performance improvement, we need to solve the problem that most advances stakeholder values. And that problem may not fall into either of the two previous categories. We will solve the problems that are more easily solvable. And we will solve the problem that allows us to implement a solution that is personally advantageous. In both cases, we are picking the solution rather than selecting a *problem worth solving*. We will choose the solution, instead of the value problem. And why would we do that? Because in the absence of anything else, the solution is the reward.

A problem must first be detected. Then we must evaluate what it would mean to the organization—all the stakeholders—to solve the problem. Then we need to determine which problem would mean the most. And we need to determine what and whom it would take to solve the problem—the resources. Only then should we attempt to solve it.

Recognizing a problem is an entirely different step from finding a solution. A problem is often detected by people who had little to do with its creation. So asking them for a solution is hardly productive.

By the way, most solutions create other problems. Did you ever wonder why we refer to it as "resolving the problem"? Let me rewrite that as "re-*solving* the problem." Yes, that's right. Quite often to resolve is to re-solve or solve again. That means that it's important that a problem be solved correctly and completely; otherwise, we will be resolving it for a long time to come.

Management's job has shifted as organizations and the environment have changed. Identifying which problems are most worthy of being solved has become a top management priority and challenge. But that means that relying on functional units to identify problems for management is no longer sufficient. We need a way to identify problems whose impact goes beyond functional concerns. *That's what the framework helps us to do.*

THE APPEAL OF A UNIVERSAL METHODOLOGY

Penicillin was a great development, but you shouldn't take it for a sprain. Aspirin may be great for headaches but it won't help with overeating. Chemotherapy…Well, it isn't even a single solution. It is a whole family of solutions.

The point is that cures, treatment plans, and solutions must be paired or matched to a corresponding disease or problem. The idea that we don't need to know the problem, that there exists a universal solution, may be appealing. But it is an illusion. To the best of my knowledge, no universal solutions have yet been found in any field of endeavour and certainly not in business.

It reminds one of the ancient alchemists. One of the best-known goals of the alchemist was the transmutation of common metals into gold or silver. We could presume that the goal of turning common metals into gold was based on the fact that gold was held as more valuable than the common metals. But I can't help but wonder if anyone ever stopped to think it all the way through. If the common metals were turned into gold, then gold would become the common metal and thus would itself become less desirable than the others. No universal cure or elixir of life has ever been found. And no gold conversion chemistry has yet been discovered. But if it were, it would only be valuable if it could be kept secret from everyone else. So maybe it has been discovered, but none of us knows about it.

In the American Wild West, there were people who were referred to as snake oil salesmen. These were usually men of dubious character and credentials who sold medicines claimed to cure *whatever* ailed you. So, in a sense, they proclaimed to have succeeded where the alchemists had failed. The great thing about them was that the state of the patient was not important. They didn't need to know anything about the patient since the medicine could cure anything. The snake oil salesman usually had someone with them who would attest to the effectiveness of the product. They never had anyone with them to attest to the failure of the product. What the snake oil salesman did was create the *illusion of potential*. Many of today's TV advertisements follow the same approach. Diet commercials show scantily dressed and attractively slim men and women alongside the product. They are trying to create the illusion of potential. The attractive, thin woman may never have been fat. Or, even if she was, her genetic makeup is probably not the same as that of the viewers'. Then there is the viewers' motivation and their basic attractiveness. Most viewers could never look like the person in the commercial. But the illusion of potential is there. The approach works because the failures are hidden from us.

It is disheartening that methodologies are sometimes sold or promoted using the "snake oil" strategy. This is unfortunate. Most snake oil was in fact fake. But many methodologies, including Lean and Six Sigma, are useful. They are not fake at all. The problem is that they are sold as *a priori* universal solutions. It doesn't matter what problems or constraints your organization has, the methodology is often sold as something you must have in order to be saved. Their effectiveness is often attested to by pointing to a few organizations that are successful and have used the methodology (success by association—same strategy used to sell snake oil). Companies that don't succeed may be criticized for improper implementation (failure through *dis*association) without any kind of examination. Rarely is the true picture given out. Rarely are all the failures made known. Of course, years later, when enough organizations have tried the methodologies, the true statistics come out. Typically only a small percentage (usually less than 10% and often less than 5%) of the organizations attempting to use these methodologies are able to get and hold measurable benefits.

I'm in no way criticizing any of these methodologies. I use them myself. The methodologies themselves, like most effective treatment plans for diseases, can be quite effective but only if used to treat the right patient with the right conditions and with knowledgeable assistance. The ultimate failure of these methodologies comes because they are expected to cure everything. When this fails to happen, they are often abandoned. Companies then wait for the next false cure-all methodology to be discovered. Of course it doesn't exist. That's too bad because, properly used to address specific issues, each specific methodology can produce significant benefits.

We don't believe a universal methodology exists or ever will. Actually, even if someone did come up with one, then there would be one of two scenarios:

1. It would be used by the originator to put everyone else out of business and so you'd never find out about it until it was too late.
2. It would be used by the originator to sell it to everybody. Since everybody had it, it would not be able to give anyone a competitive advantage. Since it couldn't give anyone a competitive advantage (because everyone had it), it would, like the gold, become common and no longer would it be a universal solution.

The framework works with methodologies. It does not replace them. The framework helps to identify those problems worth solving. Once we select such a problem and understand its nature, then we can select the appropriate methodology (treatment plan). The framework then helps us to validate our solution.

To repeat a quote from the beginning of this book:

> *There are three things extremely hard: steel, a diamond, and to know one's self.*
> Benjamin Franklin, *Poor Richard's Almanack* (1750)

The hardest of the three is "to know one's self." The self that we are trying to know is our own organization. The Relational Process Model framework is primarily aimed at helping to know oneself. We need to better understand the organization if we are to be able to make changes that will result in greater value being delivered to all stakeholders, now and in the future.

In a competitive environment, there can never be such thing as a universal methodology. The framework, the Chart of Accounts, and the other concepts introduced are not meant to be some sort of cure all. They don't tell us beforehand what we must do. We have to figure that out for ourselves. We have to lift our own weights if we want to become stronger. The next step for each organization may be different.

What we have presented is a *framework* for understanding your processes and for designing *more perfect* processes inside your organization. Why do we say "more perfect" processes? We don't know how excellent your processes are and it doesn't matter. They were designed under a different set of conditions than likely exists today. So rather than trying to determine if they are excellent or not, let's just declare them perfect under the circumstances. What we want to know, then, is how much more perfect they could be under different circumstances. That's the purpose of the framework—to help you design *more perfect* processes by seeing where the opportunities may lie.

The framework is a tool for *seeing* and *understanding* the impact of our choices and for making more profitable choices. It is more widely applicable because it isn't a solution. It doesn't dictate that you should throw away what you have and exchange it for something someone else tells you to have. Instead, it highlights the areas where change is urgent, where change is needed, and where change can wait. More importantly, it allows you to evaluate when a change has led to progress and when it has not. This is of crucial importance because if you don't know if a change was progressive, then how can you evaluate the change?

The framework emphasizes the importance of progress rather than the importance of change. Change is not the endgame—progress is. Change is only the price we must pay to move from one steady state to another, more desirable steady state. Since change is a price, it's important that the new steady state will provide us with increased value. Otherwise, we are investing without a return. The *endgame* is progress as measured by the stakeholders.

Methodologies tend to revolve around solving problems. And, therefore, they are problem specific. The framework revolves around *finding problems worthy of being solved*. It is a powerful tool that can be used to expand the limits of our vision. But, just like a pair of glasses, you have to put them on to see differently.

Enduring Principles

There are no universal solutions. However, there are enduring principles. Science is about the discovery of principles. That's what science does. It observes, postulates, and experiments to establish enduring principles—laws of the universe. But even those laws always come with caveats or boundaries. It's important to understand the limits of any particular scientific principle. Sometimes a new, more widely applicable principle is discovered and it replaces an existing principle. In those cases, it's not that the old principle was necessarily wrong. It's just that the old one only applied under specified conditions.

Engineering, on the other hand, is the art, science, and practice of finding solutions to real problems. Engineering uses art—imagination. It uses practice—practical experience. And it uses science—enduring principles. It uses all three to develop innovative solutions that we then use to improve our everyday lives. Engineering used to rely mainly on practice or what worked. It was based on trial and error. And since there were many errors, many trials were required. So when something was found to work, there was great reluctance to look for something better. Engineering effectiveness really took off when science and art were added. The use of scientific principles by engineers has greatly improved engineered products.

Business processes are practical solutions to everyday business problems. So in many ways, business process engineering today is at the practice stage. The framework helps to add scientific discipline and art to business process engineering. The objective is to move the discipline beyond just practice. The concept of best practice is OK, but practice is the initial stage for a discipline. Isn't it time to advance the discipline?

The next stage is principle-based design. And for that we need a way to separate principles from practice. The framework will help us do that. As we discover business process principles, we will be in a better position to evaluate the current processes and the current process design methodologies. We can evaluate which principles are there and which are missing. More importantly, we can evaluate which principle, when applied inside a process solution, improves the solution and which does not.

It is the discovery and application of enduring principles that can provide an organization with an advantage over its competition. Principles take time to discover, time to verify, and time to incorporate into business processes. Anyone can copy a method (recipe). But it takes practice to master it. The framework is not a solution. It is a tool that can help us achieve mastery. How does it do that?

An organization should always be learning. And learning means changing. But change can be regressive or it can be progressive. The framework helps us to determine which changes are progressive. It helps us to validate our discoveries and our ideas. It helps to remove personal preferences by providing us with a means of evaluation that isn't based on personal opinion but rather on demonstrated facts. It helps us because it provides us with a mechanism to detect drifts. It helps us by providing a framework for better understanding how the processes are currently designed.

WHY IS CHANGE DIFFICULT?

The move away from personal preferences and away from dogmatic methodologies may certainly be resisted by a few whose vision doesn't allow them to see beyond their current personal stake in continuing on as is. To those I would say "move over before you get run over."

It will require a greater level of discipline to develop a principle-based management system instead of a personal preference-based management system. But the benefits can be huge.

First of all, principles change less frequently than personal opinions. Every time there is a change of manager, employee, or supervisor, there is potentially going to be a change in how things are done, but not necessarily an improvement. So when business processes are designed based on personal preferences, the volume of changes far exceeds the amount of progress. And change costs. On the other hand, when business processes are designed based on enduring principles, the volume of changes will diminish and the volume of progress will increase. The gap between the volume of changes and the amount of progress will be reduced and tend towards zero, although it will never reach zero. We will always have some changes that prove to provide no value and must be reversed. But the volume of such changes will become quite small.

Change will never become easy. But using the framework will eliminate many changes. And that means that total difficulty and effort associated with change will be dramatically reduced. We say that change is difficult. So is lifting weights. But lifting weights or resistance builds muscle mass. So change can build organizational flexibility in the same way as exercise builds physical flexibility.

Yes, this framework is *designed* to be more sophisticated than what most people are using. That's the opportunity. Those professionals within the disciplines related to organizational process improvement have tried to keep their tools simple enough for the subject matter experts to understand. This is pursued as a positive goal. But, in fact, it is a limiting factor. Imagine if doctors limited their treatments and their diagnostic procedures to only what a patient could understand. Imagine if an automotive engineer only designed cars that the driver could fully comprehend. Imagine if we applied the concept that the user of a product must fully understand its functioning to everything. Then medical treatments would never have progressed beyond those of the middle ages. Most of us would still be driving a horse and buggy. Phones, computers, the internet, microwaves, etc., would not exist. And books would only be available to a few privileged people because they would have to be copied by hand.

Up until now, it has been the subject matter experts (SME) who, based solely on their subject matter expertise, have designed the business processes. I think that this has limited the potential of our business processes. Subject matter experts are the executors of a process. The ability to execute a process does not automatically make one able to design the process. This is like the assembly worker designing the assembly line. It may have worked well 100 years ago, but no modern manufacturing organization works this way today. Assembly line workers must certainly participate and be engaged in improving current operations. However, no assembly worker could possibly design a modern automotive factory. The additional knowledge and skill required represents a volume of knowledge that can't be obtained just by working on the assembly line. This is not to say that design is more important than execution or that execution is more important than design. They are different disciplines that require different knowledge, skills, and temperament. To compete we must excel in both. Unfortunately, there is too much knowledge, too much skill, and too much experience required for any one person to master both. And so in many disciplines design has been separated from execution

It is time we extend this separation to business processes if we are to deliver maximum stakeholder value, regardless of whether an organization is manufacturing or service oriented.

This framework is a start in that direction. It is intended to be understood and embraced by subject matter experts, but not mastered by them. It is intended to be mastered as part of a design discipline for business analysts, process analysts, process designers, systems analysts, and even project managers—people for whom process design comprises an important part of their job. The level of sophistication is high enough that it will require thousands of hours to master the use of the knowledge.

If we limit the sophistication of the tools to that which can be understood by the "customers," we will be doomed to underperform—to forever design horse-drawn carts. Our processes will perform like a horse and buggy rather than like an automobile.

I believe that this is an approach that is more likely to produce lasting results because it provides people with the opportunity to improve the organization for all stakeholders. And, by making things more visible, it will also make it easier to see those who are standing in the way of improving delivered value to serve their own interests.

The Relational Process Model with the Chart of Accounts provides us with a strong foundation around which an organization can develop and improve its own methodologies, processes, and management systems. It is part of a framework for managing and for engaging people for the benefit of all. It is not a solution, but rather a way to develop *your* own customized solutions. It is a framework that takes days to learn, but years to master.

Days to learn. Years to master.

It is an opportunity to become more sophisticated and move the discipline forward. It is an opportunity to put the *engineering* in business process engineering.

SUMMARY

There are no universal solutions. Yet everyone wants to believe that they exist. Why is that? There is the illusion that if they did exist, then "my" problem would be solved. The problem is that organizations operate in a competitive environment. That means that some will succeed while others must be culled out. This may be unfortunate but it is inescapable.

We can hold on to the illusions of the universal solution—silver bullet—or we can create our own advantage. This requires us to truly understand the organization and what makes our processes perform. Of course, we will want to take advantage of technologies and approaches developed by others, such as this framework, but we must also distinguish ourselves in some unique way that provides an advantage over the competition.

The framework is not presented as a solution. It is not an answer. It is a way to better see where we need to focus our attention in order to build that advantage. It is a tool for expanding the limits of our vision. Naturally this is a challenge. But along with that challenge comes the opportunity to develop both the organization and the people in it. The greatest advantage is mastery because it takes time. And time is always an advantage if you are in the lead. If you aren't in the lead, then you need to think about how to close the gap. The framework is all about identifying where the gaps are and which need to be closed first.

There will always be those who attempt to sell us a universal solution. They will imply that all we need to do is to apply it and success is guaranteed. Of course this has great appeal. It saves us work and effort and if it fails, then it's the methodology that fails and not us. The first time we believe such a claim it's "shame on them." But the second time we believe such a claim it's "shame on us." We are well beyond the first, second, or even third time. So we're definitely in "shame on us" territory.

Some continue to try to sell us universal, guaranteed solutions. The framework proposed here *is not* such a solution. It doesn't guarantee success through blind adherence to a recipe. Such a guarantee is both an *illusion* and a *delusion*. Success is up to you. It does require you to lift your own weights. However, if you need to learn and grow, if you need an edge on your competitors, then the framework will help you to achieve that. That is a claim I will make. Change is difficult. And so it should be. But enterprise failure is worse.

So, stop trying to make change easy.
Instead, make change count.

Glossary of Terms

1ST NF:	First normal form
2ND NF:	Second normal form
3RD NF:	Third normal form
4TH NF:	Fourth normal form
CoA:	Chart of Accounts
CVA:	Customer value-add
DPMO:	Defects per million opportunities
DPMR:	Defects per million requests
FMEA:	Failure Modes & Effects Analysis
NVA:	Non-Value-Add
NF:	Normal Form
NPM:	Normalized Process Model
NPT:	Non-Product-Transform
PT:	Product-Transform
PDCA:	Plan, Do, Check, Act
RPM:	Relational Process Model
TA:	Throughput Add
TS:	Throughput Subtract
VA:	Value-Add
WIIM:	What Is of Interest to Me
WIVM:	What Is of Value to Me

RECOMMENDED READING

Akao, Yoji, ed. *Hoshin Kanri: Policy Deployment For Successful TQM*. New York: Productivity, 2004.

Apgar, David. *Risk Intelligence: Learning to Manage What We Don't Know*. Boston: Harvard Business School, 2006.

Balle, Freddy, and Michael Balle. *The Gold Mine: A Novel of Lean Turnaround*. Brookline: Lean Enterprises Inst Inc, 2005.

Barker, Joel Arthur. *Paradigms: the Business of Discovering the Future*. New York: Harper Collins, 1992.

Brache, Alan P., and Geary A. Rummler. *Improving Performance: How to Manage the White Space in the Organization Chart (Jossey Bass Business and Management Series)*. 2 Sub ed. San Francisco: Jossey-Bass, 1995.

Burlton, Roger T. *Business Process Management: Profiting from Process*. Indianapolis: Sams, 2001.

Cavanagh, Roland R., Robert P. Neuman, and Peter S. Pande. *What is Design for Six Sigma*. New York: McGraw-Hill, 2005.

Chabris, Christopher F., and Daniel J. Simons. *The Invisible Gorilla: and Other Ways Our Intuitions Deceive Us*. New York: Crown, 2010.

Clausing, Don. *Total Quality Development: A Step-By-Step Guide to World-Class Concurrent Engineering*. New York: American Society Of Mechanical Engineers Press, 1994.

Collins, James C. *Good to Great: Why Some Companies Make the Leap--and Others Don't*. New York: HarperBusiness, 2001.

Connors, Roger, Tom Smith, and Craig Hickman. *The Oz Principle: Getting Results Through Individual and Organizational Accountability.* Paramus: Prentice Hall, 1994.

Covey, Stephen R. *The Seven Habits of Highly Effective People: Restoring the Character Ethic.* New York: Simon and Schuster, 1989.

Fleming, Quentin W., and Joel M. Koppelman. *Earned Value Project Management.* 2nd ed. Newtown Square: Project Management Institute, 2000.

Garland, Ross. *Project Governance: a Practical Guide to Effective Project Decision Making.* London: Kogan Page, 2009.

Galsworth, Gwendolyn D. *Visual Workplace, Visual Thinking: Creating Enterprise Excellence Through the Technologies of the Visual Workplace.* Portland: Visual-Lean Enterprise Press, 2005.

Gerber, Michael E. *The E Myth Revisited: Why Most Small Businesses Don't Work and What to Do About It.* New York: HarperCollins, 1995.

Gerber, Michael E. *E Myth Mastery.* New York: HarperCollins, 2005.

Gladwell, Malcolm. *Outliers: The Story of Success.* New York: Little, Brown and Company, 2008.

Goldratt, Eliyahu M. *Critical Chain: A Business Novel.* Great Barrington: North River Press, 1997.

Goldratt, Elihahu M. *The Goal: A Process of Ongoing Improvement Second revised Edition.* 2nd ed. Great Barrington: North River Press, 1992.

Hammer, Michael, and James Champy. *Reengineering the Corporation: a Manifesto for Business Revolution.* New York: HarperBusiness, 1993.

Harrington, H. James. *Business Process Improvement: The Breakthrough Strategy for Total Quality, Productivity, and Competitiveness.* United States: McGraw-Hill, 1991.

Harris, Chris, Rick Harris, and Earl Wilson. *Making Materials Flow: A Lean Material-Handling Guide for Operations, Production-Control, and Engineering Professionals.* Brookline: Lean Enterprise Institute, 2003.

Harris, Rick, and Mike Rother. *Creating Continuous Flow: An Action Guide for Managers, Engineers & Production Associates.* Brookline: Lean Enterprise Institute, 2001.

Imai, Masaaki. *Kaizen: the Key to Japan's Competitive Success.* New York: McGraw-Hill, 1986.

Imai, Masaaki. *Gemba Kaizen: A Commonsense, Low-Cost Approach to Management*. New York: McGraw-Hill, 1997.

Jackson, Thomas L.. *Hoshin Kanri for the Lean Enterprise: Developing Competitive Capabilities and Managing Profit*. New York: Productivity Press, 2006.

Japan Management Association, ed. *Kanban, Just-in-time at Toyota: Management Begins at the Workplace*. Trans. David J. Lu. Revised ed. Portland: Productivity, 1989.

Jeston, John, and Johan Nelis. *Business Process Management, Second Edition: Practical Guidelines to Successful Implementations*. 2 ed. Oxford: Butterworth-Heinemann, 2008.

Jones, Dan, and Jim Womack. *Seeing the Whole: Mapping the Extended Value Stream*. Brookline: Lean Enterprise Institute, 2003.

Jones, Laurie Beth. *Teach Your Team to Fish: Using Ancient Wisdom for Inspired Teamwork*. New York: Crown Business, 2002.

Kaplan, Robert S., and David P. Norton. *The Balanced Scorecard: Translating Strategy into Action*. Boston, MA: Harvard Business School, 1996.

Keyte, Beau, and Drew Locher. *The Complete Lean Enterprise: Value Stream Mapping for Administrative and Office Processes*. New York: Productivity Press, 2004.

Lamsweerde, Axel van. *Requirements Engineering: From System Goals to UML Models to Software Specifications*. Chichester: Wiley, 2009.

Lepore, Domenico, and Oded Cohen. *Deming and Goldratt: The Theory of Constraints and the System of Profound Knowledge*. Great Barrington: North River Press, 1999.

Levinson, William A. *Henry Ford's Lean Vision: Enduring Principles from the First Ford Motor Plant*. New York: Productivity, 2002.

Liker, Jeffrey K. *The Toyota Way: 14 Management Principles from the World's Greatest Manufacturer*. New York: McGraw-Hill, 2004.

Liker, Jeffrey K., and Michael Hoseus. *Toyota Culture: the Heart and Soul of the Toyota Way*. New York: McGraw-Hill, 2008.

Liker, Jeffrey K., and David P. Meier. *The Toyota Way Fieldbook: a Practical Guide for Implementing Toyota's 4Ps*. New York: McGraw-Hill, 2006.

Liker, Jeffrey K., and David P. Meier. *Toyota Talent: Developing Your People the Toyota Way*. New York: McGraw-Hill, 2007.

Liker, Jeffrey K., and James M. Morgan. *The Toyota Product Development System: Integrating People, Process, and Technology.* New York: Productivity, 2006.

Luyster, Tom, and Don Tapping. *Creating Your Lean Future State: How to Move from Seeing to Doing.* New York: Productivity Press, 2006.

McDermott, Robin E., Raymond J. Mikulak, and Michael R. Beauregard. *The Basics of FMEA.* Portland: Productivity, Inc., 1996.

Miller, Lawrence M.. *Design for Total Quality: A Workbook for Socio-Technical Design.* Atlanta: The Miller Consulting Group, 1991.

Niven, Paul R.. *Balanced Scorecard Step-by-Step: Maximizing Performance and Maintaining Results.* New York: John Wiley & Sons, 2002.

Ohno, Taiichi. *Toyota Production System: Beyond Large-Scale Production.* Portland: Productivity Press, 1988.

Page-Jones, Meilir. *The Practical Guide to Structured Systems Design.* New York: Yourdon, 1980.

Rother, Mike, and John Shook. *Learning to See: Value Stream Mapping to Add Value and Eliminate Muda.* Brookline: Lean Enterprise Institute, 1999.

Rubrich, Larry. *How to Prevent Lean Implementation Failures: 10 Reasons Why Failures Occur (Making Companies Globally Competitive).* Fort Wayne: WCM Associates, 2004.

Seddon, John. *Freedom from Command & Control: Rethinking Management for Lean Service.* New York: Productivity Press, 2005.

Senge, Peter M. *The Fifth Discipline: the Art and Practice of the Learning Organization.* New York: Doubleday, 1990.

Shingo, Shigeo. *A Study of the Toyota Production System From an Industrial Engineering Viewpoint.* Trans. Andrew P. Dillon. Revised ed. Portland: Productivity, 1989.

Shingo, Shigeo. *Kaizen and the Art of Creative Thinking: the Scientific Thinking Mechanism.* Trans. Enna Products Corporation. Bellingham: Enna Products Corporation, 2007.

Smalley, Art. *Creating Level Pull: A Lean Production-System Improvement Guide for Production-Control, Operations, and Engineering Professionals (Lean Tool Kit).* Brookline: Lean Enterprise Institute, 2004.

Smith, Preston G., and Guy M. Merritt. *Proactive Risk Management: Controlling Uncertainty in Product Development*. Portland: Productivity Press, 2002.

Sobek II, Durward K. , and Art Smalley. *Understanding A3 Thinking: A Critical Component of Toyota's PDCA Management System*. Boca Raton: Productivity Press, 2008.

Tapping, Don, Tom Luyster, and Tom Shuker. *Value Stream Management*. New York: Productivity Press, 2002.

Thaler, Richard H., and Cass R. Sunstein. *Nudge: Improving Decisions About Health, Wealth, and Happiness*. New Haven: Yale University Press, 2008.

White, Stephen A., and Derek Miers. *BPMN Modeling and Reference Guide: Understanding and Using BPMN: Develop Rigorous Yet Understandable Graphical Representations of Business Processes*. Lighthouse Point: Future Strategies, 2008.

Zachman, J.A. "A Framework for Information System Architecture." *IBM Systems Journal* 26, no. 3 (1987): 276-292.

INDEX

W

CPSIA information can be obtained at www.ICGtesting.com
Printed in the USA
LVOW121834100812

293858LV00014B/184/P